Worlds Within

WORLDS WITHIN

Probing
The Christos Experience

G. M. GLASKIN

WILDWOOD HOUSE LONDON

FIRST PUBLISHED IN GREAT BRITAIN 1976

© 1976 BY G. M. GLASKIN

WILDWOOD HOUSE LTD, 29 KING STREET LONDON WC2E 8JD

ISBN 0 7045 0215 1

●

The author and publishers gratefully acknowledge permission to reproduce extracts from copyright material which appear on the following pages:

pp. 9, 10, 11-14, 15 from *A General Introductory Guide to the Egyptian Collections in the British Museum,* printed by permission of the Trustees of the British Museum

p. 42 from the *Encyclopaedia Britannica* (Encyclopaedia Britannica, Chicago, 1964) © *Encyclopaedia Britannica* 1964

pp. 149, 152, from *Creative and Mental Growth* by Viktor Lowenfeld and W. Lambert Brittain (Cassell & Collier Macmillan, 2nd edition, 1964).

Computer typeset by Input Typesetting Ltd, London SE1
Printed and bound in Great Britain by
Biddles Ltd, Guildford, Surrey, and
Western Book Co, Maesteg, Glamorgan

For AMBER ROOIJAKKERS-WATTS
who has long been the kindest of kindred spirits, especially in the more common sense of the worlds within.

There is another world, but it is in this one.

Paul Eluard

It is not outside, it is inside: wholly within.

Meister Eckhart

He looked at his own soul with a Telescope. What seemed all irregular, he saw and shewed to be beautiful Constellations: and he added to the Consciousness hidden worlds within worlds.

Notebooks, *S. T. Coleridge*

Contents

Warning

The procedure given in this book, which makes it possible to dream while one is fully awake, and which possibly even reveals past lives and/or future events, is not to be treated lightly, and particularly not as some new and intriguing party game, exciting as the experience may be. As in dreams experienced during normal necessary sleep, nightmares and unpleasant experiences can and do occur, which may cause distress to some subjects despite their being able to terminate the experiment at any time, something not possible when they have a nightmare during normal sleep. Such unpleasant experiences have occurred when the experiment was carried out in both New York and London – without the author's presence, of course. On the other hand, most experimentees have expressed their astonishment at what a pleasant, marvellous, experience it is; a considerable number, incredulous as they may have been beforehand, have claimed to have benefited greatly from it both psychologically and through revelations of future events as well as of experiences indisputably before their present lifetimes.

GERALD M. GLASKIN, *author*
WILDWOOD HOUSE, *publishers*

Part One
Beyond the First Window

The mind is free, whate'er afflict the man
MICHAEL DRAYTON

    I first encountered the Christos Experiment in May 1971, exactly two years before writing this, my second book on the subject.

In my first book, *Windows of the Mind,* I related my initial scepticism which for several months made me reluctant even to consider the matter, until finally I felt that I could avoid it no longer. My own experiment with it proved to be quite shattering and I was immediately convinced that it was a most extraordinary experience and perhaps an entirely new human phenomenon, though not that it revealed past lives or previous incarnations. I could see that it could have a great deal of benefit for mankind, especially in these times of such troubled confusion. I gave my various reasons for this conviction in that book, so I think it would be quite superfluous to give them all again here.

It would seem superfluous, too, to repeat an account of my first Christos Experience; however, a little over a year later, in London, I came across some details concerning the time and location of the circumstances I had so clearly seen depicted in my experience. This, together with some further quite extraordinary experiments, made me decide that I needed both to investigate the matter much further and, consequently, write another book about it.

To explain briefly what this Christos Experiment is for those readers who are encountering it for the first time: it is a procedure for enabling one to dream consciously, and might even be a method for revealing glimpses of past lives or previous incarnations for those who can at least have an open mind of inquiry towards such matters. I was introduced to this procedure in a most unlikely locality for such phenomena – isolated Western Australia – through an organization calling itself 'The Christos Experiment' in Mahogany Creek. (Inquiries should be addressed to 'Open Mind' Publications, care of the Post Office.) The organization had published several volumes of a magazine entitled *Open Mind*, copies of which are kept in the archives of the Western Australian State Public Library.

The procedure is given in detail at the end of this book, but briefly it consists of simple massage simultaneously to the forehead and ankles for two or three minutes, followed by an easy imaginative exercise a child could perform, a memory-visual exercise, and an imaginative-visual exercise that also utilizes memory. The element of memory, however, gradually decreases as pure visualization increases. After this procedure an experience very much like dreaming is induced – but a conscious dreaming which can be recounted as it happens, and terminated at will. In some cases, including my own, it was extraordinarily like being given a glimpse into what might have been a past life or previous incarnation, if there be such a thing. My two experiences of the experiment have been the most extraordinary of what I consider to have been quite an eventful lifetime; and I must also admit that they have indeed helped, as the author of *Open Mind* claimed, to overcome problems or psychological blockages 'in this lifetime' by revealing a similar and pertinent predicament in a previous incarnation.

In my case, I had reached not so much a 'writer's block' as a feeling of the futility of writing: so many books are published, let alone written, that one could not read a fraction of them even if one spent an entire lifetime trying to do so. So why go to so much trouble just to add a few more, or even one more, to the heap?

In the very first experiment I did not achieve the visual exercises after the massaging and 'stretching and shrinking' exercises had been accomplished. Instead, I found myself having already begun the visualization purported to occur and felt compelled to continue watching it, much as one is fascinated by a television or cinema screen.

Instead of visualizing my own front door as I had been asked to do as part of the preliminaries, I was already seeing a massive stone construction that at first appeared to be a wall, though it was possibly hewn out of living rock in a cliff. This wall had a very tall doorway with double doors which, despite their great size and apparent weight, were probably counterweighted so that they could be opened with ease – or at least by 'me' they could.

When I say 'by "me"', it was certainly not the 'me' as I am today or have been at any time in my present lifetime; and prior to this experience I had not even considered, let alone been convinced of, the possibility of reincarnation. But now I could quite clearly see myself with dark skin, long thin limbs, a body well over six feet tall and the long and very different features of a man in his thirties (instead of almost fifty). I was dressed in a garment and headgear that I could only conjecture to be Egyptian, and at one stage was wearing thonged leather sandals.

What was perhaps even stranger than this apparition was the intuitive conviction that I was indeed in Egypt; more precisely at a point where a rocky escarpment of mountains or high hills rises up from a tawny-coloured plateau through which the Nile flows to the Mediterranean. I could see the coastline far in the distance beyond this brilliantly lit plain, and the river winding towards it. It was a locality I have never seen in real life.

But first I was to go through the doors and find myself in the deep shadow of an interior which I knew intuitively to be some kind of mausoleum, in which I myself would be buried, in one of the flat, plain stone sarcophagi I could dimly discern against the circular walls which rose up in a dome to the apex of this cavern-like interior. Moisture dripped from this apex into a circular hole in the floor, about eighteen inches in diameter and six or nine inches deep. From this a channel of about six inches wide and deep carried the water through the doors to the outside.

There were several sarcophagi in this mausoleum, some still empty and some containing the wrapped and crudely mummified remains of my 'forebears'; forebears not by ancestry but election, for I *knew* I was the elected leader of a small settlement immediately below the mausoleum. I had come from a community up in the mountains where, like monks, we were trained for just such a specific appointment. Eventually, when I died, I too would be mummified and placed in one of these sarcophagi. Such a fate did not distress or even concern the 'me' who was observing all this, for I believed in a life after death. Until that time I would continue my duties of ruling and recording the history of my small community.

Turning to leave the mausoleum, I could visualize a long flight of stone steps, while at the same time I gazed out on to the brilliantly clear plateau cleft by the river-valley which wound its way to the coast.

The settlement which I ruled was bigger than a village but far from being a city. Its white, rounded houses were clustered close together, each with modest doorways and small unpaned window-holes. Brown-skinned people, scantily clothed because of the warm climate, moved around the streets bent upon their various occupations.

One building was larger than all the others, with two storeys instead of the usual one. This was where I lived and worked; it was my 'palace', although I did not think of it as such, for there was certainly no grandeur about it. It was larger than the other houses and remarkably light and airy, but there was little in the way of furniture inside.

Some four or five servants appeared from dim recesses to bow and inquire if I needed anything. I indicated with a gesture that I wanted nothing, for I was bent upon walking straight through the large inner hall, oval in shape, to a doorway (without any actual door) to the left, through which I passed to my 'office' or 'study'. This contained a stone or marble table and an oblong stool of similar material. On the table was a stone tablet at which I was continually working, using sharp instruments to carve figures a few inches high in stylized forms of human beings, animals, birds, simple objects and such, and then brushes and pots of prepared 'paint' to colour these with a vivid and gleaming enamel finish. This oblong tablet – about thirty inches tall by eighteen inches wide, and four or five inches thick – was up-ended against supports and not yet completed.

I did not attempt to continue my work. Instead, I felt not despair, but a profound kind of regret that the medium in which I had to express myself was still so primitive, able only to record the factual and visual aspects of life; that man could not yet record any of his abstract ideas, let alone his most noble aspirations. Some day, I sensed, man would conceive and evolve more complicated hieroglyphics, and later an alphabet; but this would not occur in my present lifetime and I would have to make do with the primitive hieroglyphics and instruments that I had, and the simple subjects to which they confined me.

Behind me was an unpaned window through which the sun streamed brightly, lighting up the colourfully tiled floor and a corner of the stone or marble 'desk'. Standing up, I crossed to lean on the sill and gaze down on to the small courtyard with its primitive water-jars, a small pond, a potted palm or two. And there I did nothing but think of my predicament. Yet life was pleasant enough, and I was determined to enjoy whatever I had left of it.

The 'experience' then faded and ended, much as a film or a dream fades and ends. Now there was only the room in which I was lying in actuality to have this 'experience', of which I had been perfectly, and *consciously,* aware the entire time (a little over an hour).

I could immediately see the 'moral' of this visualization. After publishing fourteen books, I had suddenly felt an overwhelming futility in writing any more and had not done so for five years. The experience reminded me that I now had a perfectly workable alphabet and vocabulary at my disposal, with which to express any thought that might come into my head. I also had a life free of the duties of 'ruling and recording' a particular community. I was far from rich, but my books had provided me with enough to live on for a number of years – with luck, even for the rest of my life.

Yet I had not wanted to write. Only a few days later, however, I felt a compulsion at least to record this unusual and extraordinarily vivid experience, if only in an article of two or three thousand words. This I did. Yet somehow the matter would not rest there, and I found myself trying what transpired to be an equally vivid and extraordinary experiment (but which will only confuse matters if I recount it here). Subsequently, I tried the experiment on a number of other people – about twenty of them altogether, of differing ages, occupations and degrees of intelligence. The results varied from one complete failure (my assistant, Leo van de Pas) through rather ordinary visualizations or dreams (if any such results can be considered *ordinary*) to what appeared, in about a third of the subjects, to be revelations of past lives or incarnations (some involving change of race, colour and/or sex, and at least one taking a non-human form). And so a book was written after all – and now six more after it – at a pace and with a compulsion which I had never known hitherto.

This alone was sufficient result for me, and over the months that followed I did not forget the experience. The details remained as real, if not more so, as in any event in real life. Yet there was more to follow.

A little over a year later, having finished the first draft of a novel set in Australia, I went to see my literary agent in London. Having an afternoon free, after delivering my manuscript to a publisher whose offices were near the British Museum, I decided to visit the exhibition of relics from Tutankhamun's tomb with my assistant, Leo van de Pas. However, on arrival we found we would have to queue for several hours and even then might not be admitted before closing time. I was about to turn away when I saw that usual entry to the British Museum was still possible without waiting and so, as I had not visited it before, we decided to go in.

A mere cursory glance at the books and manuscripts showed all too clearly that one needed not just hours but days, weeks, even months to make a visit worthwhile. Wondering if such an opportunity would ever come my way, I decided to adopt my usual procedure with museums and art galleries and walk rapidly through as much of the entire building as was possible, with the intention of returning to study, at a much more leisurely pace, those particular exhibitions which appealed to me.

It might not have been possible to see the Tutankhamun exhibition that day, though I did later on, but the main hall of Egyptian monuments and relics was a considerable consolation for the meantime. But how fortunate it was that I had decided to follow my usual procedure of almost striding through room after room, otherwise we would never have discovered the very much smaller room upstairs containing more modestly-sized examples of early Egyptian art. Here I suddenly stopped.

The first thing to arrest my attention was a stone tablet of almost the exact dimensions of the one at which I had seen myself working in my 'experience', but the hieroglyphics were only carved into the stone and were not brilliantly painted as on my tablet. Also, these hieroglyphics were much more sophisticated than the simple figures depicting human beings, animals, birds, insects and so on which I had been carving.

I knew very little about Egyptology, so it was perhaps not surprising that I had not heard the word 'stele' until that afternoon in the British Museum. A stele, or 'stela', is 'an upright stone slab or tablet' as well as, botanically, the central cylinder (vascular bundles with pith and pericycle) in stems and roots of the higher plants. In Egyptology the term applies particularly to a funerary tablet like the one I had been so occupied with in my experience.

There were many stelae in this room where I had come to so abrupt a halt, but the one which had first caught my eye was exhibit number 1820 with the legend: 'Limestone panel from the tomb of NEBUNENEF, high priest of AMUN at THEBES in early years of KING RAMESES II (1304-1237 B.C.).' Nor was this all. Near by were a pair of leather-thonged sandals very similar in style to those I had seen as my own in the experience, though more elaborate. At the time I had a most uncanny feeling, a kind of intuition, that I somehow *belonged* to these articles, and that they equally belonged to me, or had at least been associated with me at some time.

However, like the near-by sandals, this particular stele was much more elaborate than the one at which I had seen myself working. Besides, it was merely *carved* from the sandstone or limestone, although I later read that many stelae, although they might look as though they have only been carved, have also had the hieroglyphic figures painted in brilliant colours, often with glistening, enamel-like finishes. I was also arrested before some primitive tools, made of copper and other materials, used for carving and painting the stelae.

The date of that particular stele was between 1304 and 1237 B.C., which made it at least 3,300 years old – surely quite a

time span for anyone to have 'glimpsed', if indeed this is what
I had actually done. Yet the stele still looked too recent in
time, and was also much too elaborate. And so I looked back
to exhibit number 1818, dated 2100 B.C. – just as I had
conjectured in my experience, about four thousand years ago.

It was a limestone panel which had been found just north of
Luxor at a place called Nag ed-Deir and was said to have been
worked by a high official called Nyhebsedpepy. Could this
possibly be the period, and the place? But the hieroglyphics,
and the Egyptian progress with writing, were still too
advanced. Even the reign of Nebhepetre Mentuhotpe II was
still too recent – and the site's distance of some five hundred
miles from the Mediterranean Sea was beyond consideration.
I had so clearly looked down from the mountains over a
sand-coloured plateau with the sea glittering in the brilliant
sunlight only some twenty miles away – thirty at the most.
Even if I had been facing east, towards the Red Sea instead of
the Mediterranean, the coast would have been well over a
hundred miles away. Besides there were no rivers there – the
Nubian desert rises up between the valley of the Nile and the
Red Sea coast. So that was that.

Were there earlier stelae on exhibit? An attendant said
there were, on the floor below; but these were only about a
hundred years older. The hieroglyphics were nevertheless
becoming less ornate.

The stelae most like the one I had seen in my experience all
seemed to be of this period of the Middle Kingdom, but then
these were about the earliest finds the museum had – except
for a 'hunter's palette' of the Late Predynastic period dating
back to 3300-3100 B.C., over five thousand years ago, surely
much too early for the standard of civilization I had so clearly
seen? The hieroglyphics on the palette, however, were very
similar to those I had seen on my tablet. But the object on
which they were carved was curved and oblong, not at all the
rectangular tablet I had so clearly seen.

There was very little else of the period which I instinctively
felt to be the one I had visualized in my experience, so we left
the Egyptian rooms and went to look at postcards and
pamphlets. Eventually, inquiry produced *A General Introductory
Guide to the Egyptian Collections in the British Museum,* published
by the Trustees. There were numerous photographs and

illustrations, maps and samples of hieroglyphics, and I had only to turn the pages to know almost instantly that this was the best place to begin what might be a very long search.

After reading the first paragraph of the book's outline of ancient Egyptian history, I found myself drawn to the time of the Middle Kingdom, *circa* 2050-1750 B.C. Then the country was divided into over twenty 'nomes' or provinces, each ruled by a high official called a 'nomarch' – which seemed to apply to the circumstances of my experience – but the standard of writing on funerary stelae of those times was much too advanced. Locations were also too distant from the coast for me to have possibly seen the sea. Yet perhaps the distant expanse of water I had seen was not the sea at all, but a lake – such as Birket Qarun near the Faiyum. It could even have been the Nile itself, and the river one of its numerous tributaries. The circumstances of government seemed applicable, though perhaps even more so to a period just a little earlier, the *Late* Old Kingdom (the Old Kingdom being from the Third to Sixth Dynasties, *circa* 2686-2181 B.C.). At this time . . .

It became customary for high local officials, the nomarchs, to be buried in their provincial localities and not in the neighbourhood of the royal pyramid . . . A new type of tomb was evolved which made use of the cliffs which were near the Nile in Upper Egypt. In such rock-cut tombs no superstructure was built, but the chapel and other rooms in which the mastabas were included in the superstructure were excavated in the cliff-face . . . In the case of very important people the tombs were often provided with terrace platforms, sometimes incorporating elaborate architectural features and formal façades. The approach to the tomb might be . . . by a flight of steps . . . Frequently, inasmuch as the provincial noble felt himself more independent than the noble at court, he showed this independence by including in his tomb [a stela depicting] an account of his [often fulsome] career and personal achievements. (Page 167)

Much of this, together with the way of life at the time –

subsistence from crops and domestic herds – seemed to apply in every detail to what I had visualized. Also, any number of locations would have fitted into 'the picture' I had so vividly seen. But the Egyptians had already developed a calligraphy, though admittedly hieroglyphic, with an alphabet consisting of figures not only for syllables but also for consonants (though vowels were omitted) from as early as about 3100 B.C., the time of the very first Dynasty. Therefore, I had visualized myself at a time prior to any precisely recorded history – this must have been so for me to have felt so despondent about humanity, as I knew it, not having an alphabet which allowed me to express my *abstract* thoughts.

Naturally, very little is known about the unlettered cultures which flourished in Egypt before the 'first truly historical' (Dynastic) period; however, some relics show that there were already some of the characteristics which marked the earliest phases of Egyptian culture in the Dynastic Period. This earlier and almost unrecorded period is termed 'Predynastic' and is described in the terms of European Prehistory as Palaeolithic, Mesolithic and Neolithic. The first possibility for my own visualization seemed contained in . . .

> The first positive evidence of such cultivation comes with the first remains of settlements in the Neolithic period. Occupation-sites of this period have been discovered on the western edge of the Delta, in the Faiyum [so I was brought to the Faiyum again, but much earlier in time] and in Middle Egypt. The inhabitants of these sites clearly lived a settled agricultural life growing crops of cereals and flax, making linen and baskets, crude pottery, and a wide variety of stone and flint tools. Objects from a particularly fruitful site on the northern edge of the Faiyum form the Museum's most important group of Egyptian Neolithic material. (Page 23)

And that is all I have. But life at that time was evidently much as I had seen it depicted. Communities were ruled by 'nomarchs' or their equivalents, though it does not seem to be known whether they became nomarchs by election, appointment or inheritance. The northern cliffs of the Faiyum face almost south-east, but the western end of the escarpment curls in a considerable bay so that it faces north of east at the far extremity. And this, during my search, had suddenly become most important – for I realized that I had visualized the sky and landscape as in the mid-morning, around nine o'clock, and the sea or water had been glittering, so that I must have been facing east. For a long time I searched for possible sites within twenty or thirty miles of the Red Sea, facing east instead of north, but again I could find nothing. So I turned back to that part of the map where the Faiyum was marked and almost at its westernmost end I found that if I turned from the cliffs to descend to a possible village I would be facing a little south of east and, no doubt at that latitude of almost thirty degrees north, into the sun at around nine in the morning. I would also be looking across what is described as a tawny-coloured plateau, between the cliffs of the Faiyum, to an expanse of the Birket Qarun, a lake that on the calm and brilliantly sunny day I had envisaged would no doubt have been glittering even more than the sea itself. And the Birket Qarun is marked between twenty and thirty miles from the western escarpment of the Faiyum, shaped somewhat like a smiling mouth, with the village of Qarun a few miles from its western tip. To the north-west, but only about ten miles from the shores of this lake below sea-level, is the escarpment Gebel Qatrani with a peak of 353 metres (just over 1,100 feet). About twenty miles from the western point of the lake is another peak, Qaret Gahannam, which rises to 224 metres (over 700 feet). Between both is a plateau, Soknopaios, which gradually ranges from near-desert to the rich grounds surrounding the lake. Furthermore, the area is shown to be studded with a number of 'seasonal watercourses'.

And so I now felt convinced that the location of my experience was on the outskirts of the Faiyum, and I had only to look on the second page of my book to find a description of it.

The twenty-first nome comprised the region known as the Faiyum, a natural depression lying a few miles from the Nile Valley to the west of Aphroditopolis and watered by an offshoot of the Nile called the Bahr Yusuf, 'Joseph's River'. The Faiyum, which today has an area of about 850 square miles, was first exploited by the kings of the Middle Kingdom who established their capital not far from its entrance at Itj-towy near the modern El-Lisht. In the north of the Faiyum is a lake, the Birket Qarun, which has always been a haunt of wild fowl and a centre for hunting.

On page 14 . . .

The marshes, which figure so largely in tomb scenes as the haunts of wild fowl and the places for hunting expeditions, were located in the Delta, round the lake in the Faiyum and in those depressions in the Nile Valley near the desert edge in which the flood-waters were trapped after the inundation.

So that my glittering sea could have been not only a lake, but also great expanses of flood-water.

On page 16 . . . 'From Cairo to Edfu the cliffs are mostly limestone.' Thus there were not only cliffs, but limestone from which tablets could easily be cut for stelae. Also . . .

Other stones used to a certain extent as building material were to be found in the immediate neighbourhood of the Nile Valley; chief among these were alabaster, the principal quarry of which was at Hatnub near Al-Amarna in Middle Egypt, basalt, which is found in a number of places throughout the land and which was worked mostly in the Faiyum in the Old Kingdom, and quartzite, a very hard compact species of sandstone, most conveniently quarried in the Gebel Ahmar, to the north-east of Cairo.

The geographical details of the location and the living conditions of the time appeared to fit perfectly; now there was just the matter of timing. It had to be the Neolithic period for . . .

The Early Dynastic Period, in spite of the paucity of its material remains, was undoubtedly a great formative time in which the bases of Egyptian civilization were firmly established. By the end of the Second Dynasty

artistic conventions had been evolved, *hieroglyphic writing
had advanced so far that it quickly became a flexible vehicle for the
transmission of continuous narrative.* (Page 30)

That was at least five thousand years ago. I had sensed that
the time of my experience was at least four thousand years
ago. It had been a figure which had just, as though of its own
accord, come into my head. Had the figure perhaps pertained
to *circa* 4,000 B.C.? Was that any more unlikely than the
incredible confirmation of detail and circumstance I had
discovered so far?

There was one more small detail which might still affect the
timing – some of my tools, small and crude as they might have
been, had been made of copper with wooden and/or ivory
handles. As this was comparable with the late Stone Age in
Europe, was it too early for me to have been using such
implements? The Neolithic culture discovered by Guy
Brunton when excavating Neolithic cemeteries along the Nile
almost nine hundred miles south of the Faiyum is described
as . . .

distinguished by the well-developed types of pottery
produced, the great variety in the tools used, the
extensive use of ivory and shell for ornaments and small
tools, and the burial customs. Burial of the dead was
effected in separate cemeteries away from the village,
whereas in earlier periods the dead were buried in or
near the houses in which they lived. (Page 24)

A little further on the same page . . . 'From graves, the earliest
copper objects found in Egypt have been recovered. The use of
copper was, however, still in its infancy and efficient smelting
of ore had probably not yet begun.'

And so there were my collection of tools, my ivory handle,
at least one copper implement – and burial in rock-tombs
away from the village.

There was still my personal appearance left – tall and slim
with long features and a high forehead, brown skin and a
garment made of a rough linen-like material. They were
already producing linen and leather and other such wear, and
on page 25 I found that . . . 'The bodies found in the early

predynastic cemeteries of *Upper* Egypt show that the typical Egyptian of the time was slimly built with long delicate features ... the men wore beards and long penis-sheaths, features which connect them ethnically with the Libyans.' I had *not* worn a beard, nor a penis-sheath. But in *Lower* Egypt the inhabitants were in many ways similar, 'but their heads were broader. Their burial customs were more elaborate.' On page 26 ... 'The fine flint tools, copper implements, beads of hard stone, and of crude glazed composition which have been found in Lower Egyptian predynastic graves, all testify to a higher standard of culture than that existing contemporaneously in the south.' And again, as though to confirm what had already been written for me before ... 'Nothing certain is known about the political organization in Upper or Lower Egypt during the Early Predynastic Period. It is generally thought that there existed two loose confederations made up of communities which correspond to some extent with later nomes.'

I think I have now quoted enough to show the extraordinary coincidence in detail of historical records and the circumstances in which I saw myself living and working in my Christos Experience – from a 'dream' induced by a simple procedure which takes about twenty minutes. There is, of course, no scientific proof that I had 'remembered an actual past incarnation'; but I have never experienced such a detailed dream in sleep, let alone detail that could be related to an actual time and place in history. If it should be no more than an illusion, at best a type of *conscious* dream, from where did all that detail come, and for what reason? A visualization of some incident in the present, whether factual or fictitious, would have been startling enough; but to have been provided with an 'entertainment' set several thousand miles from where I happened to be, and some four to five thousand years ago, now appears to me to have a good deal more behind it than mere coincidence. The very process of 'dreaming' such cinematic-like visualization is extraordinary, let alone finding that one can afterwards determine its locality and time in history – something that I, at least, have not been able to do with any ordinary dream. That the visualization contained religious conviction was even more overwhelming, for in a section about Neolithic cemeteries on page 24 I found ... 'It is clear that even at that early date the Egyptian idea of life-after-death existed.'

I cannot, of course, prove that it was a revelation or remembrance of a previous incarnation; nor, as with any prophesy of the future, can I await the passing of time to see if any equivalent of a reversed 'foresight' will eventuate. One cannot return to the past in the normally accepted dimension of actual time; one cannot go from the future via the present to the past, for that would be like a river running against its own course. At least, this is the condition that applies to time in the *actual* or outer world; but in that world within, is it possible for the present to revert from the future back into the past, like a river reversing in its own course? Perhaps it is rather like the famous sentence on the Tombos stele of Tuthmosis I (page 4) which describes the Euphrates, a river that flows from north to south instead of south to north like the Nile, as 'that reversed water that goes downstream in going upstream'.

Whether it is a revelation of a previous incarnation or not, I felt after writing *Windows of the Mind* that I wanted to continue investigating the matter, to conduct more experiments with people of considerable intelligence, and perhaps even discover why the procedure did not induce some kind of a visualized experience with *everyone* who tried it. Here then are more examples of those 'worlds within' which I have discovered can confront us – at the same time as man is taking steps to explore outer space and the 'worlds beyond'. We may know a great deal about the universe around us, but what is to be learnt of that possible universe within?

Author's Note

I wrote this second account of my first experience two years after the event, without recourse to my original account (written within a month of the experiment). When the manuscript had been typed into fair copy, the original article arrived from my London agent, but it was too late for my original purpose. However, after reading it through I decided it would be an interesting exercise to compare the two accounts (as I had done once before with Mrs Tedye McDiven; see page 29) to reveal not only how vividly the conscious memory retains this extraordinary experience (in contrast with the elusive quality of the normal dream during sleep), but also how the experience is retained by memory long after ordinary dreams and indeed even most actual events are forgotten.

Naturally, there are a few small discrepancies in detail between the two and I shall comment on these at the end of the piece. But far from detracting from the apparent authenticity (or perhaps I should say verisimilitude, or even veridicality) of the experience, they reveal instead that details can subsequently both appear or 'occur' to the experimentee long after the actual 'event' of the experience – not necessarily all at once, but whenever the experience is considered.

Here, then, is my original account of my first experience, but without most of the extraneous observations made at the time.

I could indeed see something, though it was very vague and rather brown and murky – I was looking up at the spreading tops of pillars in some dimly lit cathedral. This didn't strike me as being in the least unusual; at any time of the day you can close your eyes and all kinds of images, patterns, symbols or pictures will 'come into vision'. At first I considered my cathedral pillars as no more than some kind of auto-suggested image or a form of self-induced daydream. When I was asked, I described the picture; and at the same time it not only seemed to become clearer, though still of a rather dim interior, but either I was ascending towards the ceiling or it was descending towards me. Then I was sure it was the former. I was ascending. I was floating. I was even beginning to move rather rapidly now, though with a steadiness, even a serenity, in the speed of the motion.

Then the roof of the cathedral appeared to open and I could see the sun shining fitfully through varying layers of cloud moving slowly across the sky. Colour began to seep into my 'vision', especially the luminous golds at the edges of clouds. Now I was not just merely gliding, I was soaring, and I said so.

There was a door before me. It was not my own door, however, as the others soon found when I was asked to describe it. It was a double door, arched to a point, church-fashion, and made of vertical slats of wood three to

four inches wide and almost as thick, but roughly made, not
straight as though sawn at a mill, and bound together by
heavy but roughly-made hasps in simple curving patterns.

These doors were set in enormous and immensely thick
walls built from large and rough-hewn stones, grimed and
pitted with age and sun and desert dust. The doors were about
ten feet high and three to four feet wide (the two together).
What was odd about them was that they were the only doors,
the only opening whatsoever, in the huge expanse of wall. Not
only that: as I clearly described at the time, the left door
opened outwards and the right door inwards.

I was told to go inside, and so I prepared myself to enter.
Inside it was pitch black. My eyes had to become accustomed
to the dark after the bright sunshine outside, where I still
stood. What's more, I could *feel* the heat of the sun on my
back.

'What kind of a building is it?' Joy asked.

'Some kind of a mausoleum,' I told them. 'Or a temple.
Something like that.'

'Are you afraid?'

'No.'

'Will you go inside?'

'Yes.'

And I *went* inside. It was immediately very cold. The black
of the darkness spread all round and above me, to an
enormous height. The air was dank. The sun fell a little way
inside the doorway, but not very far; and my shadow, long
and narrow, blocked out most of what was before me – a stone
floor. The floor was not only cold but wet; water was trickling
down a groove carved in the stone floor, a groove that ran from
a bowl-shaped indenture in the centre of what I could now see
was a circular interior. And this groove gradually widened
from a few inches at the centre of the floor to almost the width
of the door, to which it ran, carrying outside the moisture
which dripped from the ceiling . . .

Around the walls were stone sarcophagi. They were not
ornately carved, but on the contrary, rather plain. Several of
them, I knew – knew without being 'told' – contained the
bodies of my predecessors, but predecessors by election and
not by familial descent of birth. My own sarcophagus was
awaiting me, for when I should die, and there were others in a

long line around the huge circumference wall, awaiting those who would succeed me.

I did not have to be told all this by 'someone' appearing in the vision; I instinctively, or intuitively, knew.

'Who do you think you are?'

I was the elected leader of a remote community.

'Are you afraid of where you are?'

'No.' I was both perfectly calm and at peace with myself. I was merely making one of my regular and routine visits to see that the mausoleum, if that's what it was, was in good order. I always did this alone. The mausoleum, or temple, was some distance from the community's 'city', but still I always went unaccompanied and on foot.

Following the book's instructions, Joy asked, 'What do you wear on your feet? Can you *see* your feet?'

I could indeed. Already I had turned, satisfied that the temple-cum-mausoleum was in perfect order, and I was approaching the open door again. Brilliant sunshine outside almost blinded me. As before, some of it fell through the doorway on to the grooved stone floor and, as I approached, it fell also on to my lower legs and feet.

'Can you *see* your feet?' Joy prompted again.

'Yes.'

'What do you have on them?'

'Nothing.'

'Nothing?'

'My feet are bare.'

'You can see them quite clearly?'

'Vividly.'

'What are they like?'

I did not hesitate, and I was not at all perturbed.

'They're black,' I told them. 'My feet are black.'

I could see this quite clearly – as clearly as I normally see my own *white* feet in actuality. I had exaggerated a little; they weren't exactly black, not as black as a Negro's or a Tamil's, say. They were more coffee-coloured. But coloured they most definitely were. I could see the pink of my toenails and also the pink of the edges of my soles and toes. The toes were very long and rather splayed, used to being bare, and coated with fine dust. There were coarse black hairs on my lower legs, and the legs themselves were very thin and very long.

'I am nearly seven feet tall,' I said.

What was I wearing? A kind of loose robe with holes for the neck and arms, knee-length, embroidered with brocade at the hem and on all edges, about three inches wide. The material was of a coarsely woven yet lightweight and soft-feeling kind of hessian. I wore nothing underneath.

'What do you have on your head?'

Nothing. At least, no hat or cap. But there was a band of the same brocade around my head. Above the band, my head was long and attenuated and covered with thick, coarse, curly black hair, fairly short-cropped. On the third finger of my right hand – brown-skinned, pink on the palms and under the fingernails – I wore a very large golden ring with the largest blue stone, probably a sapphire, I had ever seen. In my ears I wore elaborately carved ivory ear-rings inserted through pierced lobes. In my nose I wore very small carved ivory ornaments, as large as modestly sized buttons or cuff-links. These were linked together and my nose was also pierced between the nostrils to hold them. These ornaments – ring, ear-rings, nose-pieces – were, like the brocaded band around my head, insignia of my position or office. I was perfectly accustomed to wearing them without any discomfort whatsoever, and knew that I had been used to them for a good many years.

I was thin and tall, but my weight and size were normal for my kind. I could see my face quite clearly. It too was long and thin, but with finely chiselled features. The lips and eyes were very large, the nose long and narrow. It was both very different from my own 'present' face and yet at the same time still bore some resemblance to it.

I was *inside* that body and I could feel it move, and feel it 'feeling' the cold inside the mausoleum and the heat of the sun outside, just exactly as I could with my own, or present, body.

But now I was outside again. I was standing just outside the mausoleum with its huge rough-hewn walls looming up behind me. Before me the earth spread wide and flat, falling away gradually in a great expanse of near-desert that was almost blinding in the sun. And just as blinding was the narrow yet deep, dark blue, almost black river flowing, with only slight curves here and there, to the far horizon and becoming lost in the haze of heat and dust. Here and there throughout this immense landscape before me were small oases with, from this distance, toy-like fronds that were palms. Nearer, but still below me, was a 'city'.

It was *my* city. I was its elected leader. This was perfectly clear to me. I had not 'inherited' it, through any family lineage of kings or chieftains; I had been elected, as was the custom. But I was *not* one of them – I came from different stock. My 'people' were much smaller in stature, and darker in skin, than I. When I died and was buried in my sarcophagus in the mausoleum behind me, another would be elected to take my place. And this would always be so. I did not have to be told this; I knew.

My city was a conglomeration of small, white, circular, dome-roofed, stone and mud huts clustered together so that only pedestrians could pass between, even if there had been vehicles of any kind (which there weren't). In the centre of the city was one taller building, only about twice the height of all the rest; this was my 'palace'. It was bright and clean, but spare and simple in line and design. If anything it was almost austere. And now I was walking back to it.

I walked through the 'streets' no wider than paths between the houses of my subjects who, at that time of day, were working in irrigated fields. Women and children hid themselves, as was the custom decreed by the law of the community, for only fully-grown men were permitted to look upon me.

I entered the palace, its large, oval entry-hall cool and bright and pale green all around me. Servants, perhaps half a dozen or so of them, came from outer rooms to bow with folded arms and ask me if I wanted food and water. I didn't and, with a customary gesture of one hand, bade them leave.

I walked the full length of the hall and then turned left through a narrow archway into a small antechamber, brightly lit by sunlight pouring down through a window without glass. In the centre of the room was a stone desk, about the size of an ordinary office desk, plain but beautifully made of rich and gleaming stone or marble.

A backless chair was made of the same material, placed so that the light would fall over my shoulder on to the large stone tablet on which I had been working for several of my twenty-eight or so years. The hieroglyphics were beautifully executed, in precise, neat rows, and brightly coloured.

But as I sat down to look through (rather than just *at*) them yet once again, I felt, not despair, but a kind of resigned regret that hieroglyphics served to communicate only the visual and the physical aspects of those things I wished to write about; they completely failed to cope with the abstractions which concerned me so much more. But no other form of written communication had yet been invented. There was no alphabet. I knew that there would be one some day, at some time still in the far-distant future, just as I knew that Jesus Christ had not yet been born. But there would be no way for me in that lifetime, as I was *then*, to communicate any of the many things I wanted to record. I had to content myself with the purely concrete aspects of life – and these were such a small part of my lifetime experiences, or even of myself as a person, which I craved to recount for posterity. But this would have to wait – *for some other time*.

I was not at all depressed at the thought; it was merely one more thing that I knew I must accept. Sometime, somewhere, a way would be found for mankind to write of his 'inner' life, his innermost thoughts, of his hopes and fears and aspirations. But this, as yet, was still denied me. I would lead a placid and contented enough life, living to a 'ripe old age' of about thirty-five or so, which was a good lifetime for those days in those parts.

But then a strange thing happened. Having had this revealed to me, my mind, my spirit, my other self, 'overself', call it what you will, suddenly seemed to emerge and float free from the body of my former self, withdrawing to stand in the archway and look back at my former body as it still sat there in the antechamber, head supported on clenched hand like Rodin's 'Thinker', and that body in turn still gazing at the hieroglyphic tablet. At the same time I again became aware of being, in actuality, supine on a twentieth-century living-room floor.

I was back.

In my second account, I completely omitted the first vague and 'murky' images of a cathedral's interior that I recounted in the original version. This is not just a small and fleeting detail which can easily be overlooked; in some thirty subsequent experiments several experimentees have also had such a fleeting 'image' to begin with, usually of some easily recognizable scene in the present, which seems to be a kind of 'springboard' into the actual and ensuing vision of the experience. Indeed there are sometimes two such springboards. The second is usually rather longer in duration and sometimes seems to be much earlier in time, before the experimentee's own lifetime, so that it may have the appearance of being a glimpse into what could be regarded as a fairly recent incarnation. Sometimes there is a third and even longer scene in the present time, of about the same duration as an experience in the past; so that the experimentee concludes the experiment feeling he has failed to see anything of a previous incarnation, even if he *has* succeeded in enjoying an 'entertainment' of various scenes much like an ordinary dream. If such a person were taken for a further experiment, or even several, he might eventually succeed – through numerous 'springboards' – in visualizing something in a time prior to his own present life experience.

Reverting to my own first glimpse of a cathedral, I must admit that this might have influenced my image of the doors in the cliff-face being a similar Gothic shape; at the same time, however, the familiar Gothic of the cathedral in the 'springboard' image may have prepared the way for acceptance of the doors in the cliff-face being the same shape – a shape which otherwise might have seemed unlikely or even beyond credibility. Note also that the image of the cathedral was vague and 'murky'; but once the setting of the mausoleum had appeared, vision became as brilliant as in any scene observed in the brightest of sunlight.

In the first account I had distinctly seen the double doors of the cliff-face mausoleum open in opposite directions, the right opening inwards and the left outwards. Other details of the doors' construction are also missing in the second account, probably for two reasons: first, in writing the second account I was impatient to deal with the emotional part of the experience rather than the material details; and secondly, after two years some of the less important details are bound to be overlooked.

Now come the sandals. In the first account I recorded being bare-footed. Yet, when walking through the British Museum, a pair of sandals had arrested my attention. As soon as I noticed this, I did not have to 'think it out' in any way whatsoever, for the explanation was immediately apparent. It was not a case of such sandals merely being the vogue at the time of my visualization. I *knew* – and knew instantly – that I had indeed been bare-footed as I stood outside the doors of the mausoleum, so that when I entered my feet had 'felt' the cold stone floor of the dank interior. What I had omitted in both accounts – but which I knew I had done in the experience quite automatically, and no doubt without having said so – was that I stepped out of the sandals at the entry of the mausoleum, as required by custom, then stepped back into them again when returning outside, *pausing* long enough to look down over the vivid landscape beyond me – or long enough to step back into the sandals – before proceeding down the long flight of carved stone steps to my 'city' and 'palace' below. At the time of the experiment, I had been asked about my feet as soon as I had emerged from the mausoleum, just before stepping into my sandals. Immediately afterwards I was asked a considerable number of questions concerning my apparel, finishing with my headgear, just at a time when I was astonished by the landscape before me and was 'wondrous' and impatient to describe this instead. This is something I have observed frequently in other experimentees when they are asked to describe details which have already receded beyond their present 'activity', and have been replaced by much more interesting details or events.

My height? I think there is little discrepancy here between 'about seven feet tall' and 'well over six feet'. But at the same time I am sure I would be quite astonished if I suddenly found myself, say, six-feet-three instead of my actual five-feet-eleven. These extra four inches might indeed feel a good deal more – as you will experience for yourself if you put on a pair of four-inch heeled and platformed shoes.

Lastly, the second account continues a little longer than the first. I see myself walk to the window of my study or antechamber and look down into the small courtyard with its pool and potted palm or two (actually two), whereas in the first account 'my mind, my spirit, my other self, "overself", call it what you will, suddenly seemed to emerge and float free from the body of my former self, withdrawing to stand in the archway and look back at my former body as it still sat there in the antechamber, head supported on clenched hand like Rodin's "Thinker", and that body in turn still gazing at the hieroglyphic tablet.' In the more recent *consideration* of the experience, this 'other self' had waited a little longer and had seen that 'former body' rise from the stone stool at the stone desk, walk over to the paneless window, lean on its sill and gaze down into the courtyard. It is now interesting to consider whether, if I dwelt on this apparent ending of the experience a little longer again, I would 'see' some *fresh* activity, or have further circumstances revealed to me. Somehow I doubt it. I *feel* that this proceeding to the window was the *final* end of the scene, which had previously been interrupted by two factors: my interrogator asking what else I could see and my becoming acutely aware of 'being, in actuality, supine on a twentieth-century living-room floor'.

But now we must pass on to other experimentees, who are no doubt not only still sifting and interpreting the recollected details of their own experiences but are also finding that new details are continually being revealed to them.

Part Two
Windows of Other Mansions

Casting the body's vest aside,
My soul into the boughs doth glide.
ANDREW MARVELL, *An Historical Poem*

Mrs Tedye McDiven

I had already carried out all the experiments I felt I needed for my one book on the Christos Experience, when two good friends of mine expressed their interest in the matter and their desire to try it for themselves. Both are artists of considerable talent and reputation here in Western Australia – Bryant paints and teaches art at a teachers' training college and Tedye is known for her ceramics and sculpture – and it occurred to me that I should indeed avail myself of this double opportunity, if only to see if the artistic temperament and talent would provide any significant difference in the type or quality of visualizations experienced. When Leo and I arrived at their new and artistically decorated home, we found a mutual friend there – Dr Salek Minc, a heart physician, art collector and critic of note in Western Australia. Salek, I well knew, was sceptical about the experiment; but he promised in his rather whimsical way that he would not interfere if he were allowed to stay as an observer, with a certain amount of scientific interest in the procedure. Naturally, we agreed.

Mrs Tedye McDiven, née Elkington, was born in Perth, Western Australia, on May 20th, 1925. She is of slim build and average height with delicate features and gracefully feminine movements, and she looks a good ten years younger than her actual age. During the Second World War she served in the Signals Section of the Women's Australian Auxiliary Air Force for two and a half years, before meeting and marrying her husband, Bryant McDiven, from the state of Victoria, who was also in the Australian Air Force. They now have two sons, both married and talented in their own particular fields.

Tedye was the most eager of my three volunteers, but despite their willingness and genuine interest, I was afraid that the experiments would not succeed that evening, for a heavy storm – with torrential rain, thunder and lightning and great howling gusts of wind – was raging. The noise at times was almost deafening and, knowing how the voices of experimentees usually become very low during their experience, I wondered if anything much would be audible on the tape-recorder when we came to replay it. I also feared that such noisy weather might well be suggestive to the experimentees and induce them to 'see' the same kind of weather, though perhaps by day as well as by the actual night, instead of entirely different skies. Moreover, I had never attempted even two experiments in the one evening before, and so I felt at the outset that attempting three would be unwise and might prove impossible. However, we were all present and the equipment was ready, so I decided to make one attempt in any case, hoping the others might be prepared to wait for another occasion if necessary. Dr Minc went first (see page 43), but Tedye's was such an unusual experience that I have chosen to record it before the others.

It was a little after nine o'clock when we began with Tedye. She lay on the thick pile of the white carpet in their heated living-room, while Leo massaged her ankles and I massaged her forehead. She managed the preliminary exercises with ease, though at first she was a little hesitant, even apprehensive. However, in very little time she felt accustomed to the stretching and shrinking exercises, and she appeared quite self-confident and unafraid by the time the visualization exercises commenced. She was a little uncertain with details at first, perhaps because she had chosen to describe the front door of their new home, but she soon progressed with descriptions which, of course, we were able to verify later. Her subsequent description of the house's surroundings was even more vivid.

Despite the weather – the occasional peals of thunder and vivid flashes of lightning, the whining wind and the gusts of rain hurtling against the window panes – she then made the 'ascent' not only with ease but on a 'calm and sunny day', describing her widening surroundings as she ascended.

She had no difficulty in changing the entire city of Perth and its environs from day to night and back again to day, and had no sooner started the 'descent' than she said she could see land. The Indian Ocean which she had visualized previously had now entirely disappeared and she could no longer see water at all – only the land. When I told her she could now let herself go just wherever she wished, she had the extraordinary feeling that without any effort at all she could instantly leave Earth altogether, and it was only by restraining herself that she descended to the land she could still 'see'. This, however, she only told me now at the time of writing.

Having descended, she found what appeared to be a safe place for her to set foot on. It was somewhere in a very old city, she said, which had appeared below her. The streets were all old and there were no signs of such things as automobiles or electric light wires or any of the paraphernalia of modern times. The particular street she found herself in was wide, with trees planted at regular intervals along its pavements. When I asked her to describe some of the buildings she could see, she said that she felt she was in the Italian city of Florence. She was wearing a pale blue dress of light material, made rather loosely into a garment tied at the waist. Her feet were bare and she didn't think she had any other kind of apparel. She said she was fourteen years of age.

She was walking along the street, almost skipping rather, at first she thought by herself, but then she knew, and could actually see, that she had a little dog with her. She was not, however, accompanied by any other human being, even though there were many other people dressed rather like her in the street. She was carrying some kind of a toy that she played with as she went along; from her description of it, no matter how puzzled she seemed by both its appearance and the manner in which it worked, we others listening to her presumed it to be a yoyo. However, when this was suggested to her, she said no, not at all, it was something entirely different that she had never seen in actuality and she could not tell us properly how it worked. It was just that she was playing with it, she said, and it was a very pleasing kind of toy to have.

By this time she was quite sure that she was in Florence – though not the modern Florence she had visited briefly a short time before – for she was able, she said, to recognize some of the main buildings. The actual street she was in, however, was not at all familiar to her from her visit and could have been in any number of cities in Europe. But, though she could not explain why, she just *knew* it to be Florence. It was a beautiful evening and she was enjoying herself walking and skipping along the street which was quite unfamiliar to her in reality, but which in her 'experience' she obviously knew very well (although she did feel an urge to allow herself to be drawn up and off again, in a north-eastly direction she thought).

She was puzzled by the fact that although she felt she knew a good many of the people passing by, she did not speak to any of them, nor they to her. Indeed, she said, she could not *hear* anything at all, but on the contrary found everything extraordinarily silent, like a film without sound. At first I thought this was probably due to the noise of the storm raging outside in actuality; but when I suggested this, she immediately discounted it, saying she could hear *that* noise all right, but she felt that she could hear nothing at all of what she was so clearly seeing in an entirely different location and time. Even the dog was silent alongside her; surely, she added, this was rather unusual for a dog of any kind.

At this point, I wish to say that I have not yet quoted anything from the tape-recording we made of one of the best and most unusual experiences I have witnessed. I had wanted to include Tedye's experience in my first book on the Christos Experiment, *Windows of the Mind,* even if it had to be inserted while the book was in preparation, but I was prevented by illness from doing this straight away. Afterwards there was other work to do and somehow the matter was overlooked.

Then, in 1972, bound for The Netherlands under the auspices of an Australian Literary Fund Fellowship, I resolved to see to the inclusion of Tedye's experience in the book during the long sea voyage. But once at sea I found I had not put the tape in the luggage; and so with great regret I decided that I would have to omit it after all.

Later in the voyage, however, it occurred to me that it

would be a valid and worthwhile test of the experience if I wrote to Tedye telling her what had happened and asking her if she would write out an account of her experience. At least this would show that the experience could be remembered over a period of six to eight months, whereas an ordinary dream is usually forgotten well before six to eight days, or even in less than six to eight hours.

This she consented to do, and eventually I received her letter in Holland. As I had hoped, it was of great interest, for it showed that the experience was not only much more durable than any dream but also than most actual incidents that take place during a lifetime.

In a covering letter dated Monday, February 7th, 1972, when we were on board the *Achille Lauro* in the Pacific between Wellington in New Zealand and Punta Arenas in Chile, she wrote: 'Gerry, I wrote this immediately on receiving your first letter, but thought there was no point in sending it weeks before you arrived in Holland.'

In a moment I will quote her description verbatim, but first a word about a small sketch, which she also sent me, of the main surroundings in which she remembered having 'found' herself during the experience (see page 31). It is interesting to note that at the time of writing, fifteen months later, she does not remember having previously made the sketch – but said that she could, if required, draw it all again in every detail. In other words, her memory of the 'place' she was sketching remained unblemished, whereas her memory of the actual deed of making the sketch had already vanished.

But here now is her written description:

Gerry, I shall attempt to retell you in a reasonably coherent manner (I hope) of my experience. This will not be easy because I already find I want to tell you everything at the one moment.

From the time when you suggested I might fly, I found this sensation extremely easy – not in the sense of a Chagall figure flying over housetops, etc., more of a feeling of the releasing of one's essence, soul, essential self – whatever you might like to term it.

In retrospect I feel there may have been a slightly conscious desire to go to Florence, which I did, but the eventual withdrawal (north-east was the feeling) of going to Greece was completely uncontrolled is the only way I can perhaps describe it.

My awareness of Florence, however, and myself being there was quite different from (no, before saying that, perhaps it was not) I was going to say when one is actually in a place, they are not aware of themselves from the back and the side – you are aware of your physical being but not quite so three-dimensionally perhaps. And yet when you actually think back to an occasion – whether it be in the butcher's shop or Teheran – I suppose your memory of the occasion is of your complete self – back, front, sides and all – know what I mean? Anyway, my awareness of myself on that occasion was a sense of being an observer of myself as well as the participant. My blue frock had a delightful floating quality which I could feel and also see. My dog was a puppy, a joyful carefree animal, but the whole experience was virtually without sound. By that I mean the dog did not bark and, although there were people around – in Greece many, many of them – nobody spoke to me directly, although I had a feeling of belonging and the knowledge that they knew I was there.

In Florence (I use this name because that was where I thought I was, but it did not resemble any place I had actually seen when in Florence) – the street was quite long – tall trees on either side – a made roadway but for walking – no motor car or vehicle whatsoever, and my feeling was that although I enjoyed being there, I was being drawn away north-east as I said before – here again I say Greece because that was my identification of it at the time – but here again it was no place within my experience, actual experience! I was a young girl in Florence and I seemed to remain that way.

In Greece the place I entered was very beautiful – at the top of a rise – walled around – with what I then called a water-bath – within the walls – rectangular in shape.

From the grounds near the gate where I entered, I could see the surrounding countryside – there were purple grapes hanging on the vines which looked really luscious, but I did not eat them. On entering the building

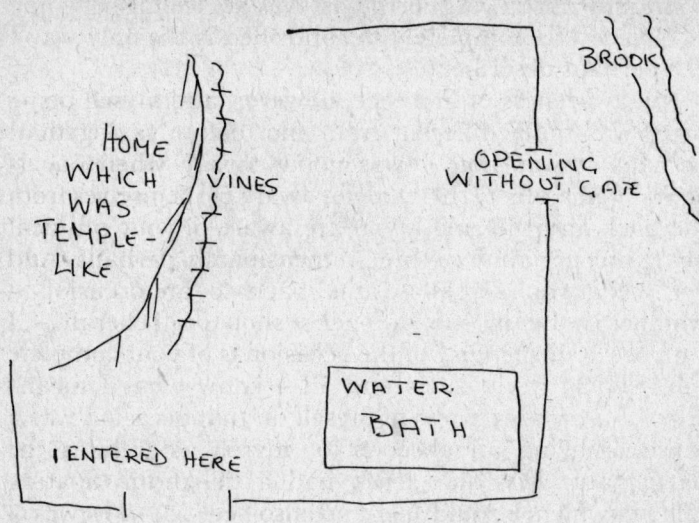

or temple, my intention seemed to be to go to *my* room
which was most beautiful – very high ceiling with
exquisite gold scroll-work upon the walls – which were
marble, also the floor. There was a single bed in the room
– and a tall window looking out over the water-bath. A
book with a delightful inscription upon it was here, but if
I knew then what it was I cannot remember now. Also a
delightful little animal was resident but not a known one
to me. A feeling of happiness and freedom was very
strong all this time until I went out through the wall to
the brook, but I then had a sensation of not wanting to go
beyond that point, and returned to the security of the
walled garden (perhaps symbolic of our home at this
time – I really couldn't say). Although I didn't want to
go beyond the brook, I still felt a drawing to the north-
east as although any place was open or available for
my enjoyment and inspection – not really 'inspection',
just pleasure I suppose. All this time I was still aware of
lying upon the floor but conscious of not wanting to
impose my experiences upon others, who were not also
enjoying them – a little as one might feel after travelling
and not wanting to bore one's friends with stories of
places they have never been to. When the knowledge is

there that the others have also seen these places the situation is rather different. The memory of that experience is exactly the same, I now realize, as it would be after an actual journey or sojourn in a place. One recalls the overall scene very clearly, and certain details very clearly, just as I can recall the Monet lily-pond (or painting of it) so very well, and the stairs leading down to it in the gallery in Paris, but I cannot recall the front façade of that building, only the side – although I am sure I went in through a front doorway – so it is when I recall this (or that) experience – but it is more as if I didn't take notice of it then than that I cannot remember it now.

It is now well over a year since this was written and very nearly two years since the experiment was performed and it is interesting to compare the account with the tape-recording of the experiment – which was found a few days ago. The beginning, unfortunately, has been wiped out; but luckily this is only a little of Tedye's description of what she was 'seeing' in the Florentine street while she was skipping along with her dog and playing with her toy.

The tape begins . . .

'. . . and it goes up and down as I go along.'

'You're running along, are you?' I asked.

'Yes.' She was still by herself, she said; still not hearing sounds of any kind, though her dog was still with her.

'Do you think the dog has a name?'

She was silent for some little while, thinking about this. I was about to tell her not to bother about it, fearing that it might terminate what was obviously proving a very vivid and interesting experience, when she said, 'I don't know, really. He doesn't need a name. But if he does have one, I think I call him "Tooli".'

(I telephoned her just a few days ago about this, and – without any preamble whatsoever, not even referring to the experience – I asked her how she would spell the name, presuming it could be spelt Tooly, or Tooley, or something like that. She knew instantly what I was referring to and, again with little hesitation, said that if it was spelt at all in the modern way, *Tooli* was how she saw it. As for the animal itself, she said that it was still as vivid in her memory as if it had actually lived in her present lifetime. This, she also said, was how the entire experience seemed to her in retrospect – not only much more vivid in every detail than any dream, but also far more than most actual experiences or events. It was, she said, even more a part of what she would consider a 'life experience' than most of her present life's events, whole blocks of which were already beyond recall or only a dim memory.)

She had not had the dog in actuality; indeed, she had never had a dog.

'And you're just playing with him?' I had asked on the tape.

'Yes,' she replied.

'Do you live near here?'

'I don't think I live anywhere, really.'

At this point, the sound of their cuckoo-clock striking ten times is clearly audible on the tape, indicating that about three-quarters of an hour had already passed since we had begun the preliminaries of the experiment. It did not affect her in the slightest; she was concentrating hard on answering my query. Finally she said, 'I think I had better go back to Greece. It's safer.'

This vacillation came as a surprise from someone so practical as Tedye; she had mentioned earlier that the 'landscape' towards which she had found herself descending might have been Greece, but a little later had resolved that it was Italy and, more specifically, Florence. However, I was used to such rapid transpositions and I had long since learned that it was far better to concentrate on any emotion that was being described rather than details, even details which might possibly help to determine a locality. Other indications of this are invariably provided, but the precise sense of any particular emotion can be quickly lost.

So, 'In what way is it safer?' I asked.

'I'm not alone there. My family is there to look after me.'

At one stage, she had mentioned vaguely visualizing people around her, wearing the same kind of garments and hairstyle as she herself, but in white instead of blue; and most of them (the women and girls at any rate) had long hair. And so I asked, 'Are these the same people you saw before?'

'Yes.'

'Still in white, with this long hair?'

'Yes.'

'Is it a city, a courtyard, or what?'

'It's on top of a hill.'

'And the ground you are standing on, what is it like?'

'White.'

'White? It's marble?' She had also mentioned standing on marble before.

'Yes.'

'In slabs? Or even?'

'Yes.'

'No steps up or down?'

'Tiles.'

These few words show that she was not to be diverted, let alone have anything suggested to her.

'And the people there, are they looking at you?'

'It is just – I belong to them.'

'Oh, I see. Yes. How old are you there?'

'I'm still wearing the blue frock.'

'Is it the *same* blue frock?'

'Yes.'

'Do you have shoes with it?' I deliberately tried to suggest them to her, but her reply was . . .

'No. I am bare-footed.'

'And can you see your feet? Are they pale, or brown, or . . .'

'Pale pink.'

They were also, she said, much smaller than they were in reality. She had no rings or bracelets on her fingers or wrists, although in actuality she was wearing both and also a wristwatch. She had pink cheeks, she said, which she does not have in actuality; and long hair which again she does not have. Its colour was brown; which does happen to be the colour of her hair in real life. Could she see the colour of her eyes at all? She thought about this for a moment or two, but the answer was no.

'And the features, are they still the same?'

'It isn't *me*!' She meant as she was in actual life.

'It *isn't* you?'

'It doesn't *look* like *me*.'

'It feels familiar, even if it isn't you?'

'Oh yes,' she said instantly. 'It *is* me, yes.'

She explained afterwards that she meant that she herself

was embodied in the little girl she could see so clearly, but who bore no resemblance whatsoever to her in the present reality.

'When you say long hair, how long is it? To your shoulders, or to your waist?'

'No, it is a little past my shoulders.'

'What are you doing now, standing still or walking along?'

'No. Still skipping, running.'

'And are you alone?'

'Yes.'

'Or with anybody in particular?'

'No, I'm by myself.'

'Do you see anybody you know?'

She was silent for a while; then said, 'No.'

'They are all strangers?'

'No. No, they're not *strangers*. I know them.'

'Oh, you do know them? But there is nobody you know particularly? No family, no parents? Or brothers and sisters?'

'Oh, yes. They are *all* family.'

There were a lot of them, she said, all around a pool that was more an ornamental pool than a swimming pool, although it was used as a water-bath. It was oblong in shape, set apart from the house with its oblong walls, and the whole establishment overlooked wide rolling plains. It was spring, or summer, for there was a lot of green in the landscape. There was also white which was the outcroppings of rock. Then she said, with sudden delight, 'I can go up and down *any*where!'

I had thought she had meant in the air while skipping or running, but she had meant that she could go backwards and forwards, wherever she wanted to, over the landscape.

'But I don't think I'll go,' she said. 'Where I was, it's safer.'

'Where? In Greece?'

'Yes.'

'Have you seen this place in Greece before?'

'No.'

'Have you seen anything like it?'

'No.'

'You don't know whereabouts it is? Is it Athens? Over to the east? The west? Or to the north?'

Almost instantly she said, 'To the north.' For a moment she thought she could see ocean, but then she said, 'No. No, it's

not. There's all land around. There is no ocean anywhere.'
She couldn't see if there were any other towns or villages in the
area because of the wall all round. So I said, 'Oh, I see. You
can't go to the exit, say? If you wanted to go home, where
would you go?'

'I *am* home,' she said firmly.

Then, after a little while, she went on to say that if she went
out of the door 'a terribly big door, much bigger than I am',
she would come to a very large hall. 'It's a very happy place,'
she said. 'Everybody is terribly confident and secure.' When I
asked her how many people she could see, she said, 'Just two
sitting on a . . . I don't know what it is. It is just part of the
marble, and it is all shaped.' There were no cushions; the two
people were just sitting on the carved marble. But then she
said there were more people in the place, men outside, women
inside. They didn't take much notice of her. 'They just sort of
know I am there, and *I* know that *they* are there.' One of them
made her a doll, very soft, with fair curly hair, shortish, that
must have been real hair as it was so soft. When I asked her
how big the doll was, she merely gestured with her hands and
said ambiguously, 'The right size.' Yes, it was dressed – in
pink. 'But I think I'd rather have my dog.' It was still there?
And was it the same dog? 'Yes' to both questions.

Again she was quiet for a while, as though completely
preoccupied with both doll and dog; but then she suddenly
said, 'I can go *any*where and see *any*thing!' And she was
obviously delighted. 'There is a beautiful book, and it has got
exquisite drawings in it. But nothing that I have ever seen
before. They're drawings, but they're . . . *foreign*. An angel,
and a fairy.'

'You have never seen those kind of drawings, or have you?'

'No. But it is a beautiful book, and it's got a beautiful cover
– sort of very soft leather.'

'A big one, or small?'

'Big. A bit too big.'

'Has it been printed, or are all these drawings originals?'

'No, they are originals.'

'And do you know what they are on? On paper, or
papyrus?'

'On *beaut*iful paper. On very uneven paper, uneven at the
edges.'

'Is the paper white, or not?'

'It is a creamy colour, and they have sewn it together in the middle.'

'Do these drawings have any captions under them or . . .'

'No.'

'Is there any text with them?'

'No. I can't read it.'

'So you can't see if there is any text with them?'

'No.'

'Just drawings. On the leather cover, is there a title or not?'

'Yes,' she said, quite readily. 'It's in gold. But I can't read it.' She was silent for a moment; and then, quite suddenly, like a young girl rather pleased with herself, she said, 'Yes, I can! It is something like "Linnen", but I don't know what it means.' The title was in letters she could read, like our present alphabet, and she could see each one as clearly as if it were a real book in her real hands. But she couldn't read it or spell it, she only *knew* it.

Was that the only book, or were there others?

'There are lots of others; but I haven't looked at them yet, because I like this one.'

'Have you looked in this one before?'

'Yes, often.'

'It's familiar to you?'

'Oh, yes.'

'Do you think many of the others are familiar, or is this one your favourite?'

'Yes, I like this one best, because I know what it is.'

'Do these books belong to your family?'

'They belong to this house. And I am living in it.'

'And you have your parents with you?'

'I don't know.'

'Do you know who owns this house?'

'No.'

'Do you think you are a servant there?'

'I don't know. I just live there.'

'Do you have to do anything in the house? A particular duty? Or do you have to study?'

'Yes, sometimes I have to study, but I like to play with my dog. What I have to study is very difficult,' she said, 'but I don't think I enjoy it.'

'Is it menial or mental?'

'Mental.'

Could she see who taught her?

'No, but there are more who are being taught.' She thought that it could possibly be a kind of school, like a boarding school. There were other pupils, both boys and girls, but they were all older than she. They were all, also, related to her, though some of them were only distantly related. If it was a family establishment, then it was a 'family' in the larger sense of the word, including uncles and aunts and cousins, 'because I know them all well, I like them, but I don't take much notice of them.'

Did she think she had a name? There was silence for a while, and she looked puzzled.

'No,' she finally said. 'I don't hear anyone call.' It was not only that she didn't hear anyone call her, she then said, but she still didn't hear any sounds. Then it suddenly occurred to her that it was as though she were deaf and wouldn't hear anything even if they did call her.

Did she know the names of any of the others or not?

'I would have to try,' she said, and for some little while she was obviously doing this, but with no result.

'Are you happy where you are?' I asked her.

'Oh, yes,' she said instantly.

'And you are still about fourteen?'

She was. Did she have a particular room in the building? She did. Could she describe it?

'It's all white. And I like being there.' It was not a very big room, 'just the right size', and it contained only a bed; but the room was very beautiful, overlooking water and the rolling plains. It was her very own room; she didn't share it with anyone. (This was not wishful thinking, for she had been an only child and, as she said afterwards, she would have been only too happy in her actual life to have had a brother or sister share her room with her. In this other life, however, this did not apply, although she was still conscious of her real self in her actual life; here she was totally different, and she did not want to share her room with anyone else.)

Did it have any other special things in it?

'No. Only on the wall. There were beautiful things on the wall. They are sort of drawings in gold, on all the walls.'

Would she be able to draw them in actuality?

'Yes,' she said. 'They are so beautiful.'

They were in gold, and not any other colour. Where would she put her clothes? She didn't have any, only those she had on. It was still the same blue frock. If she had to change it, for it to be laundered, then she would have to put on a white one, like the others wore. She did not own the white one, only the blue. She felt that the blue one was intended to set her apart somehow, perhaps because she didn't hear. That was why only the blue one was hers, and only she had a blue one. The others were always all the same, in white robes. And then, quite suddenly, she said, 'I brought my blue one from Florence.'

So there was obviously a reason for Florence appearing to her after all. Yes, she said, she had gone there for a holiday. She had stayed with friends there, but somehow it was 'dark'. She had liked being in Florence, but she preferred to be in Greece. She was happier in Greece, in this establishment. She could, if she wished, return to Florence, where now she thought she had come from originally, but she was a little frightened of doing so. She was quite at home, and content, where she was here in Greece. And then, again quite suddenly, she made a rather strange statement.

'I don't want to go to England either.'

'You don't?' I asked, and she shook her head. 'If you went to England, how would you go?' I was curious to hear what mode of transport she would describe.

'I'd have to walk,' she said.

'Oh? And how did you get to Florence?'

She went by ship, a tiny one that stayed close to the shore. No, it didn't have engines, it had oars. It was rather beautiful, but she didn't like ships.

She was silent again for a while, and so I said, 'You don't?' And then I thought I would try to find out more about the establishment in Greece in which she so obviously spent most of her time. 'Do you know what you are studying?'

'It seems to have something to do with the stars, but it is awfully difficult.'

'Do you think it is a kind of navigation, or astronomy? Or astrology?'

'Yes,' she said ambiguously, 'but I don't like it.'

When I tried to make her be a little more specific, she said that it didn't have anything to do with prediction. 'It is very serious. You have to learn it, otherwise I wouldn't know.'

Did she learn anything else? No. Did she do any ballet, or dancing? No, although the others danced. Did she play music of any kind? No, she couldn't hear it, which was also why she didn't dance like the others did. 'But I play,' she said. 'I have a marvellous time.' And then, without a pause, she suddenly said, 'There are lots of grapes, but I don't eat them.'

'White grapes, or red grapes?'

'No, they are dark. Purple.'

Didn't she like them? Or wasn't she allowed to eat them?

'They are just beautiful to look at. I can see another animal.'

'What kind of animal?'

This perplexed her and for a moment she didn't know what to answer. Eventually she said, 'I don't know. He's rather lovely. He's got a tail, and he's got ears. And he's got a soft brown . . . but I don't know what he is! He's got little hoofs.'

I had become accustomed to experimentees seeing unusual, unfamiliar animals of all kinds and sizes. A later experiment with a Moroccan friend revealed enormous monsters unlike any animals he had ever seen, even in illustrations of prehistoric animals.

'What colour is his skin?' I asked.

'Brown. Soft brown. Softish, short hair.'

'You haven't seen this kind of animal in reality?'

'No.'

'You think it is a local animal, or . . .'

'Oh, yes! He lives here. He didn't really come through the gate. But I'm not frightened either.'

'Is the animal big or small?'

And again she said ambiguously, 'He is a good size,' meaning, she told me afterwards, that he was fairly large, about the size of a deer.

'What is a good size?' I asked at the time.

'Well, he is just about up to me,' she said, meaning that it was almost as tall as she was.

'Is it your own? Your pet?'

'No, but he is a nice animal – he's friendly. And I'd rather go down the road. I'm going there, through the gate. Yet I really think that I should stay.'

'Is it still day-time, or is it night-time?'

'Day-time, but I don't think I'll stay there.'

'What kind of day?'

'Very pleasantly bright .green.' And I couldn't help wondering if that would be an apt description for a Greek early summer day.

'But you don't think you'll stay there?'

She was silent again for a while; then, almost reluctantly, she said, 'I'd better go back.'

'You've been there before?'

'I can come back to *here,*' she said, meaning the present and her own house in real life, 'but I don't want to.'

I told her she must please herself, especially if she thought she had seen enough. She said she could go on and on, as she very much wanted to do, but she was also aware that Bryant was awaiting his turn, and that perhaps the other three of us might – of all things – be finding her account becoming tiresome.

'I'll go again another day,' she said.

'You'll come back here now?'

'I don't want to.'

'What do you see?'

'I'm going to my bedroom,' she said, meaning the bedroom in the Greek establishment. 'I'm very tired. I want to go to sleep.'

'Are you still awake?' I asked, a little afraid that she might go to sleep and be embarrassed if we had to wake her. Apart from this, it would be a pity for any experimentee to fall asleep, so losing awareness of his whereabouts and circumstances.

'Yes,' she said. 'But I'd rather go to sleep to come back.'

I thought I would have one more try just before she chose to end the experiment.

'You still haven't got a name?' I asked.

'No,' she said, and shortly afterwards she opened her eyes.

That is the end of the tape. She thought she had been undergoing the actual experience for ten to fifteen minutes, not counting the time for the preliminary exercises. She could hardly believe that an hour had lapsed since she had first 'descended' into what, she felt convinced, must have been a glimpse of a previous life – it had been so real, more so than any dream or many actual events in her present life.

Author's Note

While writing this account, I telephoned Tedye McDiven to ask if she still remembered the inscription or title of the book she had seen. She instantly answered yes, that it had appeared to be something like 'Linnen'. She could not find anything like it in her dictionary and, knowing how thorough she is in such matters, I didn't bother to look up any of my own. The following day, however, she telephoned back to say that she had found the word 'Linnean', and even 'Linnaean', in the index of their *Encyclopaedia Britannica* in a reference to the Royal Society. Although this reference to the Swedish botanist Linnaeus, or Linné (1707-78) and his artificial system of classification seems more recent than the details she saw so vividly in her Grecian environment, she considers that this may not be so; she had distinctly seen several present-day buildings in Florence, and the building where she had lived in Greece had been isolated in the countryside and had looked as much like a kind of temple or institution as a residence. She also said that when I had considered her answer to be ambiguous after asking which of three possible subjects she thought she had been studying, she had not really been vague – her answer of 'yes' had been intended to encompass all three subjects: navigation (particularly astro-navigation), astronomy and perhaps a scientific form of astrology as well. The *Encyclopaedia Britannica* states . . . 'The founding of the Linnean Society in 1788 under the auspices of several fellows of the Royal Society was the first instant of the establishment of a distinct scientific association under Royal charter; and this has been followed by the formation of the large number of societies now active in the promotion of special branches of science.' She had never heard of the society before and now the association with its aims and her apparent occupation in her experience seemed to coincide to an uncanny degree. She had also consulted two friends who aspired to the practice of theosophy, but they informed her that most theosophists believed that a period of about a thousand years was necessary between incarnations. She herself, however, did not feel that the period she had seen had been anywhere near so long ago, and that the late eighteenth century or early nineteenth century could well have been the period she had envisaged.

In a further discussion, after she had read this account and a copy of the tape-recording transcript, Tedye McDiven told me that many details of the experience were still missing. She had not related them to me during the experience because she had been preoccupied with seeing everything that appeared before her, often at a pace difficult to follow. One such detail, which she considered not only important but also pertinent to her present character, was that when she had described her studies as being 'difficult' she should also have said that she had been acutely aware of a resistance towards learning her subjects and she considered that, even though allowances could be made for her being so much younger than the other students in the institution, she had been 'a rather silly little thing' for not having wanted to learn such interesting and important matters. This, she had since come to believe, was possibly why she now had such an incessantly inquiring mind, particularly for those specific subjects, and why she formulated for herself some kind of 'philosophy' which would spare her the customary dogma to which, whether rightly or wrongly, she still felt an inherent and considerable resistance.

Dr Salek Minc

Earlier in the same evening we tried the Christos Experiment with Dr Salek Minc. Before commencing, he told me that he did not believe it would work with him, for two main reasons. First, he said he was quite unable to visualize anything at all, no matter how much he might try; secondly, although he is Jewish by birth, he considers himself an agnostic, perhaps even an atheist, and this together with his medical background, he averred, made him quite incredulous of any suggestion of previous incarnations.

Nevertheless, despite what I can only describe as a kind of polite but whimsical scepticism, he was quite willing, indeed eagerly curious, to try the experiment and even be the first volunteer. I thought this would be a pity as I anticipated failure, and feared that both Bryant's and Tedye's experiments might also fail as a result. However, I am recording the experience here, considerably paraphrased but still quoting Dr Minc's exact words from the tape, for two reasons: first, to show that Tedye's experience (recorded in the previous chapter) is all the more remarkable coming after Dr Salek Minc's; and secondly, to show that, for a man who professes to be incapable normally of any kind of visualization, his 'seeing' long past experiences must have been very rewarding for him – a feeling which he does indeed express in his recorded account.

Dr Salek Minc, M.D. (from Rome) was born in 1906 in the town of Siedlce, which was then in Russia but is now in Poland. His youth was spent in Dniepropietrovsk and Charkov in the Ukraine. From here he went to Poland for two and a half years, to gain his *Matura,* equivalent to matriculation for a university. After this he went to Ghent for a year, and then to Naples for another, before going to Rome for thirteen years; and all the time he paid regular visits to Paris to see his mother and brother. In 1939 he gained an appointment for nine months as ship's doctor on the *Centaur* travelling between Singapore and Fremantle. He made Australia his home in 1940 and eventually brought his mother here in 1947. He has an extensive practice in Perth as a physician specializing in heart complaints, but is also an acknowledged art critic, publishing papers on both medical and art subjects in academic publications. He has, as well, one of the largest private art collections in Perth and has had a long friendship with the Italian artist, Corrado Cagli.

His preliminaries were managed with a certain amount of dubiousness on my part as I was not at all convinced that he was actually feeling, let alone visualizing, even the very simple exercises at the beginning. However, we continued with the procedure and I became much more hopeful when he gave excellent detailed descriptions of the front door of his home and of its immediate surroundings which, despite his previous disclaimers, he said he could visualize quite clearly.

The ascent was achieved only with difficulty, for he said he could not imagine himself ascending without the use of an aeroplane or some such vehicle to convey him, although I pointed out that even a child can 'imagine' itself in such circumstances without much difficulty. Eventually he was able to visualize and describe the resulting 'horizons' he would have viewed had he been ascending in actuality, but his scepticism, which really amounted to a determined resistance, became even more pronounced once he commenced the descent and was asked if he could see a particular place on the ground which had appeared beneath him on which he could land. His reply was, 'If I imagine it.' And when asked if he *could* come down, he said obligingly, 'I prepare for myself a piece of beach to land on.' When I asked him to tell us when he had landed, he eventually said, 'Well, I *can* of course – still in my imagination. Well, I stand on the sand.' Furthermore, he said, it was indeed sand on which he was standing as 'I wouldn't pick a rock to land on.' What kind of sand, coarse or fine? 'I picked fine.'

With this kind of resistance, I felt there was little point in continuing except, perhaps, to record such resistance; but shortly afterwards I began to feel a little differently when I asked him, while he was 'looking down at the sand', if he could see his feet. He could, he said, and they were bare – even though on such a wintry evening he was naturally still wearing his socks. His feet, he said, were neither pale nor brown (in actuality they were very white) but 'not a very nice colour'. When asked if could look up his bare legs to see what he might possibly be wearing, he said, 'I can *put* something on.'

'No,' I said, 'I don't want you to *put* something on. *If* you *haven't* anything on, then stay like that. Tell me just as you see it.'

'I wear shorts. Just little shorts, and a white shirt. It's warm.'

In actuality, of course, he was wearing a suit although he had removed his jacket.

When asked if he could see any surroundings and describe them, he said, 'I shall pick on some landscape and – hmmm – Fiji.'

I told him to do whatever he liked and just describe what he saw.

He said, 'Well, it is very close to the beach, and to the trees. And the trees are palms, and they all bend as the wind goes through them.' He wasn't moving around, he was 'just looking'. Asked if he could see any habitation or people, he replied, 'Not on this particular beach.' It was quite deserted. 'Matter of factly (*sic*), I'm looking at a landscape I've seen before, a few years ago.' There were no people, no animals, no birds. Sounds? 'The sound of the sea, that's all.' What kind of a day was it? 'Ah! The Fiji sun!' While in actuality it was, of course, storming outside. Did he want to stay there, or attempt to go somewhere else where he might not have been in actuality? He replied, 'If that is being suggested to me.'

I let him stay where he was, wondering if it might change of its own accord, either by rapid transposition or gradually. And so he said he could see the landscape he had seen a few years previously, 'and I am just there'. And then he said, 'I can't remember what they (*sic*) have done after I had gone.' His eyelids were moving, but only slowly, like a blinking with the lids already closed – not at all the rapid eye movements I was looking for.

'No, you are not to *remember*,' I tried again. 'Can you still visualize yourself standing there now?'

He could. He could see only palm-trees, in clumps or groups, all looking much the same, with straight smooth trunks, permanently leaning in different directions from previous winds and somehow looking very much like ballet dancers. He was still at a distance from them and did not know what they were called, not even when I suggested 'royal palms'; but he did not know the names of any palms. Was there any other kind of growth? 'There is a bush with some greenery underneath.' Mountains were also visible in the distance. Asked if there were any people or habitation as yet, he said, 'I could imagine the thing like anything else. I can imagine to be halfway (*sic*) in Fiji, in the place where I lived.'

He was then going along a road he had been on before, but he was no longer walking, he was being driven in a car by a Fijian. When asked if his feet were still bare, he replied, 'I can *put* a pair of shoes on.' Again I told him he did not have to *put* on anything at all, but merely see it as it appeared to him, to which he replied, 'When you ask, I have some alternatives; and until I have decided what I'm going to see, I can't describe what I *will* see.' So I again let him continue with whatever he chose to see himself doing. He was still in the car. It was day-time as he saw it but, he said, 'In actuality this journey was made at night.' However, he was now seeing the journey in day-time. He did not speak to the Fijian driver as 'he is not a very spiritually inclined person. I had better discard him.'

Where was he going? The name sounded like a Polish name, he said, between Nandi and Suva. He was going to stay in a hotel; but all of this was recollection. Was he *just* recollecting? Or was he also visualizing these places as he described them? 'Well, this is the same situation, you know. When you imagine (them), you can visualize them. But I don't feel the *tang* of reality. No, not at all. This happens all my life. I pick one or two main points, and that is on what I orientate myself.'

[The McDivens told me afterwards, in his presence, that he was notorious for losing himself, having an almost complete lack of directional sense.] 'It is very bad,' he continued, 'and I neglect and by-pass most of the surroundings unless I concentrate on them. I remember only the hotels where I lived, and their surroundings, the parts of the room, and that's all there is. And as I turn around to look, now, there is a window and a bed. And there are socks on the bed. I remember very well, because I had to wash them.' And this, just as I had thought he was seeing more specific details around him, led him only to recall that he remembered the socks well because he had, in actuality, had to wash them. He had wrapped them in a towel and squeezed them so that they would dry quickly.

What, then, was beyond the window? He could *imagine* there was vegetation, because the hotel was in the 'bush' – the middle of the bush – but again he was not definite. He said, 'It is as I remember.'

Did he want to stay there? If I asked him lots of questions about the place, would he be content? Or would he like to try somewhere else? 'In my imagination,' he said, 'I could pick some other place, something else, and go there.' He had *chosen* Fiji in the first place, he then said, because I had asked him to land somewhere. 'And to land, I thought from so high, [the best place] would probably be the beach. There was just water, and the sea, and the mountains, and so on. I *suggested* to myself that *if* I had to land there, it would probably be the beach.'

I was tempted to point out to him that he could not expect

anything to result from the experiment if he were constantly reminding himself of his own act of imagining. However, I felt sure he would realize this for himself, being a fairly intelligent man, and so I let him continue under his own conditions to see if he might eventually divulge some reason for so obviously wanting to resist the experiment – or at least approach it without an open mind or a desire to reveal something to himself, which is said to be a prerequisite of the experiment if it is to have any degree of success.

'Did I suggest the sea and the mountains?' I asked him.

'No,' he admitted. 'You suggested me flying high. And obviously I was to find something, an interesting place.'

Did he want to stay where he was, or try again?

'Yes. There is nothing [here]. There is no potential there.'

He was able to imagine or visualize himself ascending again, going very high on a grey day in autumn – in comparison with the previous brightness of the Fijian sun – until he was eventually above the clouds and could no longer see anything else below him. But without visualizing another descent, he found himself, when asked, seeing 'mainly the top of the water-tank. I used to sit there when I was – now let me see – nine years of age.'

Where was this?

'Not far from Minsk, actually.' And he gave the name, Bobruisk – though it is difficult to distinguish it above the noise, like static, on the tape. Was he above this town? No, he was already in one of the streets. 'Terrible, they are. Unpaved. And oh, it is muddy! Muddy! And there are animals in the street. There are even pigs in the street, enjoying themselves. When you cross the road, you jump from one puddle to another.' He could see his shoes as he jumped, he said – shoes, not boots, as he had never owned boots. Leather shoes, shiny, and laced up. 'They were polished by a maid when I was a child, and I was still a child then. My trousers are well below the knee, as I was on (sic) a gymnasium then. We had to wear long trousers. They are long trousers. And a Russian kind of shirt. Blue, dark blue. And a jacket, because it was cold.'

'Are you cold?'

'No, I'm not cold. But it is in Russia.'

Were there people around him? His brother? 'I remember this particular scene. My brother is in front of me, still jumping across. There are small houses, usually one storey, [though] some are two-storey houses. There is a kind of footpath; there are just long boards of wood. Occasionally a kind of chariot will pass, drawn by a horse.'

He didn't recognize any of the people in the street, only his brother who was about a year and a half older and at the same college. They were not going *to* school then; they were going home *from* school, looking at the shops they were passing.

'And what do you expect when you get home?'

'Never thought about it yet. My mother will be there; my father will be there.'

'Can you see them?'

'They're not there just now. No, I can visualize them in a different way.' Did he see the house? 'It's an ordinary house, a country house. Brick. Just an ordinary house. I know it very well. We lived only three months there, and then we moved on. I'm just reminiscing, you know.'

But why should he choose to reminisce about a house in which he had lived for only three months? It was almost as though he could not bear to relinquish himself to visualizing any one thing continually; as soon as he found himself doing so, he would immediately resist it by reminding himself of the mere mechanics of the exercise rather than what it might produce.

Was there a garden? 'There is a few feet (*sic*). There's a three-storey house opposite. I still can't remember inside the house at all. I can't place myself there, not at all. It was only three months we lived there. It's very hazy. I can't remember the previous one either. But I can go ahead, go to somewhere Russian, in Siedlce.

'There are flats, big flats. They have about five big rooms. And on the third floor is a salon, very nicely furnished in about that particular time. There was a telephone in the house. There was also a telephone in the bank where my father was. My father was the owner of the bank. It was a family bank, and they were in three cities. And you put out the switch over to the phone from the house to the bank, from both sides [presumably 'ways'], and so on. There were two servants – one was the cook and one was the maid. The cook was an oldish woman, the maid was the youngish one.'

Did he see his mother there?

'Well, she comes here occasionally. I can remember it, the big – now what do they call it? The big – container? A "botchka". [A barrel, he explained later.] It was in the kitchen, and the water – it was well-water – and it was for keeping it up on the second floor. There was no power obviously. No water. Only well-water. And in the house there was no electricity, no gas. And there was a magnificent lamp in the drawing-room. And it was just recently acquired and furnished, in red mahogany, but not heavy, very light. There was a gramophone, also a recent acquisition, I think a present from Grandfather. With the double, er – you know, the loudspeakers were extended, with a big opening. These were probably the best [available]. There was a balcony, with lace curtains, French patterns, and silk. And what was the most important, there was a piano there, a black piano. I played the piano. And mother used to play the piano. Only classical music. She was very proficient at that time, also in speaking French and German. I liked the piano, but my brother had a better ear. And the other rooms – my brother's and my room – when we moved in, it was a bit humid. We used to stand kerosene lamps in the corners by the walls to dry up the humidity. And the beds had nickel knobs. And on the walls were tapestries with scenes of the Coliseum – Dante and Beatrice, and – but these are all recollections.'

Again, it was almost as though he had deliberately reminded himself of this.

'Do you visualize them as you recollect them?'

'Yes. Oh yes. I *can* visualize them.'

'Is it quite clear?'

'*Fairly* clear.'

'Is it happy for you to be there, to recollect these things?'

'Oh, yes! It was very pleasant, although I remember occasionally my parents used to go out and the maids weren't there, they were out, and I used to say to my brother, "Isn't it dreadful! We're left here, and we're always frightened. We shouldn't be left here." *He* was frightened, and *I* was frightened. And if I fell asleep, he would be left with his fear all by himself.'

He had been so impatient to continue with this anecdote that, mere recollection or not, it was as though his visualization of it, or even just the mere remembering of it, was

trying to overcome the obvious resistance he was still
maintaining to the whole exercise.

'There were just the two of you, were there?' I asked.

'Yes. I and my brother.' Were there no pets or animals?
'No, no. Not at all. It was very difficult to keep pets in these
flats.' Did he have any special friends? 'Well, I was great
friends with my brother. And there was another couple, or
another family. Their father used to work in our bank. Mother
used to do all the social things – on certain days, collect the
money for charity. And that was life. I used to read a lot all the
time. Always sitting with a book, swallowing one book after
another.' He couldn't remember a particular favourite at the
time, but perhaps Jules Verne, 'and one about Red Indians'.
In what language was he reading then? 'English. No, Russian.
All my knowledge of world literature was in Russian. And I
used to study Hebrew. That was another thing; I was quite
good. Father used to study with us. He learnt the language
and so on, but he hadn't had enough education. We got new
books, popular books, and he used to read them with us. And
he and Mother told us we could never learn enough at school,
that was part of our education.

'In the summer we used to go to Germany. My father was
fat, and all we had to do was bathe with him and walk for
miles to lose weight. And, well, it was a very pleasant way of
passing the time. My brother and I dearly wanted a little boat
to sail in the water, in the "see" [lake], and we told our
governess and she bought one for us. Then Father found out
that we had asked for it, and broke up the boat. Terrible!
Terribly cross with us, he was – for asking somebody else for
something. Well, I can go on reminiscing and recollecting and
thinking back. But I *can* see them, especially my father, and
the broken boat.'

'You *can* see the broken boat all right?'

'Yes. It vividly stayed in my mind. Yes.'

'Are you happy there? Or do you want to move again?'

'It doesn't matter. I'm quite happy reminiscing. But it is all
out of myself. I would have liked it to be more interesting.'

If he wanted to try once more, I told him he must again
ascend and descend as before.

'It is very difficult,' he said, 'but I don't think you can apply
this in my case, because for all my recollections and so on

which should be interesting I never went up in the air. For the image of me being up in the clouds, I put myself in a plane and then I'm all right. And I'm on the way to New York, or somewhere else. But the more significant memories, of other places, I remember going by train, by train through Russia, and walking in the streets and so on. But I cannot *descend* upon them, because I never had this view. *This* is difficult. It is not difficult that you tell me to go up and down, it is just that it is like a plane or a parachute for a certain height.' No, he could not imagine himself as a bird at all, nor of being up in the air without an aeroplane. 'I never actually had the feeling,' he now confessed.

'You still realize you are here on the floor?'

This, of course, he should have done all the time in any case, while also feeling that he was ascending and descending.

'Yes,' he replied.

'If you are lying horizontally, can you turn to look down and tell us what you see?'

'Yes, I will try. And for some reason or other, I see Egypt – I don't know why – Egypt, and the Nile. I can obviously imagine the pyramids and the Sphinx.' He always reminded himself of the mechanics of visualizing, rather than just observing the result. If he came down to land, he said, it would be near Port Said – 'because it was interesting there'! 'This is of course a recollection of my 1954 voyage. You asked me to look down, and this was the first thing which came to my mind. But now – now the river is the Dniepr, in Russia. I am wearing long trousers, and again a Russian shirt, buttoned up because it is the week-end. Again I'm with my brother, and another cousin. He [the cousin] is now still in Russia; he is a professor.'

So once again, reminiscences displaced his concentration on the mere mechanics of remembering.

'It's midsummer. We are hiring a boat. We're rowing down. It is a very small boat. The area is very beautiful. The Dniepr *is* very beautiful. There were other boats, and other people. And there is an island or two. This was when I was the age of twelve or thirteen. This was the quiet time before the revolution. There was a "summer time", and this summer time was four hours ahead. This meant that when the time was officially midnight, it was eight o'clock before it was dark, and the sun had just started settling down. This was the quiet time before the revolution,' he said again. 'I was wearing a long shirt. In this time we were not very well dressed. [As most families had to do at that time] Mother had taken all our possessions in a couple of sheets, or a table-cloth, and gone to the market and exchanged it all for a couple of loaves of bread, or a bag of potatoes, or onions – and that was our main sustenance for the week. And actually we were, here, all working. I was thirteen, and doing cultural work [as a librarian in a cultural centre]. At this time I was also at a special school, "The Home of Free Creation". There we were with other young children, and we picked our teachers for the subject that we were going to study, and we discussed things in a very serious manner. We learned the essence of many things. We learned to know the essence of literature, psychology and philosophy; the essence of history, of economics. And we were always to study late at home. And we boys and girls were always discussing and thinking. But we were also young, and we sang and danced, and fell in love, and were romantic. And if I think of all the other places in the world? I used to read Marx and his theories of economics, recite poetry by Mayakovski. But this was later, when I was fourteen, fifteen . . .'

He stopped – just, I think, as we all wanted him to go on. Moreover, his eyelids had at long last developed the rapid movements for which I had been waiting. However . . .

'And do you feel happy remembering these things?' I asked him.

'Oh, yes!'

'Do you see more of it, or have you stopped?'

'I've stopped.' And opening his eyes, he struggled up into a sitting position.

'Do you know how long you have been altogether?'

'Yes. It must have been an hour and a quarter.'

Apart from the preliminaries, his reminiscing had taken precisely seventy-five minutes.

Dr Minc had certainly not seen anything that was not from his own memories of his lifetime. He had certainly not seen himself in any circumstances unfamiliar to him in actuality. But for a man who confessed that he was never able to visualize anything, he admitted to having 'seen' what he recounted with, at times, extraordinary clarity. However, the scientific aspect of his mind compelled him to wonder if he might not 'see' such reminiscences as vividly were he merely to sit in his own armchair and submit himself to them – although he had no doubt that, under any normal conditions, he could not possibly reminisce for so long. But this was all he was prepared to concede about the matter – this and the fact that the effect was a very pleasant one indeed, one of the most pleasant he had experienced.

Immediately after this Tedye McDiven took her place, with very different and much more intriguing results.

If Dr Minc's attempt had been a comparative failure, however, then the third attempt of the evening, with Bryant McDiven, was a complete failure. Although he managed the preliminaries with average facility, when the time came for him to commence the ascent he reported to us that all vision had vanished. He could see nothing whatsoever. And before I could make another attempt, he sat up with open eyes. It was very late and I was tired after a long day and the two experiments I had already conducted, so we resolved to try again another time. This seemed a pity for – knowing the highly imaginative nature of his art, especially in his paintings depicting future civilizations in decay – we had all, I think, expected something quite exceptional from his experiment. It came as a complete surprise, therefore, and quite an anticlimax as well, to find that so creative and imaginative a man could not even imagine himself ascending from the roof of his own house.

Mrs Rae van Aalen

For someone who was so eager to try the experiment, the results of Mrs Rae van Aalen's experience – although successful visually to begin with, and certainly vivid enough so far as emotion was concerned – were disappointing. This was the first experiment I had recorded where the overall 'feeling' experienced by the experimentee was an almost overwhelming sadness, 'a terrible melancholy', which was quite unexpected from such a personality.

Mrs Rae van Aalen, the wife of a Dutchman, is Australian-born – née Dinsdale on July 31st, 1939, in Perth, Western Australia. She is the mother of three children – two sons and a daughter – all at school. As well as being a very capable and somewhat artistic housewife, she was a private secretary by profession and is still competent in shorthand and typing. After her marriage, she helped her husband considerably in various business projects. I came to know them both in 1965, when I returned from a three-year stay in Europe. As chance would have it, we all (the five van Aalens and myself) embarked on the same freighter carrying twelve passengers when I decided to go back to Europe in September 1965. I would not have been at all surprised, therefore, if something of Holland or elsewhere in Europe had appeared in her experience, but not at all. Nor did any of the varying occupations she has had since her marriage: first, running a successful florist shop based on stock from her husband's nursery; and secondly, instructing horse-riding at the converted flower nursery, where they had about thirty horses.

Rae is small in build, with a vivacious personality and a rare charm of spontaneous friendliness. She almost always seems in exceptionally good spirits, even in times of adversity. This made her experience of an almost insupportable melancholy all the more unexpected. It was performed without her husband present, as he was 'wary of things like that', in my apartment on the evening of November 11th, 1971. Leo as usual massaged her ankles and then manipulated the tape-recorder, while I massaged her forehead and 'ran the trip'.

She had little difficulty with the stretching and shrinking preliminaries, nor with describing and visualizing her front door. She did have difficulty, however, in being able to 'transport' herself on to the roof of her home, where she had lived for a good many years. Eventually this was accomplished, only to encounter more difficulty in ascending into the air. It was not until the experiment was over that she informed me that she had only been able to achieve the ascent by 'cheating in a way', by imagining herself to be in an aeroplane. She chose to do this rather than end the experiment for she felt, if not convinced, at least open-minded about the possibility of glimpsing some former life. Having at last accomplished the ascent, she had even greater difficulty in descending. Although at times she did manage to come closer to the earth's surface than the great heights she mostly envisaged, she was quite unable to land – no matter how many attempts were made.

Oddly enough, although she found herself at 'a great height', she said it was a very clear day (although it was night in reality) and she could clearly, even vividly, see the ocean far below her, and then a stretch of coastline. The sea was calm, glittering, with waves breaking close to the shore. The beach was very white, a long curve coming to a very pronounced point. There were reefs some way out to sea and she could clearly see the white streaks of foam appear and disappear exactly as in reality. There were no boats, no birds, no signs of animals or people. The country inland, far below, was predominantly yellow and orange.

She could descend *towards* it all, but she would reach a certain point and then stop. She couldn't descend any further, let alone land, no matter how hard she tried. It was still a bright sunny day so she could see features of the beach quite clearly. There were no rocks to cause her concern; indeed, the beach looked ideal for her to land on safely, but she just couldn't manage it. Was there any wind? Just a little, she said, though of course there was no wind at all in the apartment. She was neither cool nor warm, but 'comfortable'. She could see no vegetation on the arid land, and no signs of habitation either, not even the smallest and simplest building of any kind. 'And still no animals, no birds, nothing.' Close to the beach, however, she could see trees with large exposed roots – mangrove-trees.

While looking down, she could also see her feet. They were clearly white and bare, although in actuality she was still wearing stockings, and were about the same size as her actual feet. Try as she would, however, she could not bring them down on to the ground. She felt that she was suspended, perfectly still and quite unable to move. And, apart from the sea, there was no sign of movement around her.

Was she happy being there, or did it worry her?

'I don't like it,' she said. 'I can't move.'

But then in fact she did feel herself beginning to move, although instead of going downwards she was going up. In

very little time she was back at the great height where she had
been previously. The day was still 'quite bright' and she could
now see even more of the coastline than before. The land
beyond the coast had become a mixture of greens and browns
and yellows, though still quite arid, and she could now
distinguish a river 'in the browns' – a river *with* water, she told
us when I asked her this particularly, in case it was an area
where the rivers, as often in arid country, sometimes ran dry.
She was looking down at it all 'from the north', she said; she
quite clearly had this definite sense of direction. She was
looking south, with the long curve of the beach still far below
her, though she could distinguish reefs and foam and breaking
waves. She located another river, also with water; but if she
could manage to land, she would not choose to come down
anywhere near either of them, and certainly not on the delta
between them. However, she couldn't even descend, let alone
land.

'What are you doing then?'

'Nothing.'

Yet soon she was able to descend again, though it was more
like a downward floating, she said, until she was only five or
six feet above the sand on the beach – yet she still couldn't
land. Was she *afraid* to land? She didn't know; she was just
incapable of coming any lower. Yes, she could still see her
feet; they were quite bare, and much like her own feet.
However, she couldn't see for sure if she was wearing
anything. When she visualized stretching out her arms with
her hands before her, she could see her hands as clearly as in
reality.

'Have you got anything on your hands at all?'

'No. Just my hands. Bare.'

In actuality she was wearing a wristwatch and four rings.

She could view herself 'from a normal sort of perspective'
and could see now that she was wearing a kind of flowing,
billowy white gown, perhaps a nightgown. She could also see
that, instead of her normal self, she was a little girl. As she
looked down at her feet, could she now attempt to land again?
There is a long silence on the tape, until I ask her if she had at
last succeeded. But no.

'I don't seem to want to come down on to the beach.'

Did she know what she wanted to do? Land, or just fly

around, looking at whatever presented itself?

'I want to lie on the beach, but I can't.'

If she tried to move at all, in any direction, she only went up. Did she *want* to go up again? Yes. And so she ascended again, very easily, until once more she was at a great height where, except for the solitude, she thought she felt more comfortable. Was she perhaps a bird, as an experimentee had been once before? But no, she had seen her own hands and feet, and she thought she was clearly herself. It was cool up where she was, but not cold, and there were no clouds. It was a clear, bright blue sky.

But then, quite gradually so that she could watch the change of colour, it became dark. The sky became a night sky, yet as though it was completely overcast with indiscernible clouds, for she could see no stars or moon, though she thought there was 'something' a bit higher than she herself was. This 'something' was at first just a kind of hazy light, with a few other individual lights contained within it; perhaps stars, she couldn't be certain, but she was going towards it all. Then the light seemed to become a very large building, suspended up in the starless night sky – a building of light-coloured stone which did not appear to have any foundations on the ground whatsoever. Was it round or square? But her only answer was, 'It is high.' Was she far away from it? 'I'm coming to it.'

She could then see a big door, or at least a doorway, an opening, which she was approaching. The whole building was effulgent with light, both inside and out, *'very* light' and shiny. There was so much light that she could no longer distinguish the walls nor say definitely any more what they were made of. And then she was no longer approaching it; she had stopped. It was still night, she said, and when I asked her if perhaps she could change the night to day, if only to be able to see more clearly, she immediately said, 'The building has gone.' There was nothing of it left, only the night. It was not completely black, only dark, and still without stars.

'And can you see any parts of yourself?'

'No.'

'Are you quite happy just floating there.'

'I'm very sad.'

'Do you know what you are sad about?'

'No.'

'Can't you see any part of yourself?'

She was silent for quite a long while, then she said, 'I'm floating.'

'Oh. You see *all* of you floating?'

'Yes.'

'Is it as you are now, or not?'

'I'm – billowy.'

Was she wearing anything? 'A gown.' Could she see anything else of herself? 'No.' Was she moving?

'I'm very sad.'

'Are you able to think at all, or do know what you are doing there?'

'I don't know why I'm here.' Was there anyone else there? 'No. I'm by myself.' After a long silence, I asked if anything had happened. 'Nothing.' Did she have any idea what kind of place it was? 'No. It seems to be just sky, but somehow I think it isn't.' Was she warm or cold? 'I can't feel anything, but there is a breeze. I can feel it in my clothes.'

There was, of course, no chance of a breeze in the apartment, nor was she wearing the kind of clothes through which any breeze could be felt.

'Do you want to stay there?'

'I don't like it.'

But did she want to stop?

'No.'

'While you are there,' I decided to try, 'do you know you are in this room?'

'Yes.'

'What do you hear?'

'A fly.'

I couldn't have been more surprised.

'A fly, do you? Or is it the tape-recorder?'

'It's a fly.' She was quite adamant about it, though I could see no fly about.

'And do you hear anything else apart from that?'

Cars had just driven up the cul-de-sac outside, one of them hooting.

'It is quiet,' she said, 'except for the fly.'

And then I saw it – one solitary fly that had evidently flown away and was now returning towards her. I got up and killed it with fly-spray while she lay there, patiently, in her melancholy solitude. Only then did I realize that she had been covering her eyes most of the time. I had forgotten to look for any rapid eye movements, probably because she had not managed to land and commence an actual 'trip'.

'If you take your hands away from your eyes, what happens?'

'It's lighter.'

This was of course to be expected. But did she see anything else?

'Nothing.'

She was still floating. Did she still see herself in the billowy gown? No, it had gone. There was only herself, a mind contained within nothing, with no embodiment whatsoever, endlessly floating in a solitude of ineffable sadness, a kind of terrifying limbo. She didn't want any more of it.

'You feel that you're back here in the room?'

'The actual me is.'

'The other?'

'Just floating.'

'I think you'd better stop.'

'Yes.'

'If you don't want to move straight away,' I said to her, 'just move slowly. Stretch yourself.' Then, 'If you saw anything at all clearly, what was it?'

'Oh, the coast!' she said cheerfully, her former self again. The coast had been quite vivid, just as in reality. Had she seen that particular piece of coast before?

'About eight years ago, I think. It is the Hundred Miles Beach.' She meant the Eighty Mile Beach in the north of Western Australia, between Port Hedland and Broome, where the country is as arid as she had described it, and where rivers either flow as torrents in 'the wet' or are just dry riverbeds in 'the dry'. She had been actually flying over it, in a plane (and it was then that she had confessed that, to be able to ascend from the roof of her house, she had been compelled to imagine herself in a plane). She agreed that this was probably why she couldn't come down again, although it was only a short while before the plane she had imagined had entirely disappeared, leaving her just floating in space, at times with her hands and feet visible and at times quite disembodied. It was then, particularly, that she had been beset by her melancholy. But before this had happened, she had clearly seen the delta of the two rivers, and the mangrove-trees.

'So that it was just a memory of something you saw eight years ago?'

'Yes.'

'Did you choose it particularly?' I asked, remembering Dr Salek Minc and his deliberate choice of Fiji.

'No, it just came. Probably because I was trying to think about a plane. I had the *impression* of a plane, and that's where we were.'

'You could see your front door quite clearly, but you had trouble getting up on to the roof.'

'Yes. A peculiar feeling.'

'But when you did get on to the roof, you saw it quite clearly?'

'Yes.'

'Then you had trouble getting into the air?'

But she was much more concerned with the recent part of what little experience she had had, for she said, 'That terrible feeling of melancholy! Terrible! Most *dreadful* feeling! A *horrible* feeling! I couldn't think why it was, this terrible feeling of melancholy. Most peculiar!' She had shivered at the thought of it, but had now shaken it off with a typical gesture – laughing it away.

'There was nothing else?'

'Nothing. Just this funny feeling.'

'Have you ever dreamt that?'

'No, never.'

'You've never had the feeling of being *nothing* before?'

'No. *No!*' she repeated vehemently. 'But it was a peculiar feeling – I *knew* it was *me!*'

'Incidentally,' I asked her, 'how long do you think you have been?'

'Not long,' she immediately said.

'What is "not long"?'

'About twenty minutes.'

'It has been an hour and eight minutes,' I told her, '*not* counting the time spent on the preliminaries.'

'Really!' She could hardly have been more incredulous. She had spent all that time doing and seeing so very little compared with most other experimentees, yet the time had never dragged at all; on the contrary, to the experimentee at least, time had appeared to speed at just over three times its normal rate.

Well over a year later, Mrs Rae van Aalen still remembers the experience clearly, in detail, no matter how little seemed to occur. The overwhelming sense of melancholy, she said, was a reflection of her feelings at the time, which she had been desperately trying to resist. It could, she admits, like her sense of solitude, have been foretelling the twelve months of depression that was about to beset her before she finally felt constrained to separate from her husband.

Author's Note, January 1976

During 1975, Mrs van Aalen acquired an oil painting for the living-room of her new home where, quite obviously, she and her three children are very much happier. When I saw it, I was immediately struck by how it so vividly portrayed the 'landscape' she had seen in her experience, both in its desert colours and awesome dimensions. Depicted above this arid landscape, which appears to be viewed from similarly coloured ocean, are two white and wraithlike figures ascending vertically, though slightly tilted against each other, into a dust-drenched sky – two aboriginal spirits of the 'dreamtime'. To me, it portrayed exactly what she had seen in her experience – either as a picture depicting the dream, or else the dream a precognition by almost four years of the painting. But when I said as much, Mrs van Aalen vehemently disagreed, saying the picture had no connection whatsoever with her experience; nor would she entertain the suggestion that the experience could possibly have been a precognition of the painting. Moreover, she still remains adamant on further consultation before returning the proofs to the publishers. I am inclined to think that her denial of any connection between her experience and the painting could be due to the experience having clearly depicted her unhappiness at the time (of which I had not then been aware), whereas the painting is a symbol of her new-found happiness since separating from her husband.

D'Arcy Ryan

D'Arcy James Ryan, forty-eight, B.A. from Sydney University, B. Litt. from Oxford and Ph.D. from Sydney University, is a lecturing anthropologist at the University of Western Australia. He has written articles in various professional and academic journals and has contributed chapters in several academic books. He is married with three daughters aged, at the time of the experience (January 14th, 1972), eighteen and (twins) sixteen.

The experiment was conducted in my apartment on a warm summer night, with raucous music from a lifesavers' dance some . quarter of a mile away all too clearly audible. Occasionally, too, we could hear the screeching of tyres as young men showed off in their cars on the near-by (about 200 yards) Marine Parade. The experiment took place from 9.58 to 11.17 p.m., and was witnessed by another guest who had called in to see us; his presence did not distract D'Arcy Ryan, even though the two had not met before.

After the preliminaries had been conducted without any difficulties, D'Arcy descended towards a coastline and then a particular part of beach, landing on coarse, whitish-yellow sand with bare feet. He couldn't distinguish any apparel except for a shortish, white garment around his loins, which could possibly be shorts or some simpler piece of clothing. He did not want to dwell on this too long as he was more interested in the fact that, although the sand he could see was a 'normal colour', his legs were 'a sort of greeny-blue colour, smooth, and as if they have been in the water for a long time.'

Toes and toenails, however, were quite normal, which made the colour of his skin all the more unusual. And when he looked at his hands stretched out before him, they were also the same greeny-blue colour. Did he *feel* as though he had been in water for a long time? 'No, not really – just the *look* of it.'

He wasn't actually standing, but was hovering just above the beach. Around him he could see 'just sand, and surf, and just miles and miles of beach.' There was a bit of scrub here and there, but no kind of habitation or roads, no people or animals, not even birds.

Could he see himself clearly? 'Only my hands and legs,'

which were still the same greeny-blue colour. He thought he was longer and thinner than actually, about eight feet tall (he is just less than six feet in actuality), and he could see nothing on his legs or arms, although he was in fact wearing a wristwatch on a leather band. He couldn't see his face, but suspected it to be the same colour. He also thought his features were different, certainly longer and thinner, with long black hair tied with a kind of string. (His actual hair *is* black, but not overlong and certainly never tied with a string.) His face was clean-shaven, whereas in actuality he wore mutton-chop side-whiskers.

He wanted to move along the beach, but he felt 'stilted' with a stiffness in the legs so that he couldn't quite control them. He thought this might have resulted from his 'being stretched' (by this he didn't mean the stretching and shrinking exercises in the preliminaries).

'I feel like a scarecrow, just moving along without complete control over the limbs and, er, feeling pretty awkward on my feet, as though they are about three feet further away than they ought to be.' They were 'bigger and flatter and with clawlike toes on them'. His fingers were the same. His fingernails were not like human fingernails, nor were they really claws, and they were a sort of dark greeny-grey.

Apart from its colour, was his skin normal? 'I don't know. It's not as *my* skin looks like. It's not scaly – but slimy!' Did he feel like a human figure or not? 'No. I feel like a *different* kind of figure.' His mind, however, felt like an ordinary normal mind. It was just that he didn't *look* like anyone else he had ever seen.

Could he see anyone else? 'No.' What was he doing – walking, looking around? 'I'm still getting used to being *me*.' He continued to feel elongated, like 'a stork on long legs'. He still couldn't control these legs, but he certainly did not have any feathers. If he were to speak, what language would he speak? 'Normally, as always.'

The beach and he himself were still much the same, but he could now distinguish particular seaweeds. He was walking east, he said, along the Great Australian Bight. Had he seen this particular landscape before? Only from the air, not like this from the ground. No, he had never walked along it in actuality as he was doing now.

As he walked along, describing the beach, he felt himself

gaining weight which his long thin legs were not designed to carry. His arms, also long and thin, reached to under his knees. He still couldn't see his body, however, but he felt, or sensed, it to be 'gawky, out of all proportion'.

To his right, breakers were coming in on the sea in great rollers. 'There is surf there, quite a lot of surf. A beautiful sea, as a matter of fact. Clean.' There were no seabirds. The sky was blue without cloud.

'When you are walking along, can you see your shadow?' This obviously surprised him, and after a pause he said, 'Er – no.' There was no shadow at all, even though it was a bright sunny day. 'Not even behind you?' I thought to ask. 'It *is* behind me, yes.' When he had turned, he said, he could see it, and this obviously intrigued him.

We then went through a lengthy business of trying to establish the time of day. As he was walking east, and his shadow was long behind him, surely it was early morning, I suggested. But no, he felt it was midday; he was quite sure it was midday.

If he looked to his left, he saw some scrub and a cliff. It was a sort of yellow sandstone cliff, with more greyish-green, dry-looking scrub on its top. He was still alone and he could not see a sign of any living thing. However, he was coming to the end of the beach where there were more rocks and scrub and where he had to climb the cliff.

'I'm on the cliff now. They're not very high cliffs. I still seem to be so long and gawky, I just seem to kind of *step* up. My hands are big, but it is very easy climbing. I just get up there, and I'm on top of it now.'

What could he see? 'Miles and miles of completely flat plains.' There was a long pause, and then, 'There's a building in the distance. It looks like a tin – corrugated-iron – shed. Not a very big one, but an odd shape. And there is a lot of machinery around it.' The shed was not only irregularly shaped, but had 'roofs jutting in all directions'. It was not at all like any building he had ever seen. 'It looks like a whole lot of rooms, but I haven't seen it before.'

When he first saw it, it had been about three miles away; but now he was going towards it, and fairly quickly.

'I'm walking along rather like an emu, in a quick kind of run, covering the ground as though I haven't got an awful lot of time. And it is just across the road.'

'Oh, there *is* a road?'

'A dirt road. A rather primitive kind of bush-track.' Were there any signs of people having been there recently? 'Nothing lately. No signs at all.' There was no one in the building, nor had there been recently.

'But there is a kind of pollen falling down, like dust. Sun shining through it, and catching the shafts of sunlight. It's like a great grain-mill of some kind, but there is nothing in there.'

Was there any grain growing around it?

'The plains are full of thistles, as a matter of fact. All *dead* thistles. The ordinary thistles that we have growing in the garden, not great big Scotch thistles but about two or three feet high. They're all around the building and in the distance. There seems to be *grain* in the distance, but there are some lower hills in the very far distance.'

There were still no signs of people and he couldn't tell how long it had been deserted. What had the mill been used for?

'It looks as though it has been a mill of *some* sort, or something to do with grain. There's a lot of pollen flying through the air.' He could feel it landing on him. What kind of a day was it? 'Very good, very hot. No clouds.' Did he feel hot? 'Not particularly.' He wasn't at all hungry either. If he *were* hungry and wanting something to eat, where would he go or what would he do? 'I can't imagine that feeling applying to me now, because I don't think I need to eat or drink.'

Did he feel himself to be quite substantial? He thought so. When he had his feet on the ground, could he feel them actually walking on it? 'No, I've got this sort of *gliding* feeling, as though I'm an inch or so above the ground.'

Had he seen this particular mill before? 'Not that I can remember. The landscape I have seen, yes.' (Though he could not ascertain exactly where, unless it had been in that area of the Nullarbor Plain which he had seen only from the air.) But he had never seen the mill nor anything like it. Did he think the mill signified anything?

'No,' he said, but rather uncertainly. 'It's a *bit* like some of those buildings you see in Lawrence Daws's [an Australian artist] paintings. But apart from that, it's just terribly desolate, and bleak, and – something rather horrible about it, in broad daylight, being so deserted. It's the kind of thing I'd imagine coming to in the *dark*, and this is in broad daylight. There is a bit of rusty machinery around. All big wheels, like ploughs and all kinds of a – all pretty rusty. No, I can't imagine what it was for.'

He was still outside the building, but he could see that there was also old disused machinery *in*side it, and something looking like work benches. Could he go inside? 'I *have* been inside. It's an enormous height, and the roof is in this very peculiar shape, and light is coming through at odd angles, as if it was designed that way; or else, looking at the shafts of sunlight, it [the building] was just damaged in the roof. The odd thing about the shafts of sunlight is that they cross each other. And they've got these grains of pollen and dust in them.'

'If they cross each other, do you think there can possibly be two sources of light?'

'Well, there *must* be.'

'Two suns?'

'It would have to be, wouldn't it. You can't get crossed shafts of light with only one sun.'

'It doesn't surprise you?'

'I've only just noticed it.'

'*Does* it surprise you, or . . .?'

'It does now. It makes the whole place just – creepier.' Did he feel frightened in there? 'Yes. I'm so bewildered, and yet I'm part of the scene.'

'You think you belong there?'

'Well, I'm not uneasy at all. It feels familiar, and yet I'm really seeing it for the first time. And there is a certain bleakness.'

He could find no printed signs giving directions, nothing saying 'Boiler Room' or something like that for instance, and no signs of books or records. 'There is nothing at all, except for those rusty bits of machinery.' The floor was covered with a thick mixture of dust and pollen, so that he couldn't tell what it was made of, 'and there is wheat growing through it'. Yet he could see no cobwebs, and the pollen was not falling inside, only outside. There was nothing alive.

'You are the only person in the whole landscape?'

'That's right.'

'Do you feel in need of company? Do you long to find

somebody else?'

'I do.'

'You think you are accustomed to being alone?'

'Yes, very much.'

'You don't think you belong to a herd, or a mob, or a small village, a group of something?'

'As I look at present, I couldn't.'

'No? Do you think you ever have?'

'Don't know. Before this all started, yes. But now, looking the way I do, it's impossible.'

'In this present form you are in, do you think you have a name?'

'I haven't thought about it. I don't know.'

Did he suppose he would still have his own name? He supposed so. 'You do, even though you haven't got your own skin or present form?' 'Yes.' Did he have an identity? 'An identity, and appearance. I don't have the *same* appearance any more.' So he had a different identity? 'Must have.' But he was quite content with the same name? 'Hmm – I don't know. I think it's the same one, but I really don't know.'

'Or is it irrelevant?'

'I've *got* to have a name!'

'Do you know what age you are?'

'The same, I think. Or a bit younger, I don't know. Age is irrelevant.'

He hadn't changed at all. He was still the same awkward form and strange colour, his black hair was still long, and he was still clean-shaven.

'Ah! If you are clean-shaven, do you think you have shaved, or is it because you don't grow hair on your face?'

'I don't grow it.'

'Are you male or female?'

'Male.'

'Quite definitely male?'

'Yes.'

'Or do you have two sexes at all? Or just one sex?'

'I'm just male.'

'Any obvious species? *Are* there females as well?'

'I don't know. A *new* species.' But he still hadn't seen anyone else, whether similar to him or not. Did it seem alarming to be a new species?

'Somebody has to be. I haven't worked it out yet.'

'Have you dreamt about this sort of thing?'

'No, never. I've dreamt about being a monster at various times, quite a lot – of being very much at home in nightmare country, because I *was* amongst it, too. I dream of it from time to time, not frequently. But in dreams, there are other creatures around. In this, I'm completely by myself.'

Which was the more disturbing: the dreams with other creatures around, or this where he was by himself?

'This one, probably. The others are rather fun.'

'Do you think this could possibly be a dream which you are now having consciously?'

'Oh yes, I could have had a dream like this.'

'Do you want to do any more with this dream? Do you want to go on? You can go on as long as you like, or stop whenever you like.'

'Er – I don't know where to go from here.'

'You are still inside the building?'

'I'm outside now. I'm walking towards the distant hills, wading through those goddam thistles!' Did they irritate his skin at all? 'A little bit. The sun is very hot. I've suddenly developed some black overalls.'

But there was still nothing on his feet, which were still greeny-blue. The black overalls covered him from shoulders to ankles, but surprisingly left his green arms bare. They were made of a sort of canvassy stuff, he said, *like* canvas yet *not* canvas, with a couple of pockets, a pair of pliers in one which, to inspect them, he had taken out and then dropped. 'I'm trying to pick them up, but my long spidery fingers can't hold them. I'm trying, in those thistles, to pick them up. I've found them, and put them back in my pocket.'

Did he know what he used them for? No. Was there anything else in his pockets? No. Did the overalls belong to him? 'I don't know where they came from – they just suddenly appeared.' Did he have anything on underneath, or just the overalls? 'Nothing underneath.' And no shoes, no hat. 'Do you wear glasses at all?' No. In actuality he did, if for reading only. Looking at his long spidery fingers, he was still wearing no rings or wristwatch. He also knew he was not wearing the black overalls in reality. 'I'm wearing slacks and a shirt. Tan and white.'

'White trousers and a tan shirt?'

'No, the other way around.'

'O.K. Now tell us what you are doing now, in your other – dimension.'

'I'm here. You brought me back to here.'

'And you can't see yourself as you were before? With the pliers? O.K. Now tell me – make the effort – what do you see when you first remember?'

'Thistles.'

It is interesting to note here that my suggestion of the pliers to induce him to resume the visualization did not work; it was his own 'connecting link' of the thistles which appeared to him. I had deliberately interrupted his experience to see if it *could* be resumed.

He still had the black overalls on, the day was still hot and dry 'with piercing sunshine', and the thistles were still there. Had he seen this landscape before, in reality? Yes. Where was it? In New South Wales, near a place called Cootamundra. (This was at least a thousand miles from the landing point on the Great Australian Bight he had first seen.) Were there thistles for miles and miles there? Yes. He was aware that this landscape was nowhere near the Great Australian Bight? Of course. Would the building have been there too? 'No. Probably not. No, not that I remember.'

Was the building like anything at Cootamundra?

'No. That was an Air Force station.'

But was it a real, a natural landscape?

'I *think* it was Cootamundra – but *I* didn't look like *that* in Cootamundra.'

'Does it seem unusual to have such an unrealistic shape?'

'I've got used to it now.'

'Do you think it will change, or do you want to stop?'

'I don't particularly want to stop, but I think I would like to change the shape.'

I began to tell him that he could just let it change of its own accord or, if he had difficulty with this, he could ascend into the air again; but he said, 'Well, I *have*.' And he sounded very surprised when he then said, 'Yes, I just suddenly took *off*! I'm right up in the air and flying around now. Just flying with my arms, (but) I can't actually control them. I took right off above the country.' Now, when he looked, everything he had seen before was gone. 'I'm going through the clouds now. They're sort of cumulus clouds.' What form did he have now? 'I'm stripped of the overalls. I don't seem to wear anything at all, hovering over the clouds.' The colour of his feet? 'They seem to be normal again – a bit paler than usual, but they're normal. But I'm being tossed around in these clouds all the time. Just me, still by myself. Now I'm falling.'

'And what's below?'

'A lake. A lake or – a lake, I think. Very rough. Very green and very rough.' The shores of this lake were just jungle. He was falling on his back into the water, and then was suddenly *in* the water, quite deep down, but then was coming up slowly.

'Any trouble getting up to the surface?'

'Er – I *hit* the surface all right. I'm above the water. On the shore is a small lovely beach. The jungle goes right down to the edge of the beach. Just a sort of a dirty kind of sand on it, though – yellow-grey, dirty. Nothing like the other beach. Fine sand. The jungle is real rain-forest. Big trees, and lots of vines. I'm stuck on this beach, just crawling up out of the water.'

His hands and feet were still normal in shape and colour. Was there anything on them now?

He was quite surprised. 'They have a whole string of pearl rings. One on each finger. Silver or platinum, set with pearls. Big pearls. And I don't like pearls particularly. One ring on each finger.' He had eight rings altogether? He appeared to be counting them before he said, 'Yes.' Anything else on the wrists?

'Trouble is, as you say them, the things appear. That's what happened with the rings, too. When you said so, they appeared.'

'I just asked . . .'

'And they suddenly appeared.'

'They did? What appeared on your wrists when I asked?'

'Big pearl bracelets.'

'And you don't like pearls?'

'No. And they're as big as pigeon eggs.' Were they well polished, or rough and primitive? 'Quite sophisticated. I don't like them. You put them there!'

This was said with a note of facetiousness, so I adopted the same attitude. (Later, after reading the transcript from his

tape-recording, he said he was *not* being facetious; that I *had*
been suggesting. From my own point of view, I may have
inadvertently suggested rings by asking if he saw himself
wearing anything, but I certainly had not mentioned pearls,
nor so many pearl rings. Besides, rings had not appeared on
the two previous occasions I had asked him to describe his
hands. I think that this is the typical annoyance many
experimentees feel when they consider that they are being
asked inconsequential questions.)

'*I* put them there? I don't want to put *any*thing there. But
what else do you see about yourself?'

He was naked, he said. 'Completely naked, except for the
pearl rings. You can take them off now. I'm still on the beach,
propped on my elbows.' And his brief period of facetiousness
was gone, even when he said, 'It sounds silly, but there are still
those damned pearls.'

'You haven't taken them off?'

'*I* can't take them off. *You* take them off.' His facetiousness
was back, but I did not return it this time. I was curious to see
if it would terminate the experiment.

'No,' I said. 'I can't. I just merely ask you things.'

But he still persisted with, '*You* put them there, *you* take
them off!' (In his corrigenda he again says he had no intention
of being facetious and that I could 'make what you like out of
that one, chum.')

'Are there any people there?' I continued.

'No.' Nor were there signs of people having ever been there.
Moreover, he did not think there was a village near by. And so
he was completely serious again, reabsorbed with the
experience.

He could recognize some of the trees as big tropical
rain-forest trees. It was very dark inside the jungle, he said,
just like a lot of rain-forest jungle he had seen. Yet there was
no sound whatsoever, even though, when asked, he *could* hear
the hum and occasional squeak from the tape-recorder. He felt
drawn towards the rain-forest, and yet at the same time was a
little apprehensive about entering it, it looked so dark and
forbidding. However, soon he said, 'I'm going in – and it's
suddenly very, very cold. Suddenly it is as though a wet
blanket has been thrown over me, wet and cold. And now I'm
walking through a patch of mushrooms. There – there *is* a

village, a kind of native village. But there is no one there, not a soul. It's a village of huts, made of thatch, and wood. But there's not a soul. They [the huts] are in very good condition. They have all their cooking utensils, things, all around. But there is just *nobody* around.'

Asked to describe some of the cooking utensils if he could, he said they were 'long, sort of wooden spoons, long handles, about four feet long. And ladles, and barrels, and great big wooden bowls and drums. Everything is wooden, and just an ordinary brown wooden colour.' But then he could see some metal drums and pots. What kind of metal? 'Galvanized iron, aluminium, tin.' Primitive? 'European. They are used by the natives, but they [the metal drums and pots] must be European.' Had the natives bought them, or acquired them some other way? He didn't know. What kind of natives did he think would be there?

'They're coming out now. They are big, and brown. Black, curly hair. And they are just sort of surrounding me, and standing around.' Did they look hostile? 'They look *hungry*, as a matter of fact. I think they *are* hungry. Just like animals, they are – coming in for the kill.'

Did he feel alarmed at this? Quite matter-of-factly, he replied, 'No.' Did he try to escape? Also no. 'You're just going to stand there?' Yes. 'If they do come in for the kill, how will they kill you?'

'With spears.'

'And you don't try to escape at all?'

'No, there would be no point, I wouldn't make it.'

'Have any of them actually started to throw at all?'

'No,' he said at first, quite factually. But then he said, 'Yes, they have,' and mumbled something more that was too incoherent for us to catch, or even to be decipherable from the tape. Then quite clearly, he said, 'They have stabbed me.' Yet he remained motionless where, in actuality, he was lying in my apartment.

'Can you feel it?' I asked. There were certainly no signs on him of the assault, nor did he seem at all perturbed by it.

'No,' he said.

'And what is happening to you now?'

'Nothing.'

'It doesn't kill you?'

'Oh, yes.'

'Does it hurt?'

'No.' A little later he explained to us that by this he had meant it did not hurt *him*, his *actual* self, as he lay there in my room.

'What is *their* reaction?'

'I don't know. They have faded out.'

'They've faded out, have they? Are you just back here? It's all finished, has it?'

'Sort of, yes. I'm drifting around underground now.'

'Underground?'

'Yes.'

'In the *ground*, or in a cavern?'

'I don't know. A big black void – a big void in the underground.' What did he think he was doing there? 'Nothing, nothing at all.' Was he alarmed, distressed? 'No.' Cold or warm? 'Warm.' Could he see anything? 'No.' Did he think he would continue there for some time? 'Probably.'

'What sort of condition do you think you are in?'

'I'm probably dead.'

'Do you want to stay there for long, or you don't know?'

'When you're dead, you're dead, aren't you?'

'I don't know. You just tell me.'

'I'm coming to the surface.'

'Yes?'

'I pop out of the ground. I'm in a terrible mess. I'm covered in vines, and creepers.' What did he think he was? 'I don't know. I'm probably a – I can't move. I'm tied up with vines and creepers.' Was he attached to the ground in any way? 'I probably am. I don't know whether I am or not, but the vines and creepers are growing *out* of *me*.'

'As though you are a tree or something?'

'Sort of, in a nasty sort of way. I think I'll finish it now.'

'You're back? Oh, good. How long do you think you've been?'

'Oh, God! Probably an hour, an hour and a half.'

'You've been an hour and seventeen minutes.'

During the usual 'post-mortem' that followed, D'Arcy said that, after falling into the lake in the latter part of his experience, he had realized that he then had a *choice* of dreams to follow, as frequently happened with him in his normal dreaming. He could have gone on down to the bottom, 'but there was a lot of unpleasant sea life down there,' he said, so he decided to surface and go ashore.

He had also thought, even hoped, that he might 'lose control of himself' during the experiment, but he hadn't at any time. He had always been aware that he could end the experiment at any time he wished. However, he did think that he had required my promptings to 'keep him going', and believed that it required my patience and leading questions for the experiment to be successful (although he conceded that it *could* be conducted by anyone with as much patience and percipience). He considered the experience an 'interactionary affair' greatly relying on me, or someone like me, to conduct it. Yet it is interesting to note that he was able to resume the 'dream' almost instantly after I had deliberately interrupted it.

On April 13th, 1972, when D'Arcy Ryan had read the transcript of the tape-recording of his experiences, he wrote to me in The Netherlands where I was then working . . .

I return here your typescript with a few trifling amendments. No, on second thoughts I've decided to keep it and just send the amendments which I hope will be clear enough. [They were.] I found it interesting reading – being about *me,* how could it not be? – and it has a number of very revealing features, if you know where to look for them. I told Pat [his wife] about the experiment, and showed her the script when it came. She said it was very dull but was relieved to find that there was nothing *queer* about it – but more about that later. [However, apart from a brief corrigenda of only ten small items – changes of words or correction of typographical errors – there was no further mention of this in what was a fairly lengthy letter of mostly personal news.] . . . It might provide a relevant appendix if I mention two dreams I have had since. I'm no sadist; I'll be brief:
1. I dreamt I was a vampire, teamed up, aux Musketeers, with a witch and a werewolf. I could transmogrify and fly. After a lovely fracas on a rooftop in

which we killed numerous policemen (armed, but we were bulletproof) we set out for Transylvania but we got trapped on a mountain pass where my companions were captured. I was just about to rescue them (after a quick snack off the guard's throat) when I awoke.

2. I was in St George's Cathedral. Crowd of tough-looking hippies (middle-aged) in front of the altar, putting on fancy head-gear and chanting. In among the chants I heard 'Tie him tighter', and then a balding, grey-headed man was hauled up by his feet and, while he hung there, they proceeded to gouge his eye out and fluid like washing-up water spurted out. Everyone else was very shocked, and I woke up just as I was telling a distraught Dean Hazlewood '*Now* see what you've done with your Rock Masses!' So you see, the monster theme does recur, although I don't really get two of them as close together as that.

I personally can see little connection really between his experience and what appear to me as perhaps rather concocted 'dreams'. D'Arcy's suggestion that I myself played an essential part in the success of the experiment, however, was reiterated in October 1972, in London, by a Jamaican psychiatrist/doctor practising there. He witnessed an abortive experiment on a friend of long-standing, whom I had thought would prove an excellent experimentee, particularly as he was so eager to try the experience for himself once told of the procedure. The failure was immediate once I suggested the ascent, as he was afraid of heights; he wouldn't even consider continuing the experiment, even though I explained he would be lying safe on his bed all the time. Although he believed that I had hurried the experimentee too quickly through the preliminaries, the psychiatrist also thought that my 'type of personality' was essential as conductor of the experiment. He also felt convinced that the experimentee was subject, even if inadvertently on my part, to a form of suggestive, even 'auto-suggestively induced', hypnotism. As a psychiatrist, he practised hypnotism himself, he told me, and although this possible aspect of it was far from obvious, he had nevertheless suspected it at the beginning of the experiment. Although he soon changed his mind about this, it did make him wonder how much more successful the procedure might be if hypnotism were included, if only to allay the apprehensions of experimentees like this one, but at the same time without interfering with the 'subject matter' of the resulting dream. He said that he found the entire experiment potentially a tremendous aid to psychiatry and intended practising the experiment himself.

Abdeljalil Bouzoubaá

Even before we had left Australian shores on board the *Achille Lauro*, en route for northern Europe, we had met and become close friends with a young man whom I at first thought Latin but who surprised us by being Moroccan; he was called Abdeljalil Bouzoubaá.

He was the eldest of a family of ten, who lived at Meknes. He had undergone a Jesuit education before going on to the University of Paris, where he obtained his *Diploma de Lettres*. He then went to the University of Melbourne to study English. He has a very pleasing and friendly appearance, is short but stocky in build and quite athletic, playing mainly soccer and handball. His hobbies are classical music and reading.

Abdeljalil was naturally apprehensive about returning to a Moslem way of life, which would suddenly impose so many restrictions on him. Not only would there be few unattached European girls of his age in Meknes, but he would be unable to take out a Moroccan girl unless he was already committed to marrying her. Worse than this, he suspected that his family had already, as was the custom, arranged a marriage for him.

During his spare time, Leo told Abdeljalil about the Christos Experiment and Abdeljalil wanted to try it. I, however, was reluctant to do it with him, firstly, because I was engrossed in writing a long and difficult novel under conditions that were far from conducive to writing, and secondly, because the cabin was narrow and cramped with all our luggage. And where else could such an experiment be held aboard ship? There were also the ship's constant noises, making the reception of any tape-recording rather poor in quality, and possible interruptions from stewards to contend with.

But Abdeljalil was persistent, and I had to admit he was

both an unusual and rather specialized person to have as a candidate for the Christos Experiment. He might be Moroccan, but his English was excellent, with only the trace of an accent. However, his voice was naturally soft and I knew from experience that voices became very low indeed once the experiment was well under way, sometimes becoming little more than a whisper. Consequently, I feared that whatever he might have to tell us would be drowned by the constant hum of the ship's engines and air-conditioning. I also felt that he might easily lapse into French, of which I have only a very basic knowledge, and I knew that I would not be able to cope at all were he to lapse, as was even more likely, into his native Moroccan.

But after a month of being such good friends, I could hardly refuse. And so on February 24th, 1972, just three evenings before he was to disembark at Tenerife, we commenced his experiment in our cabin, at 8.10 p.m. Atlantic Ocean Ship's Time. And I am now very glad we did.

Although it is lengthy, I have decided not to paraphrase Abdeljalil's experience completely, but only here and there. However, I would ask the reader to bear in mind that the actual passage of time, except in the case of rapid transitions, is naturally longer and more leisurely than that taken to read this account. The dialogue is inevitably punctuated with pauses of varying lengths and does not indicate the vividness of vision or degree of interest that the experimentee may be experiencing. On the contrary, the experimentee's descriptions of a particularly vivid scene or event are often poor, sometimes with both voice and words diminishing to almost nothing, or even nothing at all if the person conducting the 'run' does not prompt him to keep recounting what he is seeing. If he does stop talking, the experimentee can all too easily fall asleep, though he no doubt continues his 'dream' in the *unconscious* condition in which we normally dream. In this case, like most ordinary dreams, the experience is invariably lost.

After the massaging, with myself at his forehead and Leo at his ankles, Abdeljalil progressed through the imaginative stretching and shrinking exercises without any difficulty and at the normal pace of about a minute for each separate visualization. When asked to imagine himself standing in front of the door of anywhere he had lived – in Morocco, France or Australia – he chose the front door of the flat he had rented in Melbourne, describing it in such detail that it became quite familiar to both Leo and me. He was able to 'ascend' with ease to the roof of the building and 'see' and recount to us, in considerable detail, the buildings and near-by surroundings.

I then asked him to commence the ascent, and he did so almost without any hesitation at all.

He descended to what he could only describe as a very dark place, then a jungle, 'really a forest, dirty-looking water that was not the sea, maybe a river, maybe a lake', he didn't know. But he was coming down towards the jungle or forest, which was becoming increasingly clear, very beautiful, with big palm-trees. It was a clear day and distinctly a tropical climate, hot and moist. There were many trees around him and now, surprisingly, he saw the sea on the left. It was really a kind of bay. No, he was not yet down on to the ground but just above it. On one side of him were very tall trees and he was still about thirty metres above the ground. He was looking for a firm place to land, perhaps on the beach.

'Is the beach made of sand or rock?'

'Sand. Very clean sand. But I've left it. I've gone inland. There is only jungle beneath me. And it's *real* jungle. There is no way – no way for me to go. I have to hack my own. I'm wearing a skirt!'

He was genuinely surprised at this, his hands moving down as though to feel it, but of course encountering the trousers he was wearing in reality.

'A skirt?' I asked him.

'Yes. Made of leaves of trees. Big trees. And I'm very dark! I'm *black*!'

At this he was obviously even more astonished than he had been by his skirt, and this was quite understandable as, although a Moroccan, he was in actuality quite fair with dark brown hair rather than black. He was no darker, indeed he was a good deal fairer, than most Latins.

'Black?' I said.

'Yes.'

'And your hair?'

'Also black. Black, curly hair.'

No, there was nothing on his feet; they were bare. Moreover

he was not particularly interested in them and seemed impatient at the question. Perhaps no wonder, for he was evidently able to study his own *new* black features, almost as though he were gazing into another face, or at least observing his own in a mirror.

'My *eyes* are black!' he proclaimed with the same degree of astonishment. 'And with a white spot in them. And I've got this very, very black, curly hair!'

Was he short or tall?

'Average.'

Fat or thin?

'Thin.'

How old did he think he was?

'About thirty-five, forty years old.'

This really surprised us, for we well knew that he was then only twenty-two, although he would be twenty-three in just five days time on March 1st, the day he expected to arrive home in Meknes. He seemed just as surprised himself. Was anyone else with him, or in sight?

'I'm alone. I'm holding a kind of lance at the moment. Yes, I'm on the ground, holding this lance. It's to protect me.'

There were still no other figures around him, not even birds or animals. There was no noise, he said – nothing. Just the jungle.

'Is it a place that you feel you know?'

'No, no. I've never been there.' He seemed uncomfortable in these surroundings and soon said, 'I'm coming back to that beach. It's very nice. I like it; I like to be there. But I have to find my way to it.'

This was difficult, he said, because there were lots of trees still, though the trees were much smaller now. Just lots and lots of trees. Again I asked him if there were any other people – or animals, birds, or perhaps just insects. 'No,' he replied, 'no,' if anything a little shortly, as though irritated at this questioning – something I have frequently experienced when experimentees are absorbed in whatever they are seeing.

'Is the grass . . .' I started to ask, but was immediately cut short. He was almost indignant when he said, 'I'm not giving any false description! I'm standing and turning my feet.'

No, he didn't know what part of the world he was in. He had never been there before.

Did it feel real?

'Yes. Very real. I think it is a jungle in Africa. I don't know it, but . . .'

'It could be anywhere?'

'Yes.'

'And can you find your way back to that beach, or not?'

'No, I'm kneeling on my knee.'

'Kneeling on your knee? And what are you doing with your lance?'

'I'm holding it. I'm in front of a cave.'

'A cave?'

'Yes, a cave. It's very dark. I'm going in. I'm down, but I can't get in. It — it goes *down*. I think it was used by some people. I *can't* get in. I have to jump.'

'Do you want to jump, or stay where you are?'

'No, no. I'm going. I'm walking now. My feet are really black.' Then he grinned. 'And the sides are red. I'm wearing another skirt now — white. A piece of cloth.'

Why the sudden change? Or, instead of somewhere in Africa, was he perhaps in a place like Fiji?

'What is the hem of it?' I asked him.

'What do you mean?'

'Is it a straight skirt, or is it . . .'

I had been about to ask him if it was flared in the Fijian style, but he was again becoming impatient with my interruption, as though I should just accept whatever he had to tell me and not ask him for other information. He even frowned as a person does when annoyed at being distracted.

'It's just like a towel you put around you,' he said, 'above my knees.'

Did he wear anything else?

'No. I'm wearing a sort of hat at the moment, made of a thick, er — some sort of material, I don't know what. And I have got a collar around my neck as well. And very, *very* long nails. Terribly long.'

'While you are looking at your hands, do you wear any rings? Or any bracelets on your arms?'

'On my left arm. Silver. I can recognize one, anyway.'

'You can?'

'Yes. It belongs to Moudanlah.'

'It belongs to . . .?'

Again he interrupted impatiently. 'Moudanlah! It is a woman – a slave woman, you know – that we had at our house.'

'A *real* slave woman?' By which, of course, I meant in his actual life. How disappointing now if he should suddenly revert to his present life, just as it seemed that he was observing something so entirely different. Perhaps this did happen for an instant, but certainly not for long. And possibly it had been my own reference to his actual life which had caused it as much as anything, or would some reason for this recognized bracelet emerge later?

'Yes.'

'Oh. It *was* a real slave woman,' I said.

'Yes. A real slave woman. She was my nurse before I left for school.'

Abdeljalil had already told us that he was about four years of age when he was sent to the Jesuit College de la Salle.

'It belongs to her,' he continued. 'I still remember her . . .'

'And that's with several other bracelets?'

'Yes. It is from my shoulders. It's a bit heavy. I'm – I'm walking, you know. It's a – it's a . . .'

His feet were making plodding movements, so I prompted him with, 'A steep hill?'

'No. I had to use my knife to get on the top. I want to see what's around me. I want to find someone to talk to.'

'Do you have a *name*?' I ventured, at the risk of another rebuff.

'No,' he retorted, without giving it any apparent consideration.

'No? Or don't you know yet?'

'No,' he answered ambiguously.

'If you have found someone to talk to . . .'

But of all things, it appeared that the alien landscape he had visited had already reverted to the familiar, for . . .

'I'm coming back now to my flat,' he said, obviously as surprised as we were. 'I can see the division of my flat.'

I felt disappointed, presuming the experiment already to be over. But not at all . . .

'Yet I'm still the same person,' he said, even more surprised, 'in the front of my flat. And there are people.

People. Neighbours. They can't understand it is me. Hmm . . .'

'This is the flat in Melbourne?'

'Yes, my flat. Marian, she is horrified.' Who was Marian? I didn't, at this stage, dare interrupt to ask. 'She can't – she doesn't realize it is me.'

'She doesn't?'

'No.'

'You can recognize all the people?'

'Oh, yes. Marian – she's about fifty years old – is there. And the other woman; I don't know her name. Marian – I know she is married; she is married to a doctor – she's a very nice person. We always talked together. And the other person, I never talked to her, she's closing the door.'

'She doesn't believe it is you?'

'No. No, she's closing the door, and screaming. I'm on the top of the hill now.'

'On top of the hill?'

'Yes.' And of all things, he actually giggled; I can only presume at registering my own note of astonishment at this sudden jump back to the visualized (or should I say imagined?) landscape from one that had previously been all too familiar to him. 'Oh, I can see the beach,' he said now. 'And it is beautiful. I want to run and get there quickly. I'll probably change colour.'

'Which beach is it?'

Impatiently he retorted, 'Oh, it's the beach I described before. It's *very* nice.'

'Are there any other people yet?'

'No, no. No one. I'm on my own.'

'You've still got the lance? Or not?'

'Yes.' And then, laughing, 'I have to use it now. There is a big – very big – animal coming.'

'Animal? What kind?'

His laughter suddenly stopped.

'Well – prehistorical,' he said. 'It is walking towards me.' He was now breathing deeply, stretching his head upwards and backwards as though he would press himself into the mattress and pillow of the bunk to avoid something approaching him. His hands and then his feet began moving, as though both to defend himself and run away. 'It's coming!'

he said, and seemed obviously alarmed; and so I thought it might reassure him if he heard my voice again.

'Is it bigger than you are?'

'Oh, it is *very*, very big. It's a *very*, very big animal.'

'It's not an animal you see these days?'

'Oh, no – not at all. It's coming! Huh!' And he began writing. 'I have to kill it.'

'And are you able to do it with the lance?'

'Oh, I will. I won't move, anyway. I'll let it come. It takes a long time to come in, you know. But it *is* coming. It seems to be nearly there but – it's coming. Hah!'

'How much taller than you is it?'

'It's like a fly to a car.'

'Yes?' I began to wonder if he was joking, pretending such a thing. Or else, watching the way he was now writing on the bunk, his hands and feet so active that they sometimes banged the cabin wall or the bottom of the bunk above him, was he perhaps becoming hysterical? But the Abdeljalil we had come to know in the past month had always seemed practical and well-balanced. Hysteria was the last characteristic one would have attributed to him.

'It's coming,' he went on. 'A big, big tall neck.'

'You think it can see you?'

'Oh, yes. It's coming towards me. Really.' This last word was as though to reassure me.

'Can you hide from it? Or what do you do?'

'I have to fight it. It's coming. Now.'

He was now not only writing and breathing deeply, but grunting and going through all the gestures of struggling. At one stage I feared he might even throw himself from the bunk and on to the cabin floor, perhaps injuring himself if he did. But then suddenly he stopped writing and lay still, only his chest still heaving from what had been, even on the bunk, considerable physical exertion.

'It's dead,' he said.

'Dead?'

'Yes.'

'How did you kill it?'

'I cut its neck.'

'You cut its neck?' But then, remembering how his hands had seemed to be gripping something, I also had to ask, '*And* strangled it?' But this he chose to ignore.

'Its neck is just on top of the hill. I can see a very, very big body.' Then, almost excitedly, 'I can use it to come down now, because there is no other way to come down. I can use its neck. I walk on its body. Yes, it's moving. The meat is raw, not dead yet. I'm coming down now. Hah!'

I don't know why, but I could not resist asking him a seemingly irrelevant question, perhaps because I again suspected that he might be making it all up.

'And what colour are you now?' I asked.

He was almost impatient when he replied, 'I'm still *black*.'

'Hair?'

'Pardon?'

'Your hair?'

'My *hair*!'

He seemed genuinely puzzled that I should ask him such questions. 'Yes,' I persisted.

And so he answered, 'It is brown now, but still curly. Yes, I'm getting blue. I look like a caméléon.' He pronounced the word in the French way. 'You know what a caméléon is in French?'

'Yes. Almost the same in English. A chameleon.'

'Oh. You know the animal? If you put it on red, it changes to red.'

'Yes.'

'I look like that – because I'm walking on the body, you know? So I'm blue. And I'm walking with big, big steps.' And now his feet moved as though he were indeed striding. 'I killed that big animal, you know. Now I'm running. I've left my lance behind me.'

I remember having noted during the experiment that, no doubt because his French was better than his English (no matter how good the latter might be), he called the weapon he saw himself holding and using a 'lance' rather than a spear. But he had said he was running.

'Which way are you running?'

'I'm er – I'm *not* running towards the beach. I'm running towards, er – there is a way. I can see a way down there.'

'You mean there is a footpath?'

'Yes. Flat. There are trees behind it. There are trees everywhere. Earth. It's brown. And yet it's green. You know, except the way.' By this I ascertained that by 'way' he meant path. 'You can only see that way, which I'm going now. And I'm walking.'

'Any rocks at all?'

'No, no.'

'Can you see where it is leading?'

He paused for a while before answering this time. Then 'Yes. I can see a big castle now.'

'A big *castle*?' Had I heard him correctly?

'Yes. Very white.'

'White?'

'Yes. I can recognize it. It's in Istanbul. The Blue Mosque.'

'Have you been there in reality?' I was again incredulous at how quickly he had apparently reverted to the familiar and actual.

'Yes,' he said, and I felt quite deflated; however, I decided to persist.

'And what colour are *you* now?'

'I'm wearing a white dress – a Moroccan dress, a "djelaba". I had to get him to spell it for me afterwards, as at the time it sounded more like *chidadah*.

'But what colour are *you*?'

'I'm my own colour.'

'You are yourself?'

'Yes.'

Was the experiment already over? Just as I expected him to open his eyes, perhaps even sit up, his forehead creased and he said, 'No, I look like my grandfather. I'm *with* someone. There are plenty of slaves around me.' Was this really like his early life in Morocco? In our previous normal conversations I had never heard him mention 'slaves' as such, although as his family was well-off by Moroccan standards he did indeed often mention servants.

'Slaves?'

'With red hats.'

'Are they the red fez?'

'Fez, yes. They are bending.' Presumably he meant bowing.

'And you are still near the mosque? How long ago *is* this, do you think?' But he did not reply; he seemed to be puzzling over the matter, as though it was quite difficult to understand. 'Do you think it is in modern times?' I prompted.

'Oh, no, no!' And he could hardly have been more adamant. 'You know, this castle is surrounded by a forest around it. Just by the castle is a big, big place with all the slaves standing there, bending to my grandfather. I'm coming, you know.'

'And you can see them all quite clearly?'

'Oh, yes.'

'Do you recognize any of them?'

'No.'

'No? They are *all* strangers? Are you going to buy some?'

He was quite indignant when he replied, 'They are *not* to sell!'

'They're not?'

'I'm the king, you know – of the country.'

'You are wearing a fez yourself?'

'No, no. I'm not wearing anything.'

'Not even the white skirt any more?'

'No.'

'What colour is your skin?'

'Very brown.'

'Not black as it used to be before?'

'No, I'm – I'm tanned. Sun-tanned. Not my natural colour.'

'Do you still wear the white skirt?' I prompted again.

'No, I can't see myself wearing the white skirt.'

'You can't?'

'Yes, before. But now – I'm nude.'

This seemed extraordinary before a lot of people, yet apparently not to him.

'What do you see now?'

Once again he appeared to be perplexed and did not reply for a while. Then, quite suddenly, he said, 'Oh, no more castle. Nothing. Just flat, flat plains. No trees. Nothing.'

I had not experienced this quick changing from location to location before, whether existing in reality or purely imagined. But by his expression he was already absorbed in yet another landscape, so I could only presume he was serious about it. These sudden changes were obviously quite genuine, and each time I had to start from the beginning again. So naturally I had to ask, 'What kind of day is it?'

'A very, very hot day. I can see the, er . . .' And his hands, especially his fingers, made a rapidly shimmering movement.

'Heat haze?'

'Yes. I'm sweating. It's very hot.'

'Is anybody else there?'

'No.'

'You're alone?'

I could not help wondering what had been the point of his grandfather, whether seen as actually his grandfather or as himself in his grandfather's body, and all those slaves near Istanbul's Blue Mosque if he were to leave it so quickly. What could be the point of their sudden disappearance? But there was no time for speculations, or even more questions.

'It's very scary,' he said. He offered no more, so I asked him, 'Why is it scary? Because you are alone?'

'Because I don't like that sort of place, where there are no trees, nothing. If there are trees, at least you can hide behind a tree if someone wants to attack you.'

'*Can* you see anybody?'

'A black dog.'

'A big dog, or a small dog?'

'Big. It gets bigger and bigger. It gets very big. *Very* big. It's got white feet.'

Surely not another prehistoric animal, I could not help thinking. Perhaps they were symbolic or psychological 'monsters', suitable for psychiatric analysis? This time I thought I might lead him on a little, if only to see what effect it had upon his apparent absorption. I had no doubt that he was taking it all, and therefore his various selves, quite seriously.

'Does it bark at all?' I asked.

'No, no. It's going to attack me. Really.' And once again he became agitated, then writhed and dodged some visualized foe while lying on the bunk. 'I've nothing to fight against him,' he said, throwing up his hands above his head as though to defend himself. 'It's coming.'

'Is it so *very* fierce?'

'Yes. It looks like – a wolf. Now . . .'

There was again a lot of writhing and heavy breathing, which then suddenly stopped.

'What have you done to it?' I asked.

'I pushed it away. I'm walking on it, screaming. I'm jumping on it.' And there was more heavy breathing, which again abruptly stopped. 'I need some water.'

'And you are still in the desert? Anybody around?'

He did not reply, but allowed his heavy breathing to diminish. Then he said, 'My hands are red with its blood – red of the blood of the dog.'

'And you can see the dog? The body of the dog?'

'No, it has disappeared.'

'But you've got its blood left on your hands?'

'Yes.' He paused again, and then, 'I can see all lizards coming towards me. Big ones, and many of them. They come after the smell of the blood. Very big lizards. Long ones. There are *mil*lions.'

'Have they got a name?' I had meant by this, but had put the question badly, if it were a species of lizard he knew. I suppose I deserved his impatience.

'No. Yes. Of course they've got a name.'

'Have you seen this kind of lizard before?'

'Yes. I've seen them in the Melbourne zoo.'

Obviously it is never difficult for an experimentee to refer to something in his present life-experience, no matter how unfamiliar or even removed (in time as well as in location) this other visualized experience may be.

'And now you can see them in the desert?'

'Yes. I'm running. Running, running, running, running. There is an airport. I can see an airport, but it is very far away. I can see the flag; it gives the direction of the wind. I'm running. I jumped over the fence.'

'You have been running for quite a way – and a long time. But what age are you?'

'Now I'm very young. Seventeen.'

'And you are in the airport now?'

'Yes.'

'And are there planes? Or people? Or what?'

'There's no one. Nobody. It's deserted. I'm very thirsty.'

For a moment I thought he had meant in actuality, and was about to end the experiment again if only by getting up to fetch him a drink from the water-jug. Then it occurred to me that he might have meant that he was only thirsty as this other self he was seeing in the desert airport. To make sure, I asked him, 'Can you find something to drink?'

It was a good job I had asked as it was then immediately apparent that, as he told me afterwards, he was not at all thirsty in actuality; and yet, at the same time, he could *feel* the sensation of thirst being experienced by his other self.

'No,' he said, 'I'm searching. I'm in a big – it looks like a jungle again. And there is a river. There's a bridge. But the river is dry, very dry; it looks like powder. The river, in winter, is probably very full. But now, because of summer, it is dry.'

How well I knew rivers like this in the north of my own country. Was this where he was? But what about the deserted airport? Somehow it all seemed to smack at least of the present, if not of the future. But as yet we had not even ascertained in just which part of the world he was now seeing himself.

'I can find no water,' he was saying. 'I'm walking. I can see palm-trees – tall ones. I can have some water now. Yes.'

This sounded as though he was coming to some kind of oasis, and therefore placed him still in Africa, if more to the north of it than when he had seen so much jungle, and nearer too to his native Morocco. But then again, *was* this so?

'What is it in?' I asked him.

'It's in a jar, a big jar, one that keeps the water cool.'

I don't think I could have been more surprised.

'Where *is* this jar?'

'Just to one side of the jungle,' he said, quite matter-of-factly, as though it was the most natural place for such a jar to be. 'And it's got a wooden top on it.'

'Did somebody put it there?' I asked, possibly a little incredulously, though it might seem strange for anyone to be incredulous at so ordinary-seeming a detail compared with the so much more incredible events or circumstances that are so often recounted.

'Yes,' he said. 'Probably for the people who travel, I can't tell.'

'Have you drunk of this water?'

'Not yet.'

'Are you going to?' I was already wondering if he would, in actuality, make swallowing motions when he drank, considering how expressive his hands and even feet could be at times.

'I'm very thirsty,' he repeated; and just as I had half expected, he *was* making swallowing motions, his hands to his mouth.

'Are you drinking?'

'Ah!'

'Does it taste good?'

'No, it tastes like caoutchouc!' From my stockbroking days in Singapore, I was already familiar with this French term, if rather more in the sense of the total commodity.

'Like rubber?'

'Yes. Not that it matters. In my state I can drink anything. I think I'm all right now, though I'm still hungry.'

It seemed quite rational of course that, experiencing thirst in such a 'vision' of himself, he should discover water somewhere or other; but if the travellers' jar had seemed extraordinary enough – even ingenious if any of this had been concocted – how much more extraordinary or ingenious it was for him to think of slaking his thirst, only to find the water tasting of rubber.

'How did you drink it?' I then asked him, thinking of the gesture he had made at the time. 'With your hands?'

'No. There is a cup – a white cup.'

'Made of what? Metal?'

'Metal.'

'Is it absolutely round, a round shape, or what?'

I thought that perhaps a description of this vessel might give an indication of the time-period in which he was seeing himself.

'No,' he said. 'It's got a bottom, and a handle.'

'Is it like an ordinary metal mug?'

'That's right.'

'A modern one, or an old one?' I persisted.

'Oh, it looks old.'

But as he was showing signs of impatience again, I decided not to press the matter further, as more important things might be revealed if the experiment was not interrupted by careless persistence. So, 'It doesn't matter,' I said. 'What are you doing now?'

'I'm walking towards the trees now.'

'Are you still hungry or . . .'

'Yes, I'm very hungry.'

'Do you know where to look for food?'

'Yes. There are dates.'

So this, at least, helped pin-point his locality. No doubt he was somewhere in the Sahara; it did not sound like Australia.

'Dates? Do you have to pick them, or are they already picked?'

'No. I can find them on the floor.' He meant ground. 'They are very nice – very sweet.'

'Better than the water?'

'Oh, yes.'

'And what colour is your skin?'

'Dark.'

'And are you still' – but I didn't want to put words into his mouth – 'what age?'

'I'm very old.' Yet another change.

'Are you tall or short?'

'Short. Very thin. You can count the ribs.'

'Do you think you have a name?'

He took a little while to think about this, but then shook his head on the pillow when he said, 'No.'

'Is there anybody else there?'

'No.'

'Do you think you have any family? Do you know where they would be?'

'Ah, no. I am all alone.'

'Do you like being alone, or not? Or do you want to find someone?'

'Not at my age. I think it is the end.'

'You think it's the end?' I wondered if by this he meant the end of the experiment, or the end of himself as he was then seeing himself.

'Yes. I don't want to walk any more. I'm very old.'

His voice was very low; he was quite still, and even his real face looked weary, if not on the point of exhaustion. Once again I wondered if we should bring the experiment to an end. Or should he, as had other experimentees before him, be allowed to go through a possible death experience?

'Where are you now?'

'I'm sitting.'

'Still near the palms?'

'Yes. I'm resting my head on a stick.'

'What kind of a stick?'

'Wood.'

'Short or long?' Perhaps the stick would give an indication

of the time in which he thought himself to be? But he evidently considered the matter of little, if any, importance compared with what now had him so preoccupied.

'I'm sitting in a position to rest my head,' he said.

'I see.' Then trying again, 'You've got your head on the stick?'

'Yes. I'm thinking.'

'What are you thinking of?'

What was to follow was not at all what I had been expecting.

'My age,' he said. 'All the time I've had.'

'And what did you do with it?'

'Oh, no regrets at all.'

'No regrets?'

'No. None at all.'

'You've had a good life?'

'Yes, I'm quite happy about it. Really.' This at twenty-two.

'And what do you think you will do – just stay there?'

'Oh, I don't know.' And then, quite abruptly, 'No, no, no. I *have* to go and find out.' And his arms began to move around again, though he remained silent for a while. I was about to ask him what he was doing when he said, 'I'm flying.'

'Flying?'

'Yes.'

'How high in the air have you gone?'

'It's beautiful, beautiful. I'm very athletic.'

'How *high* have you gone?' I persisted, for I wanted to know if he had transformed himself into some kind of bird or if he had merely reverted to the preliminary exercises of the experiment.

'I'm going high. There's no wind.'

'If you look down,' I persisted, 'can you see land, or sea, or anything?'

'I'm flying above the airport,' he said, in tones implying that I should have realized this. Ah, so the airport was still there.

'Have you seen any planes or people there yet?'

'No. I have *wings*! I have wings my*self*!'

'Do you?'

'Oh, yes.'

'You *have* got wings? And can you see your hands? Feet?'

'No.'

'What colour are you?'

'Green.'

'Skin?'

'Everything is green. I've got feathers.'

'You've got feathers! Do you feel like a bird?'

'No! I *know* I'm human.'

'You *are* human?'

'Yes, but – I invented that myself.'

'You invented it?'

'Yes. I got it from a legend actually – Icarus.'

'But you feel the sensation of flying?'

'Oh, yes. I don't want to go down.'

'What time of day is it?'

'It's evening.'

'Can you see a long way around you?'

'Oh, yes.'

'What kind of a country is it?'

'Meknes.' So now he was in Morocco, and presumably in the present again. 'I can see, now, the big minaret. It didn't take me long to get there. And it is very far away.'

As in ordinary dreams, conscious dreams can provide instant transposition across even vast distances.

'You got there quickly?'

'Yes. But the city is disappearing again.'

'And what do you see instead?'

'A big wall. A very big wall. A very *tall* wall. Oh . . .'

'Is it a building?'

'No, no. It is the wall surrounding the city – to protect it from war, probably.'

'And which city is it?'

'I *think* it is Meknes.' He was obviously uncertain.

'You recognize it? Meknes today, or in the future?'

'No. It's as it *used* to be. Hah, I like flying! It's a great sensation.'

'And you are high above the city?'

'I'm right above the *middle* of the city now.'

'Can you see people?'

'Yes.'

'What are they wearing?'

'Normal clothes.'

So he *was* back in the present after all, even though he felt himself to be flying.

'Are they clothes from today, or what?'

'It's mixed. Young people are wearing European clothes. I can't see many *old* people. I can't distinguish them very well. I'm very high, you know. I can't make a distinction. I *can* see a big fountain, in the middle of the square.'

'Do you recognize it?'

'No. But I've heard about it actually. But I've never seen it.'

'You've *never* seen it?'

'No.'

'But it exists in actuality?'

'Yes.'

'And are you still actually flying?'

'Yes.'

This part of his experience sounded more to me like accounts I had read of purported astral travelling. I wanted to ask him about it, but he said, 'I'm going now. It looks like a tower I'm visiting.'

'A tower?'

'Yes. It takes me a very short time to get there, you know. I see the old times, almost as if I *remember* them. I see the minarets, and a block of – like a picture, you know – houses with different colours. And it is on a hill. I'm going down. I'm leaving. I won't see it any more. I'm going – and I'm back. I'm still flying. The sunset is very red. It is beautiful.' The cabin, of course, was dimly lit with just the one light. 'Hah! I haven't got wings any more!'

'No wings?'

'No. I'm falling down.'

'Is it really the story of Icarus?'

He did not answer, but merely frowned. Had he forgotten his own reference to this already?

'Where have you fallen?' I asked.

'On the ground.'

'You're on the ground. You're quite comfortable?'

'I don't know. I feel terrible. I feel pain.'

'Actual *pain*?'

'Yes.'

'Has anybody come to you? Or are you alone, or what?'

'There are only trees around me.'

'Only trees?'

'I'm on a piece of land. Brown land.'

'The city has gone?'

'Oh, yes. I can't see the city any more. There is no one.'

'And what colour are you?'

'I'm – *black* again.' And at the time I almost expected it. Were we, if I permitted it, to start the cycle all over again?

'Do you have anything on or not?'

'No. I'm in the nude. I'm *old*! I think I'm that old man I told you about before. I'm *very* old. I'm over a hundred years, because I can't stand – my back is bent at ninety degrees. You know what I mean?'

'Yes, I know.'

'I'm very old. I'm walking now. I'm looking for someone. I want to kill!'

'You want to what?'

'To kill someone. I don't know why. I'm changing. I'm not human any more.'

'What do you think you are?'

'I don't want to be a – oh!'

'What did you become?'

'I think I'm a bird.'

'You're in transition?'

'Transition?'

'What do you think you are changing into?'

'I have feet – two feet – but they're not human feet. They are – what do you say? – like sheep's feet, with hoofs. And do you know, the bottom part is very dirty. And it is brown, and light. But up here, you know [he clasped his chest with both hands] I'm a normal human being, with a tan as well. Funny, I've got very short hands. But the feet look like a sheep's, standing. I'm walking now. But I'm changing again.'

Before yet another transition took place, I hastened to ask him something I wanted to know.

'Have you got a human head?'

'Oh no,' came the answer. 'I have a sheep's head.'

'Then what do you think you are?'

'I'm a king.'

'Do you have a name?'

But, as previously, the answer was still the same. 'No,' he said, but then went on quickly to add, 'I'm hungry.'

'Are you a king of some place?'

'No. I'm a king on my own.'

'And you are still alone?'

'Yes. And there's not much around.'

He was quiet now for some time, so that I had to prompt him.

'You're still in the same form?'

'Yes.'

'Like a sheep standing up?'

But, 'No, no!' he said impatiently. 'I can see water. I'm changing. I'm not human. I'm a – I'm a frog! A very, very small frog. And the water is dirty.'

'Is it better to be swimming than it was flying?'

'Oh no. I don't like it. There are big fish around, and they probably want . . .'

He had stopped again. 'They probably want what?'

'To eat me – I don't know. The water is green now. I'm coming up. I'm swimming. I'm human again now. I'm on the edge of a pool.'

This talk about being a frog lasted about a minute and a half, not just the few seconds it takes now to read these half a dozen or so lines. If you count out ninety long seconds to yourself, it's quite a long time, almost interminable when you are sitting waiting for this extraordinary sequence of transitions to formulate themselves into some kind of pattern, or else, after close to an hour, at least come to an end. Would a normal, stable human being under much more usual conditions have the patience to make such observations for so long, let alone be so completely absorbed in them as Abdeljalil so obviously was, even after lying there on the bunk for (counting the extra twenty minutes for the preliminaries) well over an hour? At times, I must admit that I was still suspicious that he was faking a good deal of it. Yet I never seemed to be able to catch him out in any of his details, and most experimentees can easily be caught if they start making things up. Besides, I have only to look closely at the experimentee to verify for myself: when such visions are actually being seen, the experimentee is subject to what psychologists call Rapid Eye Movements (or REMs) which cannot be faked. If the experimentee is faking, the eyes invariably remain still, or the lids squeeze with the obvious effort of concoction, or there are only slow movements of the eyes beneath the lids, almost as though the eyes are searching around inside their lids for answers to the questions being plied. And so I asked:

'Were you really a frog, or were you just imagining that?'

He was not only indignant, but I could see quite plainly that his eyes were flickering to the rapid movements. He was also impatient to continue.

'No, I was really a frog,' he retorted.

'But you are back to a human again?'

'Yes, because I could *see* the – transition, you call it? I was green and down in the water. And when I came up, I became bigger and bigger.'

'You're as big as you are now? In reality?'

'Yes.'

'And colour?'

'My colour.'

'You're in the present time?'

'Yes. I'm on the edge now – on the edge of the pool. But it's not a pool. It's a mere, a lake. A small lake. I'm reading a book.'

'Do you know what book it is?'

'It's got no name.'

'Do you know what *language* it is in?'

'English.'

'English?'

'Yes. I'm thinking – philosophy. I've just read a bit of it, and now I'm thinking.'

'And what are you dressed in?'

'Still in the nude.'

'In the nude. Aren't you wearing *any*thing? Rings? Or anything at all?'

'No, I don't like rings.'

This was an extraordinary statement for him to make, as in ordinary life he normally did wear a ring and sometimes other adornments – a bracelet or at least a wristwatch – as well as always being very conscious of dressing quite fashionably.

He was alone again. There were no buildings in view, just trees, 'a big forest' unlike anything he had ever seen in actuality. He had no idea at all where it was, nor did he know what he was doing there, apart from thinking about a book he had just been reading while sitting naked. I was beginning to

think the experiment would be interminable if I allowed it to
be, and so I decided to draw his attention back to his
immediate and actual surroundings, perhaps bringing him
out of the experience at long last.

'While you are there, can you also hear the sounds of the
ship?'

'Oh, yes.'

'And you know it is me talking?'

'Yes.'

'And what are you doing now?'

'I'm thinking.'

'Just thinking?'

'Yes. Say, my hair is short. And straight.'

'You are your normal self again?' I suggested. But he did
not reply, so I asked, 'Do you see your surroundings still?'

'Yes.'

'It looks quite clear?' He nodded. 'And what time of day is
it?'

'It's spring.'

'Are you warm or cold?'

'You know – the spring. You're not warm, you're not cold.
You know, I always liked the spring. I always enjoy it. Makes
me think.'

'And you are still reading?'

'No.'

'What are you doing now, then?' I already suspected his
activity, as his arms and legs were moving again.

'I'm running,' he said. 'Running.'

'Why are you running?'

'I'm playing with a ball, like a football, just on my own.'

'And you've got a real ball?'

'Yes. It's a real ball. I'm very tiny.'

'Are you wearing shoes, or are your feet bare?'

'I'm changing again. I'm looking like a small bird, but I
don't know the name of the bird in English. Really. It is a *very*
small bird. I have wings – two types of wings. One on the top
and one on the bottom.'

'Oh, like a humming-bird?'

'Yes, that's right. I'm young. Very, very young. I'm
dancing.'

'And are you high above the ground, or just above it?'

'No, I'm *on* the ground. Dancing. It is very nice.'

'What colour are you?'

'I'm, er – I'm wearing a hat.'

So he wasn't being at all suggestible here.

'A hat?'

'Yes. My head is round, like a ball. My neck is really very thin, and my arms are very thin as well. And I have only two fingers on each hand. And I'm wearing a black skirt; it is very wide, on the top, up here [he made movements with his hand around his hips]. And then the skirt is going down, and my legs are very thin.'

'And what colour are *you*?'

'Black. I can't see the colour of my skin, but everything is black, except here [he touched his chest and shoulders] it's white.'

'Then what form are you now? You're not a bird any more?'

'Oh, I'm still a bird, dressed up. It's a skirt I'm wearing. I'm running. Running, running, running. I'm changing green-yellow-black. And white. I'm becoming like – like a duck. I'm running – very fast.'

'You're still in the same place at the time?'

'No. I'm running. You *know* the place – where children play. Like a Luna Park. I'm there now, wearing a red hat.'

'Still as the bird?'

'Yes, it looks like a bird. A bell? A churchbell?' He was suddenly listening, but there was no sound of a bell on the ship, nor on the tape where all other ship noises are audible. But this did not distract him for more than a few seconds. 'I'm walking,' he continued. 'Walking with my hands behind my back.'

He was still in the place like a Luna Park, which he could see, he said, with incredible clarity. But just as I was about to ask him for specific details, the impetus of his visions again carried him forward before I could do so.

'I'm changing to a human now. But very little. Changing now. And getting fat. A *big* man. Red. Hair, black and grey. I'm not very old – must be sixty. [Another extraordinary statement for a young man of only twenty-two.] I'm dressed very, very formally. A uniform. Very formal. I'm walking, very much.'

'Is it modern, or is it old?'

'No, it's not modern. I'm in a court, actually. A palace on each side of it. It must be a *big* garden, you know. I've never seen it before. It is very beautiful, though. Very, very nice.'

No, he didn't know where it was, and there were no other people around. The whole scene, incredibly clear as it might be, was entirely deserted. It was eery, he said, so he kept on walking. He was then silent for some time, his eyes moving rapidly; but I was too weary to ply him with more questions. I suppose I should have asked for details of the uniform he was wearing, so that we could perhaps have traced the period in which he now saw himself. I had learnt that experimentees rarely if ever tire of their experience, whereas it soon becomes quite wearying, even exhausting, for the one 'running' the experiment. Abdeljalil was clearly reluctant to come to an end, in spite of all the running he had seen himself doing in his various forms, but I fear I was quite tired and longing for his experience to be ended.

Asked what he was doing now, Abdeljalil said he was still walking.

'And can you still hear the sound of the ship?'

'Oh, yes.'

'And can you hear the sound of people passing in the corridor?' The sound of voices and footsteps outside the cabin is quite audible on the tape.

'Yes,' he said impatiently, 'but I'm walking. I'm on a boat now, on a river.'

He was not at all interested in any actual sounds around him, nor would he be distracted. I remember that I was wondering if he *could* be distracted, or had I launched him on some interminable sequence of visionary events which he found more absorbing than actual life?

He was now in a rowing boat, a small one, still quite alone. He did not have to row the boat because it somehow went by itself. He was in midstream approaching a bridge, just a small bridge, but he still couldn't see any people no matter where he looked, on the riverbanks or the bridge. He went under the bridge and left it behind, going downstream. He was enjoying the trip very much, he said, for 'it was such a beautiful day, about noon.' In actuality, of course, it was becoming quite late in the evening. 'And it is very, very sunny, with only shadow from the near-by trees.' Once more the scene was as vivid as anything he had seen in actuality; it was, he said, as though he was actually there. All the colours were real, not 'overdone' as in a technicolor film. The details were astonishing, down to dancing spots of light from the sun falling on to grass. And when he looked at it closely, he could see every blade of that grass as though he could reach down and pluck some of it.

He paused; and then, 'I'm very hungry,' he said.

So once again I hinted at his possibly ending the experiment by asking, 'Do you think you've done enough?'

'Yes, I need something to eat.' Yet it was only two hours or so since he had eaten a sizeable ship's dinner.

'Do you think you want to stop now?'

'Yes.' And I couldn't have been more relieved. All the same, he still hadn't opened his eyes; he was still lying there.

'You *do* feel that you are back here in the cabin?' I ventured.

But no, he was still on the river, and still very hungry.

'You mean, you still want to go on?'

'Oh, yes. If I wasn't hungry, that is. I'm really very hungry, you know.' I could hardly believe this; we had all eaten the same dinner and the last thing I felt like was any more food.

'You want to stop and try it again another time?' I asked hopefully. 'Do you know how long you have been?'

But he was still disinterested in these matters. He said, 'I'm still on the river, you know . . .'

'You *haven't* come back?'

'No.'

Heaven only knew how much longer he would continue if I let him, but I decided to end the experiment even if I had to sit him up and drag him from the bunk forcibly. However, this wasn't quite necessary.

'You'll exhaust yourself if you do any more,' I said, though the only one he was likely to exhaust, I had to admit, was myself. Leo was still sufficiently intrigued to want the experiment to continue, even though it might have meant being there all night. But I had had enough. 'I think we ought to stop,' I said. And then, as though to be quite definite about it, 'You've been an hour and a quarter.'

The tape-recorder wasn't switched off yet, however, as Leo had long learned that the 'post-mortem' of the trip often takes the experimentee as long to recount as the actual experience. Experimentees almost invariably forget that they have already been recounting everything, presuming that they are the only ones who know what they have been seeing. This stems no doubt from associating the experience with actual, or unconscious, dreaming; and perhaps there is little difference between the two phenomena, except that to dream normally the dreamer must be asleep – and so is unable to recount what he is dreaming. Most experimentees take some while to realize that all this time they have been conscious, and *aware*, on at least two levels: first, with what they are 'dreaming' and second, where they are lying while having this 'dream'. Indeed, it frequently takes a reminder or two to this effect before the fact is absorbed.

However, to continue with the rest of the tape:

'Could you see everything you described very clearly?'

'Oh, yes.'

'Did it feel just like a dream?'

'Yes.'

'Did you ever have anything like it before?'

'No, never.'

'No? Was it *very* vivid?'

'Yes.'

'Had you expected it to be like this? Or is it more or less what you expected?'

'I really expected – *any*thing else.'

'Were you conscious of moving all over the bed?'

'No.'

'Moving yourself?'

'No.'

'You nearly came off, several times.'

'Oh?'

'Especially when you were flying. And you really felt the sensation of flying?'

'Oh, yes. It was beautiful.'

'And swimming?'

'Hmm.' He was much more dubious about this.

'We had to take the cushions from underneath your legs, you were moving so much. Do you think it is like a dream? An *induced* dream?'

'No. I was at so many places, and the changing was very quick.'

Here the tape ends.

However, we discussed the experience in considerable detail in the few days we had left before his disembarkation at Tenerife. I questioned him about many of the details, including the travellers' water-jug with its white metal mug. It was not at all modern, he said; on the contrary, it was very old. In replying he never faltered, the details never varied.

He considered that he had seen himself, from both outside the form he was inhabiting as well as from within it, in various forms in which he had either lived or could *possibly,* even probably, have lived. The sensations of flying, and of running and swimming for instance, had been too real to have seemed a mere illusion; they had not at all been a *memory* of such actions but rather an actual participation in them at the time, even to the extent of feeling the air passing, at times even rushing, around him. This sensation, I suppose, was much the same as that written of by Paul Brunton as proclaimed by the Chinese mystic Chuang Tzu, who after a curious dream in which he flew about as a butterfly said he did not know if he had been a butterfly imagining itself to be a man, or a man who had dreamt himself to be a butterfly.

The various scenes were not only in different locations, he averred, but also in different periods of time – though not necessarily in any strict sequence of time, either progressing or receding. He felt that he had been haphazardly seeing himself in various forms, in various periods of time, and in various locations, moving easily from one to the other much as one might do when remembering actual events in one's real lifetime. Moreover, when he had seen himself naked, he had also felt himself naked, although at the same time being aware that he was, of course, wearing clothes as he lay there on the bunk. When he had been thirsty, the mouth and throat he had *had at the time* had been thirsty, not his actual mouth and throat; the same had applied when he had said he was hungry. Once the experiment was over and he was quite at liberty to get something to eat or drink, he no longer wanted it; these sensations were no longer there. Indeed, he said, they never had been so far as his real, his *present* body was concerned; only in the body he had seen himself in at the time.

He had no doubt that he had seen himself in periods of time other than in his own actual lifetime; and in real places, near or far from his own home in Meknes, which he had never seen in actuality. He was not so much convinced, however, that he had actually lived in other forms, locations and periods as that he had experienced the *possibility* of having lived in those other forms, locations and periods.

More important, as he agreed once I pointed it out to him (especially in the early events of his experience), were the psychological attitudes and conditions which were easily translated into his present day and all too real attitudes and circumstances, and which he could easily interpret for himself much as any psychiatrist or psychologist could. The two huge beasts he had had to kill, for instance, were undoubtedly his two great fears of, firstly, not being able to readjust himself to the strictness of his family's Moslem life and, secondly, his horror of having to submit to marrying – according to the Moslem faith – someone who had been selected for him and who, he feared, would be deadly dull after the varied *affaires* he had experienced when away from home.

In his experience, he had killed both of these *monsters*. We have corresponded since, and in actuality he found that by being kind but insistent he was able to leave his family home again after a short time by taking a position as interpreter in Casablanca, thus retaining the freedom he had been afraid of losing. Also, instead of finding that his mother had arranged a marriage for him as he had suspected, within a few months he met a Moroccan girl as liberal-minded as himself. He wrote to me that he was engaged to be married on March 1st, 1973, his twenty-fourth birthday and the first anniversary of his arrival back home. His normal dreams, so far as he knew, had not provided him with such easily interpretable symbols, which might have allayed his apprehensions of his homecoming much earlier.

And the rest of it all? Well that, I suppose, is for Abdeljalil, or any reader, to interpret for himself. So far, in my own two experiences, I have seen myself only in human form. But Abdeljalil was not the only one to see himself in some other form; he was the first, however, to see himself in so many *different* animal – and human – forms. The extraordinary thing about this diversity is that there had been a fundamental and somehow permanent-seeming *self*, that was always instantly *recognizable* as himself, in each and every form he had seen himself to have assumed.

Perhaps even more extraordinary was his feeling that none of the experience seemed at all impossible, fantastic as the various forms and scenes might appear to anyone else. On the contrary, he felt that each and every form, event and location was not only possible but was somehow all too redolent of having been *probable*.

Lastly, as with most experimentees, all these events were readily memorable, unlike ordinary dreams. Furthermore, they were memorable in very great detail for very much longer than many real events in one's actual lifetime.

Paul Kluwer

The next experimentee proved the most difficult I have encountered. I had expected him to be one of the more successful ones, if only because I was sure he would want the experiment to show some degree of success, for Mr Kluwer was a very successful Dutch publisher who had read the manuscript and was interested in publishing *Windows of the Mind*.

Paul Kluwer was about forty, tall and slim, pleasant and meticulously polite. His wife, perhaps even taller than he, fair and also of slim build, had a quiet but essentially feminine charm that made one feel instantly at ease with her. Kluwer on the other hand (perhaps because of the circumstances of business being negotiated between author and publisher) appeared to be reserved, rather distant, even a little cold in attitude – although, as I have already said, he was always polite. He was co-operative up to a certain point, but thereafter he remained adamant. I would not normally have selected him as an experimentee; I felt – though quite instinctively I must admit – that he was much more interested in merely observing the experiment as a concerned and naturally interested *spectator* rather than as a participator. And I had long learned the admonition of the Christos Movement in *Open Mind* magazine that the experiment rarely, if ever, succeeded unless the experimentee was already convinced of, or at least had an open mind about, reincarnation and genuinely wanted to try to glimpse a past life. Kluwer quite obviously did not fit into this category, though strangely enough I felt that Mrs Kluwer might.

So an appointment was made for us all to meet at 5.15 p.m. on Friday, May 26th, 1972 at my literary agent's office in Hilversum. Mr and Mrs Kluwer came from Deventer and my assistant, Leo van de Pas, and I came from De Bilt. With us we had Mrs Ruby Beecham, from Western Australia, who was on a two-week visit to The Netherlands. We wanted her not only to witness this experiment, but also to talk to Mr Kluwer about her own which we had conducted almost a year before and in which she had seen herself, astonishing as it may seem, as an albatross.

So we were six altogether. The number did not bother me at all, as I had previously conducted the experiment with as many people present, and in one case even more. Nor was I concerned about the possibility of two languages being involved as it had already been agreed that any experiment with a Dutch person should be conducted in English, for my 'children's Dutch' was far from adequate.

However, to our surprise, Mr Kluwer insisted that, although I could conduct my side of the experiment and interrogate him in English, he would reply in Dutch. Needless to say I was most disappointed by this, for I feared that I might not be able to follow his Dutch well enough to understand what he was describing and so I might ask the wrong questions, or not know what to ask at all. This, sadly enough, was what was to happen. I was reluctant to conduct the experiment under these conditions, but Mr Kluwer was still keen to try, and both he and Menno Kohn (my agent) presumed that if I did not follow the Dutch then Leo, my assistant, of course would. In vain did I point out that Leo was not only rather shy with other Dutch people, where almost all classes are instantly and intuitively wary of each other until such time as some kind of *rapprochement* is established, but also, because of his own experience with three failed experiments, was reluctant to do more than the heel-massaging and managing of the tape-recording at the time, and the transcription and retyping of manuscripts afterwards.

However, as they all looked so disappointed at the mention

of abandoning the experiment, and with the Dutch publication of my book at stake, I decided that little harm could come of the matter if, as I feared, the experiment failed. Kluwer seemed the kind of person who would surely understand that to conduct a 'conscious dream' without the experimentee falling into natural sleep required a considerable amount of selection and tact on the part of the experimenter, or the person 'doing the run'. After all, in normal sleep, it takes little enough in the way of interruption for the dreamer to be awakened and the dream instantly banished.

Another argument for continuing the arrangement was that my apprehensions regarding Abdeljalil Bouzoubaá had been quite unfounded, when not just one but two other languages were involved. Abdeljalil had replied and spoken the entire time in English, and was conscious of this during his experiment when I asked him if he felt at all tempted to lapse into either French or his native Moroccan. However, Abdeljalil had just spent some time studying and working in Australia, where the majority of people speak only 'Australian'; and few on board the boat with us could speak French and none could speak Moroccan. This probably helped him to communicate so easily in English throughout his own long experience.

However, what had at first appeared a simple enough case in comparison with that of Abdeljalil Bouzoubaá was to be a disappointing failure – or at least far less of a success – mainly because Mr Kluwer, unlike the majority of Dutch, spoke German instead of English as his second language, and I speak virtually no German at all. Hence we had no common language developed to the necessary degree to cope with such an experiment.

But if these circumstances seemed most discouraging, at least the chosen surroundings (about which I had previously had greater apprehensions) proved to be ideal, for my agent's office is in an attractive house, quite large by Dutch standards, on a very beautiful street not far from the famous Radio Hilversum buildings. We had come on a pleasant early-summer day, with the sun shining and a light breeze rustling the new growth of the trees around us.

During the experiment, when I could not understand

Kluwer's responses, I gestured for Leo or my agent or Mrs Kluwer to continue the interrogation in Dutch. At the time, I felt convinced that Leo's attempts were much too shy and therefore quite inadequate, which I found both frustrating and exasperating. Mrs Kluwer made very little attempt, although she was quite obviously enrapt in the entire procedure; she gradually leant forward in her chair, her hands clasped in church-spire fashion before her, as though she was almost trying to insert herself into her husband's mind and what little vision he was experiencing. Menno Kohn, my agent, would not participate at all, not even on the several occasions when I thought that, through sheer lack of prompting, the experimentee would surely be unable to continue and would open his eyes and sit up.

The general reader may find entire transcriptions tiresome reading, especially when the experiment is considered by the experimentee to be at least a disappointment if not entirely a failure, but I have decided that in this one particular case the full transcript should be provided, including that spoken in Dutch, for it was only a few days ago – almost a year since the experiment – that I realized that Leo's promptings and inquiries were in fact perfectly adequate. The full transcript will also show how at times, because of the length of the experiment exaggerated by my tedium at not being able to follow all of it, I interjected at the wrong times and quite frequently with the wrong questions or suggestions.

Here then is Paul Kluwer's experience, which he considered a disappointment; although he had almost decided to publish *Windows of the Mind*, after the experiment he turned it down.

The preliminaries were conducted in the unprecedented time of just under ten minutes, instead of the normal twenty, so that I felt convinced that he was hurrying through them and not at all visualizing them as he proclaimed he was at the time. He described his front door, his house and the surrounding countryside at Deventer in like manner, with a description of his house that was so vivid that even I felt as though I could see it in actuality, and Leo was most certainly impressed. But long before I expected him to commence the 'ascent', perhaps because he had read my manuscript, he was already on his way. Where a 'silence' is indicated, it was more often than not a very long silence indeed, and I frequently felt that the experiment would surely falter and end.

G. Try to float up in the air, and look around you, and tell us what you see.

K. *Omhoog gekomen, zie ik in de verte heuvels die op de Veluwe moeten zijn — allemaal bossen — torens, ja. In de verte zie ik Deventer, met kerken en fabrieken.* Having come up, I see hills in the distance which must be at the Veluwe — all woods — towers, yes. In the distance I see Deventer, with churches and factories.

G. And what kind of a day is it?

K. *Middag.* Afternoon.

G. Is it a good day?

K. *Ja, een hele mooie dag.* Yes, a very beautiful day.

G. And can you still go up higher? So that you can see many miles away? And then tell me what you see.

K. *Als ik nog hoger ga, dan zie ik aan alle einders bossen, Holter- berg — stukken van de Achterhoek — en daar een heel dun kerktorentje ertussen — Heteren of Raalte of Lochem.* When I go higher again, I see woods on all horizons, the Holter Mountain — parts of the 'Achterhoek' — and in between a very slim little church-tower — Heteren or Raalte or Lochem.

G. Do you feel warm or cold?

K. *Ik voel niets van temperatuur.* I feel nothing of temperature.

G. Hmm. And can you go up still . . .

K. *Het is zonnig.* It's sunny.

G. It's sunny?

K. *Ja.* Yes.

G. And can you go up still as high as you can? Till you can't see how it is any more?

      (Silence)

K. *Ja.* Yes.

G. What kind of a day is it now? Has the day changed?

K. *Ik heb nu het idee of ik heel hoog zit, en of de aarde een heel klein bolletje in de verte is zoals wij de maan zien.* Now I have the idea that I'm sitting very high, and as though the earth is a little disc as we see the moon.

G. Now I want you to change it from . . .

K. *Als een astronaut.* As an astronaut.

G. I want you to change . . .

K. What did you say?

G. . . . from day-time to night. I want you to be looking,

instead of it being day-time, I want you to see it as though it is night-time.

K. *Ja.* Yes.

G. And tell me what you see. Is it night-time now?

      (Silence)

K. *Ik zit zo ver van de aarde weg – nu zit ik in de schaduwkant.* I'm so far away from the earth – now I'm on the shadowed side.

G. If you look at . . .

K. *Ik zie nu de aarde als een soort maan die het licht weerkaatst.* Now I see the earth as a kind of moon which reflects the light.

      (Silence)

G. But there is no light? Do you see stars above, or any little light, or anything?

K. *Nee alleen die grote maan die de aarde is.* No, only that big moon which is the earth.

G. Hmm.

K. *Ik zie geen zon.* I see no sun.

G. I want you to change . . .

K. *En de andere – de echte maan – kan ik ook zien.* And the other – the real moon – I can see, too.

G. Yes?

K. *Bijna vol.* Nearly full moon.

G. I want you to change it back to day-time again, still looking down. Get it back into day-time and tell me what you see.

K. *Nu zie ik de aarde als een hele bol – met stukken oceaan en wolken – erg veel wolken.* Now I see the earth again as a whole ball – with pieces of ocean and clouds – a lot of clouds.

G. And is it day-time again?

K. *Ja.* Yes.

G. What kind of a day?

      (Silence)

K. *Ik denk ochtend.* I think morning.

G. Clouds or . . .

K. *Ik zit boven de wolken, heel hoog. Maar er zijn veel wolken.* I'm above the clouds, very high, but there are many clouds.

G. A lot of clouds. Are you higher than the clouds? Or . . .

K. *Veel hoger, ik zie de aarde heel ver weg.* Much higher, I see the earth very far away.

G. I want you to move over the clouds as much as you like — and when you see an opening I want you then to come down.

K. *Ja.* Yes.

(Silence)

Ik zie alleen maar water. I see only water.

(Long silence. I gestured to Leo to take over the questions. He did so, but rather shyly.)

L. *U ziet geen eiland, geen schip?* You see no island, no ship?

(Silence)

G. What kind of water? Is it the sea?

K. *Ja.* Yes.

G. Is it rough or . . .

K. *Het is een heel rustige gladde blauwe zee, zoals de Middelandse Zee.* It is a very calm blue sea, like the Mediterranean.

G. Yes?

(Silence)

L. *Is het de Middelandse Zee, of is het zoals U zich de Middelandse Zee voorstelt?* Is it the Mediterranean, or is it like you imagine the Mediterranean to be?

K. *Zoals ik de Middelandse Zee weleens gezien heb, vanuit een vliegtuig.* It is as I have seen the Mediterranean, from a plane.

L. *En ziet U land of een eilandje waar U naar beneden kunt komen?* And do you see land or an island where you can come down?

G. Can you see the water clearly? As though you are looking at it?

K. *Ik ben erg hoog nog.* I'm still very high.

G. Can you come down then? Can you come down and look at the water close to the waves or — it *is* really water?

K. *Ja.* Yes.

G. No island?

K. *Ik kom ergens naar beneden, het moet haast in Italië zijn.* I am coming down somewhere, it *must* be in Italy.

L. *Is het Italië zoals U het kent? U ziet land? Het is het voornaamste dat U land ziet waar U naar benedan kunt komen.* Is it Italy as you know it? You see land? It is important that you see a place where you can land.

(Silence)

K. *Het is een kust met stenen, niet strandachting maar geen steile kusten.* It is a rocky coast, no beaches and no slopes either.

L. *Ziet U een plaats op de rotsen waar U kunt landen?* Do you see a place to land on the rocks?

     (Long silence)

Zijn het rotsen, hoge rotsen? Of is het een rotsachtig strand? Are there rocks, high rocks? Or is it a rocky beach?

K. *Het zijn meer losse keien – stenen.* They are merely loose stones – rocks.

L. *En als U nu naar beneden komt, land U daar dan?* And when you are coming down, do you land there then?

K. *Ik kan ook wel ergens anders neer komen.* I can easily land somewhere else.

     (Silence)

L. *Ziet U geen groen? Geen grasveld of . . .* Do you see any green? No fields or . . .

K. *Een beetje dor is het.* It is a bit arid.

L. *U bent nog steeds in de lucht?* You are still in the air?

K. *Ik weet niet waar ik ben.* I don't know where I am.

     (Silence)

L. *Kunt U proberen om met Uw beide voeten op de grond te komen?* Can you try to come down on to the ground with both your feet?

     (Silence)

K. *Ik heb geen duidelijk beeld op het ogenblik.* I have no clear vision at the moment.

G. Are you close to the rocks or . . .?

K. *Ik probeer om het beeld vast to houden.* I'm trying to keep the vision.

L. *U zag rotsen – U zag water.* You saw rocks – you saw water.

     (Silence)

Het is nog steeds dag? It is still day-time?

K. *Ja.* Yes.

     (Silence)

L. *De kust, is die ver weg of dichtbij?* The coast, is it close or far?

K. *Ik zie het niet meer – ik zie de rotsen ook niet meer.* I don't see it any more – I don't see the rocks any more either.

L. *Bent U weer hoog in de lucht of zo?* Are you back high in the sky or so?

K. *Ik zit bijna zonder beeld. Alles is blauw om mij heen.* I'm

almost without any view. Everything around me is blue.
    (Silence)
L. *Hoe is de lucht?* How is the sky?
K. *Moet ik weer proberen to duiken, of moet ik weer de lucht in?*
Must I try to descend, or must I go back into the sky?
    (Silence)
L. *Is het nog steeds diezelfde rotsachtige kust of is het anders?* Is it
still the same rocky coast, or is it different?
    (Silence)
G. Are you still high above?
K. *Ik weet niet waar ik ben.* I don't know where I am.
G. Are you just in the sky or where?
    (Silence)
K. *Ik kan niet helemaal een beeld krijgen — ik zit maar in de lucht,
of in het water.* I cannot get a view altogether — I'm just
sitting in the sky, or in water.
G. Do you see anything? Any light? Or anything?
K. *Het is maar blauw voor me.* It is just blue around me.
G. Just blue?
K. *Donker blauw.* Dark blue.
G. Do you feel anything? Are you cold or warm?
K. *Wel.* Well . . .
G. And when you look down below you, do you feel
anything about you? Any wind? Or anything at all?
K. *Het is warm.* It is warm.
G. Just warm?
K. *Zomernacht.* Summer night.
G. Is it a night-time scene, or just a colour?
K. *Het is te donker om te zien. Het is donker om mij heen.* It is too
dark to see. It is dark around me.
G. And there is nothing at all yet?
    (Silence)
What did you see before — some land? And you have left
that?
    (Long Silence)
K. *Het is zo vaag wat ik zie. Ik zie iets van een strand.* It is all so
vague what I see. I see something of a beach.
    (Silence)
L. *Is het wazig of* . . . Is it hazy or . . .
K. *Ja.* Yes.
    (Silence)

Het beweegt, het trilt. It moves, it vibrates.

L.   *En kunt U niet dichterbij komen?* Can't you get any closer?

>   (Silence)

K.   *Het is niet helder.* It's not clear.

>   (Silence)

Ik geloof dat ik weer een stuk terug moet om opnieuw te kunnen duiken. I believe I must go back to be able to dive again.

>   (Silence)

Ik geloof dat dat maar beter is. I believe that that is better.

>   (Silence)

Ja. Yes.

>   (Silence)

Ik ben nu niet zo hoog – een honderd meter. Ik zie een branding of schuimkoppen. Now I'm not so high – a hundred metres. I see a crest or foam.

L.   *Breekt het op de rotsen, of wat?* Does it break on rocks, or what?

K.   *Het is geen strand – een kust.* It is no beach – a coast.

G.   You can see the coast? [A pity I interrupted here, for obviously he was just beginning to visualize a coastline with improved clarity.] What we want to do is for you to understand it is as though there is a cinema in the other room, and there is only one little hole, and *you* have got your eye to it and *only* you can see it. And *we* can only see it if you tell us what *you* see. That is one thing. I don't think I will interrupt any more, because we have the two languages. But when you see the coast, or somewhere, you finish your exercise by coming down somewhere and land. And when you have landed there, I want you to tell us where you are. Is that all right? You see the coastline, and try to come down.

>   (Silence)

K.   *Het beeld is alleen niet duidelijk.* Only the view is not clear.

L.   *Maar U weet dat er rotsen zijn.* But you know there are rocks.

K.   *Ja.* Yes.

L.   *Is het mogelijk om er dichter naar toe te gaan?* Is it possible to get closer to them?

>   (Silence)

Of bent U in de branding? Or are you on the crest?

K.   *Nee, ik zit er ver boven.* No, I'm high above.

L. *Kunt U zich concentreren op een stukje grond en probeer daar dan te landen?* Can you concentrate on one piece of ground and then try to land there?

(Long silence)

K. *Al de beelden verdwijnen. Het word allemaal bruinig voor me.* All the views disappear. It is becoming brownish around me.

L. *En dat bruin – is dat alleen maar een kleur of is het zand?* And that brown – is that only a colour, or is it sand?

K. *Het is zand.* It is sand.

L. *En kunt U daarop landen?* And can you land on it?

(Long silence)

G. Can you see your feet now when you come down?

K. *Nee. Ik voel ze wel, maar ik zie ze niet!* No. I feel them, but I don't see them.

G. You only feel them – and you can see the ground?

(Silence)

Can you see any . . .

K. *Nee, niet.* No, not.

G. Can you see any part of your body?

(Silence)

K. *Nee, ik voel het alleen maar – ik zweef.* No, I only feel it – I float.

G. Do you feel that you are in your body?

(Silence)

K. *Ja, in een vliegend lichaam.* Yes, in a floating body.

G. Now can you see anything?

K. *Ja, ik zie nu – velden – rijstvelden – akkers.* Yes, I now see – fields – rice-fields – paddocks.

L. *Kunt U landen?* Can you land now?

(Silence)

Denkt U dat dit een tropische omgeving is? Do you think that it is a tropical landscape?

K. *Het beeld verdwijnt weer. Het is niet duidelijk. Ik kan het ook niet scherp stellen.* This vision disappears now. It is not clear. I can't readjust the vision.

L. *Was U hoog in de lucht erboven?* Were you high above it?

K. *Ik was er vrij dicht boven.* I was quite close above it.

(Silence)

L. *Wat ziet U nu? Nog steeds de lucht? Of wolken?* What do you see now? Still the sky? Or clouds?

K. *Het is allemaal weer bruin onder mij.* It is all brown underneath me.

L. *Kunt U proberen om op die bruine kleur te landen?* Can you try to land on this brown colour?

(Silence)

Is het land? Een grasveld? Is it land? A field of grass?

K. *Het is grond, maar . . .* It is land, but . . .

L. *U hebt maar een heel klein stukje nodig om te landen.* You need only a small piece to land on.

(Silence)

En is het bruine grond? And is it brown earth?

(Silence)

K. *Het is zo vaag. Ik zie haast niks.* It is so vague. I see almost nothing.

L. *Is het nog dag, of is het nacht?* Is it still day, or is it night?

K. *Het is nacht – avond.* It is night – evening.

L. *En U kunt het niet omzetten in dag, zodat U kunt zien waar U kunt landen?* And you can't change it into day, so that you can see where to come down?

K. *Het is zo vaag of het uberhaupt de grond is, of dat het weer bossen word.* It is not clear if it really is just land, or that it has become woods again.

L. *Maar het is grond – het is geen water?* But it is land – it isn't water?

K. *Nee.* No.

L. *Kunt U nu proberen om tussen de bomen op de grond te komen?* Can you now try to land in between the trees?

(Silence)

Is het een groot bos, of weet U het niet? Is it a big wood, or don't you know?

K. *Nee, het is oerwoudachtig, met hutten er in. Negerhutten.* No, it is jungle-like, with huts in it. Native huts.

L. *Wat voor hutten zijn het? Rond? Vierkant? En wat voor daken erop?* What kind of huts are they? Round? Square? And what kind of roofs have they got?

K. *Ronde hutten met daken van – wat is het? Het lijkt op dat cocos, harig, palmbomen erom heen.* Round huts with roofs made from – what is it? It looks like coconuts, hairy, palm-trees all around.

L. *Het is dus een tropisch bos?* It is a tropical jungle then?

K. *Ja.* Yes.

L. *Ziet U ook mensen?* Do you also see people?
K. *Ja, met zwart kroeshaar.* Yes, with black curly hair.
L. *Waar bent u nu?* Where are you now?
K. *Ik zit er vlak boven.* I'm just above them.
L. *Kunt U proberen om te landen?* Can you try to come down?
        (Silence)
Bent U dichtbij? Are you close?
        (Long Silence)
K. *Het verdwijnt weer allemaal die beelden. Ze zijn heel ver weg.*
All these views have disappeared again. They are very far
away.
L. *Bent U nu hoog in de wolken? Is het dag of nacht?* Are you
high in the clouds? Is it day or night?
K. *Het is schemerig.* It is dim.
        (Long Silence)
Ik zie niks. I see nothing.
        (Silence)
L. *Kunt U weer proberen om voor te stellen dat U in de lucht bent?*
Can you try to imagine that you are back in the sky?
        (Silence)
G. Is it all dark again? You are high in the air but it is
dark, is it?
K. *Ja.* Yes.
G. Do you feel afraid up where you are?
K. *Nee.* No.
G. Do you like being there?
K. *Nee, ook niet.* No, also not.
G. You can't see anything at all?
K. *Ik zie vaag weer iets van bossen.* I see vaguely something of
woods.
G. You can see woods? I want you to come down into
them.
        (Silence)
If you see something, you must go towards it. If you see the
trees, I want you to land there on the ground.
        (Silence)
What kind of ground is there with the trees?
K. *Bruine grond, zand, zandgrond.* Brown earth, sand, sandy
ground.
G. So it is quite safe to land there?
K. *Ja.* Yes.

G.   Can you come down and put your feet down on it?
K.   *Ja.* Yes.
G.   Now are they down on the ground?
K.   *Ja.* Yes.
G.   Can you see your feet there?
K.   Yes.
G.   What do you have on your feet?
K.   *Sandalen. Met een touwtje tussen mijn voeten erdoor.* Sandals. With a string between my toes.
G.   And what colour is your skin?
K.   Dark.
G.   And can you see up to your knees? What kind of clothes do you have?
      (Silence)
K.   *Eh, van riet.* Er, of reeds.
L.   *En wat hebt U verder aan? In Uw handen, of op Uw hoofd? Iets op Uw bovenlichaam?* And what else are you wearing? Something in your hands, or on your head? Something on your chest?
K.   *Mijn bovenlichaam is bloot.* My chest is bare.
L.   *En daar bent U ook bruin?* And there you are also brown?
K.   *Ja.* Yes.
      (Silence)
Ik heb zwart haar. I have black hair.
L.   *Hebt U iets in Uw handen? Hebt U ringen?* Do you have something in your hands? Do you wear rings?
K.   *Nee, geen versiering.* No, no ornaments.
      (Silence)
Ik zie alleen nog maar een – nee . . . All I see is a – no . . .
L.   *Hebt U iets op Uw hoofd?* Do you have something on your head?
K.   *Ik heb heel zwart haar.* I have very black hair.
L.   *Hebt U een baard?* Do you have a beard?
      (Silence)
U hebt ook niets in Uw handen wat U vasthoud? You are not holding anything in your hands?
      (Silence)
U staat met een rieten rok, maar verder niets? You stand there in your grass skirt, but further nothing?
      (Silence)

En hoe ziet de omgeving er uit? And what do the surroundings look like?

      (Silence)

Ziet U bomen? Do you see trees?

K. *Ja. Er zijn wat hutten. Ik zie geen mensen.* Yes. There are some huts. I don't see any people.

L. *Zijn dit dezelfde hutten die U eerder gezien had?* Are these the same huts you saw previously?

K. *Ja.* Yes.

L. *Zijn al die andere mensen verdwenen?* Have these people disappeared?

K. *Dat denk ik.* I think so.

L. *Kunt U naar die hutten toegaan? En ziet U daar gebruiksvoorwerpen? Kookgerei?* Can you go to those huts? Do you see any tools? Cooking utensils?

      (Silence)

Of restanten van vuur of wat dan ook? Or leftovers of a fire?

      (Silence)

K. *Ik kan niet goed dichterbij komen!* I cannot get closer easily.

L. *Durft U niet dichterbij te komen?* Or don't you dare go closer?

K. *Ik kan het beeld niet naar me toe halen.* I can't get the vision closer to me.

      (Silence)

Het is een open plaats. De bomen zijn vrij ver weg. Het is bruin. It is an open space. The trees are at a distance. It is brown.

L. *Kunt U naar die hutten toegaan? Of is er iets wat U ervan weerhoudt om er naar toe te gaan?* Can you go to those huts? Or is there something keeping you from going there?

K. *Ik zie het niet duidelijk.* I don't see them very clearly.

L. *Maar kunt U Uzelf wel duidelijk zien? Uw handen zijn bruin en . . .* But you can see yourself quite clearly? Your hands are brown and . . .

K. *Bruine huid, zand.* Brown skin, sand.

L. *Geen gras?* No grass?

K. *Nee.* No.

L. *Zijn er bomen of struiken om U heen?* Are there any trees or shrubs around you?

K. *Nee, die zie ik niet. In de verte alleen bruinige bossen.* No, I don't see any. In the distance only brownish woods.

L. *U bent dus op een open vlakte?* You are in an open space?

K. *Ja, met bossen er rondom heen.* Yes, with woods surrounding.

L. *Kunt U in een richting wandelen, naar de hutten of naar de bomen?* Can you walk in any direction, to the huts or to the trees?

    (Silence)

G. Are you standing still?

K. *Ja.* Yes.

G. You don't move at all?

K. *Nee.* No.

G. What is nearest to you?

    (Silence)

K. .*Ik weet het niet. Ik zit er niet helemaal in.* I don't know. I'm not completely part of it.

Mrs K. *Ga je naar de bomen?* Are you going to the trees?

K. *Ik zweef er een beetje boven. Alsof ik er niet helemaal in zit.* I'm floating a little above them. Just as though I'm not completely part of it.

Mrs K. *Is het warm?* What is the temperature?

K. *Ik weet het niet.* I don't know.

L. *Kunt U Uw voeten neerzetten?* Can you put your feet down?

K. *Nee, het is alsof ik naast mijn lichaam sta. Eens kijken of ik kan duiken.* No, it is as if I'm standing next to my own body. I will see if I can dive down again.

    (Silence)

L. *Voelt U dat zwarte lichaam alsof het Uw eigen lichaam is?* Do you feel that black body as though it is your own?

K. *Nee, het is nogal vreemd.* No, it is quite alien.

L. *U kijkt er dus op neer alsof het iemand anders is?* You are looking down on it as if it is someone else?

    (Silence)

Kunt U niet proberen om naast die andere persoon te gaan staan? Zolang als U maar met beide voeten op de grond gaat staan? Can't you try to go and stand next to that person and try to put both your feet back on to the ground?

K. *Het lijkt wel of dat lichaam plat ligt.* It looks as though the body is lying flat.

    (Silence)

Alles draait, en ik draai er misschien tegenin. Het duizelt een beetje. Maar het is niet duidelijk allemaal. Everything turns, and perhaps I am turning against the direction. It dazzles a bit.

But it is all not very clear.

L. *Draait Uzelf, of draait de aarde?* Do you yourself turn, or does the earth turn?

G. It is very dark?

K. *Het is vaag.* It is vague.

G. Can you see yourself clearly?

K. *Nee.* No.

G. Not any more? But you did?

K. *Niet erg helemaal, niet in details.* Not completely, not in details.

G. And what do you see now? Anything?

(Silence)

K. *Ik probeer weer om dat lichaam voor te stellen, de omgeving, maar het is te vaag. Ik geloof dat we weer opnieuw moeten beginnen ergens. Het gaat nergens heen.* I am trying to imagine that body again, the surroundings, but it is all very vague. I think we should start somewhere again. This isn't getting anywhere.

L. *Kunt U zich weer boven de wolken, hoog boven de aarde voorstellen?* Can you imagine yourself above the clouds? High above the earth?

K. *Ja. Nu zie ik alleen wolken.* Yes. Now, I see only clouds.

L. *En U bent er boven?* And you are above them?

K. *Ja.* Yes.

L. *En wat is het, dag of nacht?* And what is it, day or night?

K. *Het begint avond te worden.* It is becoming evening.

L, *En U kunt het niet volop dag maken?* And you can't make it fully day-time?

(Silence)

Is het een wolkenmassa, of kunt U er doorheen kijken naar de aarde? Are there many clouds or can you look through them to the earth?

K. *Het is allemaal wit onder mij, allemaal schuim.* Underneath me it is all white, all foam.

L. *En kunt U proberen om naar beneden te komen door de wolken heen?* And can you try to come down through the clouds?

K. *Ja.* Yes.

(Silence)

L. *Waar bent U nu? In de wolken of er boven?* Where are you now? In the clouds or above?

K. *Ik zie stukken kust ver weg, veel water onder mij.* I see coastlines and much water very far below me.

L. *En kunt U nu dichter naar die kustlijn toegaan?* Can you go closer to that coastline?
(Silence)
Is het een rotsachtige kust? Is er een branding? Is het een kalme dag? Is het een strand met zand of zijn het rotsen? Is it a rocky coast? Is there a crest? Is it a calm day? Is it a beach with sand or are there rocks?
K. *Rotsen.* Rocks.
(Silence)
Basaltachtig. Basalt.
L. *Kunt U naar beneden komen en op een van die rotsen landen?* Can you come down and land on one of those rocks?
K. *'Ik ben er vlak boven maar het beeld is niet helder.* I'm just above them but the vision is not clear.
L. *Kunt U naar beneden komen en landen?* Can you come down and land?
K. *Vaag; het lijkt of ik erop sta.* Vague; it looks as though I'm standing on one.
L. *U kunt het voelen?* You can feel it?
K. *Voelen – ik weet het meer.* Feel – it is more that I know it.
L. *Zijn het Uw eigen voeten of zijn het zwarte voeten of ziet U schoenen?* Are they your own feet or are they black feet or do you see shoes?
K. *Het is niet duidelijk.* It is not clear.
(Silence)
L. *Kunt U de omgeving zien?* Can you see the surroundings?
K. *Het verdwijnt weer allemaal.* It has all disappeared again.
(Silence)
G. You don't see anything any more? Do you feel as though you are somewhere else, or just here in the room? Is your mind up and down in clouds, or just sitting here?
K. *Ik weet niet hoe ik dat zo duidelijk kan zeggen. Ik kan me voorstellen dat ik hier lig, maar ik was wel ver weg.* I don't know how to express myself. I can imagine that, even though I'm lying here, I was far away.
G. Did you feel anything about doing this or not?
(Silence)
Have you done it before? Or seen what you saw before?
K. *Het kwam me niet helemaal onbekend voor, maar ik kan het niet goed beschrijven wat ik zie, het is allemaal te vaag.* It is not all unknown to me, but I can't describe it very well as it is all

rather vague.

G. Do you sometimes dream of yourself in one colour, like dark blue or brown?

K. *Nee.* No.

G. Do you feel as though you have been doing something? Or nothing?

K. No. I'm only looking.

[At long last he had condescended to speak in English – but, alas, too late.]

G. Just looking. You did have something to look at some of the time?

K. I try to see something, but I don't see very much.

G. How long do you think you have been trying?

K. Er – a quarter of an hour.

G. Quarter of an hour. I don't think we should go on any more. I don't see any point. You seem to start, and then you stop again. But you have been trying for an hour.

K. How long?

[Even on the tape he sounds obviously astounded, even incredulous.]

G. One hour.

K. No!

G. You have been seeing colour after colour, and absorbing it minute after minute, quite content just to lie there and look at nothing but blue or brown, till I nearly went to sleep, and she [Ruby] did go to sleep. We don't know why you haven't seen anything much; perhaps the two languages were confusing, because I didn't know what you were seeing even to be able to say '*what* colour is it?'

K. I *was* seeing things, but . . .

G. You were too far, too far. We were trying to get you closer.

K. Always too misty, too hazy.

Menno. And too far away, and couldn't move closer.

Mrs K. It was too misty.

G. Always too misty and too hazy. Do you have dreams of being too far away, and mist?

(Silence)

Did you think you were one hour?

K. No.

G. You were very quick with the exercises in the beginning.

I think too quick.

K. I think that is possible.

G. You didn't spend much time with the stretching. It is normally twenty minutes and you were only ten. After this you have been fifty minutes going up and down, but I couldn't understand. I think this was the difficulty, and Leo was shy to ask you questions. We have to ask questions, otherwise it will stop. You were clearly established somewhere, and then you would keep talking to yourself, and I couldn't help you, and he couldn't either. Your wife started to, but I think she was shy. And he [Menno Kohn] wouldn't help at all. Now you saw yourself at one stage quite clearly when you could see your feet with sandals on?

K. Yes.

G. Do you still remember the sandals?

K. Yes.

G. Do you remember if they were from leather? White, brown or black?

K. Brown leather.

G. You can still see them? Any buckles? How many bands? Then I would have asked what clothes you had. You had black hair. And you had no beard?

K. No.

G. But you do have one now.

He also remembered quite clearly having seen himself as a negro in a landscape that was quite obviously African. Yet he seemed not at all surprised at this, as though such visions of himself were not at all an extraordinary occurrence. His wife, however, was obviously astounded and was anxious to ask him questions about what he had seen. He was, admittedly, quite genuinely astonished at how much time had passed, even checking his watch and looking around the room as though to see if it had a clock, then looking out the window. Obviously the progress of evening could not be refuted.

Menno Kohn also seemed astonished at the results of the experiment. And despite the dimness of vision and restriction of what Kluwer had seen, I myself felt glad that he had at least seen something; and I felt convinced, as did Leo, that he would be content with this much for a first try under the difficult circumstances of conducting the experiment in two languages.

What I did not know until only now, almost a year later, was that he told Leo, in Dutch, that he had deliberately tried not only to avoid becoming too involved with whatever visions came before him, because he was apprehensive of the whole procedure, but that when they did begin he tried each time to 'push them away', to disinvolve himself from them and not allow himself to become absorbed in them. He had deliberately tried to avoid co-operating if only to see how much the experiment would still work when resisted.

And yet, although he was kind enough to drive the three of us to the Hilversum railway station for our return to De Bilt, he shook his head with disappointment and said it had not impressed him. *'Het was geen trip,'* he said. 'It was no trip.' And he did not contract to publish the book.

> *K. C. Redman*
> *Dr G. W. Rudd*
> *P. G. Hurford*

The next three experiments – done on the evenings of May 11th, 12th and 13th, 1973 in my apartment – are rather typical of the results that can be expected. All three experimentees were young men, ranging from the mid-twenties (Dr Gordon Rudd) to the early thirties (Ken Redman and Peter Hurford), but none of them knew each other and still do not at the time of writing. All three are notably successful in their careers, which vary from lawyer to doctor of geology to regional manager for British Airways in the United Kingdom.

None of the three had difficulty with the preliminaries; if anything, they were all a little too fast with the stretching and shrinking exercises and, with the exception of Gordon Rudd, showed impatience for the actual 'experience' to begin. At the same time all three were sceptical of the experiment to the extent that, although it might work with so many others, they were prepared for it not to succeed with them – just as they were convinced that they could not easily succumb to hypnotism. Ken Redman also thought his natural fear of heights might preclude him from 'ever getting off the ground', but this was not at all the case. One factor common to all three is that they are unmarried.

Kenneth Charles Redman, LL.B., is a successful young lawyer and the senior of three young partners in a rapidly expanding firm. Ken was born in Kuala Lumpur in Malaya, on October 31st 1940, where his father died as a prisoner of war in September 1942. With Ken in her arms, his mother escaped from the Japanese invasion, fleeing to India and from there to Australia, her native country. After the war, they returned to Malaya where his mother remarried. At the age of seven, Ken was the first witness of a highly publicized poltergeist of an extremely mischievous nature, which threw objects from onions to aubergines, footwear and knives at his mother, her servant and visitors to the house, and even at the investigating police officers, before being 'exorcized'. Ken was sent back to Western Australia for his education, and had two visits to Europe before commencing his career. Hence I would not have been at all surprised had he 'landed' somewhere in either Europe or Malaya; but the scene, the eery landscape he saw, was not identifiably in either.

One notable factor common to nearly all Australian experimentees is that they almost invariably 'land' on a coastline, whereas other nationalities more frequently land well inland and may not see ocean at all. Perhaps this is because the majority of Australians live in or around the country's half dozen major cities, all in fertile coastal areas, and know little of the hazardous inland desert ground.

Ken Redman followed this usual Australian predeliction for seeing a vast, straight coastline that consisted of little more than flat blue sea and equally flat brown land bisected by a thin line of white, like a string of cotton, that was the coast. He landed on a beach of 'clear sand, no rocks, the ocean calm but with small waves rippling in'. There were very small shells and some 'funny little crabs' being washed by the waves up the beach where they scuttled down holes, sometimes reappearing again.

'I look up the beach and there is just white sand, non stop. Now I look to my right – not very far away, twenty yards or so – and there is a ridge, roughly about not more than three or four feet high, but sharp, perpendicular, straight – a ridge of earth. Yes, the earth beyond it is three or four feet high, and this straight perpendicular ridge is chopped out of it. So the beach level is three or four feet below that. It is like erosion.

The undergrowth beyond it grows up straight; looks thorny. Then it sort of flattens out like a kind of – I don't know what it looks like. It grows three or four feet high, clear underneath, but it looks prickly. All the branches are woven together like a thick, queer mat, so that you couldn't walk *through* it. You could perhaps *crawl* through it, and you could even walk *on* it if you wanted to, but you can't walk *through* it. It's like a lot of vine branches woven together – not green – it's a kind of browny colour, brown with a slight greeny tinge to it. But it doesn't *look* green – it's dry.'

There was nothing else – no hills, no people, no animals, nothing. Out to sea there were no boats, not even seabirds. The little crabs, however, were still there, just a few yards away from where he was sitting.

So he was sitting? There was no point in walking, he said, as there was nowhere to go; one part of the beach would be the same as any other. What would he do? Just sit on the beach.

Looking at himself, he found that his legs and arms were bare, whereas in actuality he was wearing both wristwatch and signet-ring, neither of which appeared to him now. He was wearing what could possibly be shorts or more probably shortened trousers that were faded, ragged, 'not white – they never *were* white – a very light khaki colour, but tattered'. His skin was quite white and did not even look tanned. He was also wearing a kind of short-sleeved gown that was not a singlet or vest, not a sweat-shirt, not a modern garment of any kind. Its colour was creamy, like his faded trousers, both made of cotton. His hair was 'not dark' (which it is in reality), 'not blond, sort of tan-coloured, not long, but cut at the back'. Afterwards he said that his hair had not been cut at all, for the simple reason that it never grew, just as he did not need to shave. Nor did he need the thickly lensed spectacles essential to him in real life. He saw himself as young, but could not accurately determine his age between fourteen and twenty-four; it was probably nearer eighteen.

He was still sitting there, cross-legged, on the beach. If it resembled anything at all in reality, he said, it was a little like Port Dickson beach near Kuala Lumpur in Malaya, but was nowhere near as wide as Port Dickson and the undergrowth and inland landscape were not at all like that area.

With so little to occupy him, was he quite content there?
'I'm not unhappy.' He didn't know where he might have come
from, it was just that he was *there;* he felt that he had always
been there and always would be. He would never change, just
as the beach and landscape would never change. He had no
identity and, even when pressed by repeated questions and
references, absolutely no need to eat or drink in order to exist.
In this respect he was similar to D'Arcy Ryan (see page 66),
though he had been told nothing of that experience. Like
D'Arcy, he could not see himself eating or drinking in his
present form. He was not at all concerned about his
circumstances there. 'It feels quite normal to be here. I don't
want to do anything. I just want to sit.' The only activity he
could watch was that of the crabs, 'more like praying mantises
– or three matchsticks put together – than crabs; thin, about
two or three inches across.' He had never seen such crabs in
reality, and there were only about twenty of them altogether,
all just near him.

The only break in the beach was a short rocky promontory
some distance away, almost on the horizon. Yet asked if he
could go there to look at it, he immediately replied, 'I *am*
there.' There was no change in any of the scenery however;
and on the other side of the promontory, the beach again
stretched for miles and miles. Inland, it was still just flat with
the same matted growth, no sign of habitation, 'not even a
flea'. He himself had not changed in any way either.

Far away, he could then discern a very low hill, no more
than a slight rise; but he did not want to go to it because it
meant that he must crawl to it under the matted growth or
else walk on top of it. He was quite content to stay where he
was? 'I'm not lonely, not looking for anything – just content
being there.' He was neither hot nor cold, the air was neither
hot nor humid, there seemed to be no night though it did 'just
get a little dark'. But if it did, there was no moon, although he
could discern stars without recognizing any of them. There
were no clouds, nor was there bright sunshine – the air was
softened by a kind of haze. There was not even a breeze. And
furthermore there was no sun. Had he seen such a place in
reality? Not that he knew of. Was it just an imaginary
country? It wasn't a country, just a place, perhaps an island,
but if so a very large one. However, he didn't know this for

certain, yet it *felt* like an island.

'It doesn't feel as though I have been here *all* the time, but I don't feel as though I was ever *not* here. I suppose it's as though I have both always been here and yet never been here at all, both at the same time. It's as though I belong here, without questioning it. I just accept it.' And what would he do with himself there? He didn't know, because there was nothing to do. He still would not need to eat or drink, he would never get hot or cold, it would never rain – nor ever *not* rain, because there was always a kind of haze or mist. 'It just seems to be everything with nothing. There is everything you want because you don't need anything. There is the beach to go to, and the undergrowth where you can't go. I'm free – with no people, no houses. I don't want anything. I still don't want food, I don't want water. It doesn't rain, it doesn't get hot. I don't want more clothes than I've got. I haven't grown, and I don't age. It's as though I'm there for all time, and yet without being there for any time.'

'And you are quite content there?'

'I'm content.'

'You feel content without experiencing anything as in real life?'

'More content.'

'You'd quite willingly go to a place like that?'

'I don't know. When you look at it, from the outside looking in, you're frightened. But when you are *in* there, and look around you, it is peaceful. Just peaceful. You don't want anything or even need anything. It depends on which side you are to know what you feel about it.' He was on the *inside,* and was content to stay there. 'I just sit. I don't want to talk, or even move. I just sit there and look, quite content.'

Afterwards, I showed him some lines from Andrew Marvell's *An Historical Poem,* and he thought the following particularly apt for how he felt:

'Society is all but rude
To this delicious solitude.'

And also:

'What wondrous life is this I lead!'

At this point, I decided to experiment by trying to see if he could 'go' somewhere else, and he was almost immediately up high in the sky. But when he descended again, it was only to return to the very same place, the same conditions. With a great deal of effort – and time – I managed to get him inland a little by walking on the strange matted growth, but he didn't care for it very much and wanted only to return to the beach and his previous contentment.

While he was there, was he also aware of this room? 'Yes.' He could hear Leo 'fiddling with papers' (Leo was turning the pages of a magazine) and he could also hear a buzzing sound which he didn't think was the tape-recorder, although it was. Yet at the same time he did not ever leave his beach.

He was quite sure he had never seen a place like it in reality? Yes. Not in a film, or photograph? No. Had he dreamt about it? No. He saw it now for the first time? Yes. Had I suggested it to him?

'I don't know. I just disappeared from reality – not that this is an *un*reality, this is also real. This is another dimension of reality. You need nothing and nothing is provided – water, food, clothing, other than the clothes I had on. It is a place where you can live happily. You don't need anybody. And yet there is no death in it. Time has stopped still.'

He was reluctant to end the experience, but felt there was nothing more for him to learn about it, so he opened his eyes. Asked how long he thought he had been sitting on his beach, he guessed 'Fifteen minutes?' Without the twenty minutes spent on the preliminaries, he had been an hour and twenty minutes – the longest we had recorded. He was so incredulous that he checked his watch, feeling convinced that we had exaggerated by at least an hour; but of course this wasn't so. Asked if he would spend so long in such a place in actuality, he replied, 'No. I would be walking in five seconds.'

Did he think it was like having a dream consciously?

'Not really; there was nothing to have a dream about. That is the difficulty of it. To me, when you have a dream, you dream about something consciously. There is something sort of subjective about it – something you can see and visualize; something you can feel and you can touch. But this place was like a vacuum.' Was it difficult to get him out of the experiment? 'No, no.' Yet he could have gone on indefinitely, even though the whole thing *was* so indefinite.

Asked a little later about his predominant impressions of his experience, he said that first of all he remembered the awful isolation, although he was not at all afraid of it; then there was the eery feeling that he had always been in that environment, which in itself was without beginning or end; and thirdly, he felt that he had no sense of any unhappiness whatsoever, having no needs of any kind, neither emotional nor physical. Concerning his appearance, he had not been at all as he was in real life – his legs had been covered with blond instead of black hairs, he was smooth-chested instead of hairy, and he had not been balding. He had reached an idyllic age and would not grow older or change, but would remain that way in a totally static period of time. To describe this, he had at times seen himself from the viewpoint of standing just behind himself; and while experiencing this, he felt utterly convinced of his circumstances as though it was truly reality.

The final revelation came when he admitted that in real life he had developed a 'kind of self-sufficient personality'. At one time, when he had been young, he had felt an almost desperate need to have someone to depend on; but never finding anyone he had made himself independent, 'indestructible, not needing anyone or any place to continue to exist'.

And the experience, he said, seemed to depict precisely this.

Author's Note, January 1976

By chance I recently came across an illustrated article about the French possessions of Amsterdam Island and the Island of St Paul in the southern reaches of the Indian Ocean, between South Africa and Western Australia – a route frequented over several centuries by Dutch ships sailing between the homeland and the Dutch East Indies, now Indonesia. Amsterdam Island is said to have been so named because homesick or recalcitrant Dutch sailors longing to return mid-voyage to their capital city were marooned there. The island's only vegetation was a unique species precisely formed and matted like that envisaged in Redman's experience; and the only living beings, apart from insects and visiting seabirds, were a small species of shore crab. Redman had seen himself dressed in tattered 'shorts, or more probably shortened trousers' of a light khaki or creamy colour and a similar coloured 'kind of short-sleeved gown' that was 'not a modern garment'. He had been young, of an indeterminate age, perhaps as young as fourteen or so as he did not yet need to shave. With his extraordinary sense of resignation to his frightening isolation in his experience, amounting almost to melancholy, could he have seen himself as a boy seaman marooned, whether accidentally or deliberately, on the inhospitable Amsterdam Island?

At only twenty-five Gordon William Rudd has a Doctorate of Philosophy in Geology, and a Bachelor of Science degree, from the University of Newcastle in New South Wales. He is slightly but athletically built, and of average height. He has pleasant features, small yet darkly intense brown eyes and dark, thinning hair. His voice is normally soft and, during the experiment, at times became almost inaudible – making the tape-recording difficult to transcribe. His hobbies are reading, films and classical music. He has twice experimented with seances: in the first experience, with his brother and two girls, each of the girls 'contacted' a deceased relative. In the second experience, 'we' (his brother and he) contacted an aunt who had died about twelve years previously, through the medium of a girl participating with them. He has travelled extensively within Australia (although he has not been outside the country) and he now resides in Perth, though he was born in a small town called Kurri (the aboriginal word in the locality for a kookaburra) near Newcastle. He deliberated for several days before consenting to try the Christos Experiment.

The preliminaries presented no difficulty and he gave very graphic descriptions of his front door, flat-building, immediate surroundings and then the environs of Perth as he ascended to a considerable height, where the sky became a little darker than before when it had seemed to be of a late autumn afternoon (it was an autumn evening in actuality).

When returning to earth, he found himself over a coastline with the sea and land clearly discernible, but for a while he could see little else. Eventually a few roads became distinguishable. At first he thought he would land on the narrow beach, but he was drawn inland towards a couple of clear patches among the smallish trees, and then to one particular cleared patch 'with four sides, but irregular' about five miles inland from the coast. It was a lighter green than the rest of the landscape and he felt himself drawn towards it, then coming down to land. 'I'm just landing on the grass.' This grass was patchy and very short, 'as though cattle have been grazing there', but when he looked he couldn't see any cattle around, only fences made of wooden posts strung together with barbed wire. Asked to look down at the grass again, which he could still clearly see, he could not see his feet but 'just lots of cow-dung'. He couldn't see anything of himself at all.

There were no signs of habitation and no people or animals around, but there was a track leading from where he was standing to one corner of the field, just wheeltracks in the gravel earth leading out of the field. He himself was about a hundred yards from the corner. He couldn't see where the track led as there were small but fairly dense trees beyond the field's fences; he could see about fifty yards into these trees but not completely through them. To find where the track led, he had to follow it to 'a closed iron gate with a chain around and fixed over it'. When he opened this chain, he could see his hands, which were 'just normal flesh colour'. He was even more conscious of wearing a 'jump-suit', and immediately observed that 'it must be a fairly cold day' although he was not at all cold in reality. He was not wearing any rings on his hands, but only his own actual gold watch. But then the jump-suit apparently disappeared and he was wearing a green jumper and brown trousers – whereas in reality he was wearing black trousers with, admittedly, a dark green sweater.

He had gone through the gate but still could not see any specific place to go to; he could only follow the road, which was still gravel and with a few 'pot-holes here and there, no water in them'. The same trees were flanking either side until he found himself coming 'out of the woods and to a T-intersection'. What was the other road made of? 'Just gravel. It sort of goes up-hill, and then makes a right-angle following the contours of the hill. And there's a house near the junction. No fence. It's an old wooden house with concrete-type pillar foundations. Verandahs around at three sides. An old farm-house, with an old corrugated-iron roof. The house needs painting. There's a woman standing on the verandah, with a baby in her arms. She's watching me. She's in her middle thirties, with just a young child. Very tall, dark brown hair, wearing a long kind of dress, old-fashioned looking. She looks at me suspiciously. I can't see anyone else. I'm walking up towards her house, but she is making no move to come to me. She doesn't speak.'

He didn't know who she might be, he had never seen her in reality, but she was perfectly clear to him and as real as anyone he might see in real life. He wanted to ask her where he was, and how to get back to Perth, but before he could do so she turned and went inside, closing the door behind her. He had no choice but to continue further along the road; then he chose to take a new road 'to the right'.

There were still trees over to his right, but only cleared land on his left. The trees were gum-trees and he was leaving the house behind him. There were no other houses in sight, no people, no animals. It was a pleasant day but just slightly overcast with clouds forming. He would have to walk along the road for a couple of hours before coming to where he thought it ended, or perhaps just changed direction. He was now in slightly hilly country and could see a few sheep, a dozen or so, grazing near by.

He had not seen this actual country or the house before, but he had seen numerous localities and houses like them. But then, he said, the road had suddenly become bitumenized and was running off towards a railway-track, with a near-by railway-station that was just a typical country siding. There was about a mile of sealed road before it became gravel again. 'I can see a sign,' he said, 'but I can't make out the name.'

I then suggested to him that he was really just seeing things in a familiar environment and in the present time, to which he naturally agreed; I asked if he would like to ascend again and 'come down somewhere else' and see what happened. So he did.

This time he found himself descending to an enormous range of snowcapped mountain-peaks. 'I'm not in India,' he said, 'but next to it. I can't think of its name now.'

'Tibet?'

'Yes, Tibet. I'm gradually floating and coming down. Just floating around.'

The day was clear but cold. He could even feel the cold, but only as himself *there*, not as himself *here; here* he was comfortably warm. 'I see someone else floating,' he then said.

'He's not going up or down; he's just floating around.' What kind of person was he? 'A Tibetan monk. About fifty. He has a saffron-coloured robe on.' He himself was still dressed in trousers, jumper and shoes. How high were they? 'Er – a couple of thousand feet. It's in a mist. And the country is partly covered with snow. But I can see green fields further on the slopes. Er – there is a village. Small houses made out of clay and stones.'

'Any people there?'

'About twenty. Just carrying on with everyday things. One leading a donkey. Couple of women walking along the streets together.'

Where was he now? Still floating. Was he still with the monk? 'I've left him – he's still up there.' And he pointed with his finger above his horizontally placed head. If he was going to land, where would he choose?

'Probably just outside the village. There is a man ploughing the field with an old wooden plough and a horse. Only a small field, a couple of acres.' What colour was the horse? 'A small one – only brown, with some markings on the forehead. Fairly long hair.'

He was still about twenty feet above the ground. 'I don't really want to land.' Were any of the faces in the village familiar to him? 'No, I've never seen it before.' He didn't feel part of the village? 'I wouldn't be able to speak to any of them. I'm coming down. It is all close. There is only one track, one main track down the hill, with houses on either side, but not close, some further away from it than the others, say fifty yards, and even a couple of hundred yards from the road – sort of spread out.'

Were there any crops or vegetation?

'No. Mainly grassy fields, apart from the man who is ploughing.' He was still above the village and didn't really want to land. 'I feel as though I want to . . . the village is sort of high up, in the mountains, on a little plateau. I'd like to go down – further down, I mean – before I land. I'm on top of the village people now, and I'm gradually coming down. The cliff is almost hundreds of feet tall. Now I'm descending into a gully which has little creeks flowing into it. Now I'm going downstream to the bottom of the gully. It's very rocky – too rugged to come down.'

Did the scene seem familiar to him at all?

'No, it's not. I've never seen it before.'

'And what do you feel when you are looking down on it – the *you* that is floating there, I mean – is it familiar to you?'

'Er, very strange – but it's exhilarating.'

'Are the mountains high around you?'

'They have been. I'm following down the river. I've landed. I'm on a track, with a haversack-thing on my back. And I'm walking down this mountain-track and just passing a man, a woman, and a little child of about six years old.' The woman and the man were about thirty. 'The woman wears a sari and the man's dressed in a dirty white, er – linen pants and shirt.' Did they wear any headgear? 'The woman doesn't. The man has a – not actually a turban – and he has got a donkey which is all laden up . . . '

'Are they going away from you, or . . . ?'

' . . . two loads, one on either side. And they're walking up the mountain. I've passed them.'

He was now so intent, as is obvious from this declining to be interrupted, that he was adopting the familiar expression of being if not irritated then at least impatient at questions when he was preoccupied with trying to see all that was appearing before him. However, I did persevere; if the details are not elicited as they appear then all too often they are not divulged at all, being overlooked in 'post-mortems'. Sometimes, though, they are recalled after reading the transcript or a written account of the experience, and I have often been thought stupid or remiss for having omitted details or circumstances which were so vivid to the experimentees that they take some time to realize that I did not also witness them.

'Do you know them at all?' I asked.

'No.'

'Do they take any notice of you?'

'They gave me a few looks, but we make no attempt to speak to each other.' He was walking on now? 'Yes. It's still a fairly flat track, fairly easy walking. It's in the morning, about ten. I'm walking a great distance, but I don't feel tired.' Did he feel the weight of his haversack at all? 'It's not really heavy.' Did he have any idea what was in it? 'Dry clothes to change into, and a bit of bread, things to eat. And there's a sleeping bag.' Did he have a haversack like this in reality?

'Yes.' (Though afterwards he said it was not necessarily that particular one, but just a haversack.) Did he use it very often? 'Not very often – not now.'

He was still walking along the track. He was heading for a largish town, he said, where he would be able to take a train. Did he know where he wanted to go? 'Sort of travel down to India, down towards the tip. I want to catch a boat there.' What age did he think he was. After some hesitation, he said, 'Same age as I am now. I've reached the city, and I can manage to get on the train. There are six carriages, very crowded, very smelly.' What kind of people? 'I'm the only European. All the rest are Indians, and men.' Did they take any notice of him? 'No. Oh – a few.' Had the train started yet? 'Still waiting at the station.' Was he going to have a long journey or a short one? 'I'll have a long journey, and stop overnight at a couple of places. Haven't got much time to catch the boat.' And where would the boat be taking him? 'Back to Australia, to Sydney.' I noticed that it wasn't back to Perth.

'Have you actually done this?' I asked him.

'Oh, no. Never been on a sea cruise before.'

Did he have plans for doing this trip?

'No. I don't think I like boats.'

If he were going away, would he go to Tibet and India?

'I don't know. I'd like to.' But later he said he would no doubt choose Europe or South America first. On the other hand, it did occur to him now that he had always been fascinated with India, but not necessarily Tibet.

I then suggested that he had probably seen enough of this particular 'trip' unless he wanted to go for a longer journey. But he agreed that he had seen what was probably the essentials of the 'trip' and did not want to see any more. I had meant to take him up again, almost certain that his third descent would bring him somewhere not only entirely different but also in another period of time. However, I had expressed myself clumsily and he had thought that by 'trip' I had meant the entire experiment, and so he had already opened his eyes and was sitting up.

How long did he think he had been? He didn't know. But he looked at his watch, saw that it was 10.20 p.m. and was obviously dismayed. He recalled that two friends had called in for a few minutes and left again at nine o'clock, shortly after which (at 9.20 p.m.) we had commenced the experiment. 'So it must have taken about an hour,' he said. It had been exactly an hour altogether, I told him; but how long did he *think* it had been? 'Ten minutes.' Had he seen everything clearly? 'Oh, yes!' – it had been almost as though he had been actually there and seeing it with his own eyes. Had he expected to see anything as clearly as that? 'No, I don't think I did.'

It then occurred to me that we had never attempted to see if an experiment could be resumed without the preliminaries once the experimentee had opened his eyes and sat up, becoming fully aware of his actual surroundings again and discussing the experience as an incident of the past. However, when I suggested it, he said he had so much to think about already, from both 'visitations', that he didn't want any more straight away. He was also leaving a few days later to fly to an oil-rig off the north-west coast of Western Australia and wanted to think about what he had seen so far. 'Perhaps some other time,' he said.

I personally felt that there was little possibility that Dr Rudd had seen something of the past; the first scene I thought had been in the present, and the second was a kind of wishful fulfilment of fantasy. He, however, wasn't sure that the first visit was not timed shortly before he was born, if only because of the woman's long old-fashioned dress – which was not at all like a modern 'maxi' skirt. The second visit he thought was more likely a glimpse of the not too distant future.

A previous experimentee had also been convinced of this (Stephan M. in *Windows of the Mind*) when he had seen himself attending a family funeral in a suit he had bought in London – when at the time, and not only for financial reasons, it could not have seemed less likely that he would ever be able to leave Australia. Shortly afterwards, however, his circumstances changed for the better and within a few months he was sailing for Europe. He is still in England at the time of writing and, because of the great difference in climate there, has naturally had to buy new clothes. However, it will no doubt still be some time before we can know if, instead of seeing something of the past, these two experimentees really had been shown – as so often appears to happen in normal dreams – a glimpse of the future.

Author's Note, August 1974 and January 1976

After eighteen months in England, Stephan returned to Western Australia because his mother was taken dangerously ill with a spinal disease. Fortunately, she recovered and Stephan lived with her for some time till she was completely better, telling me their relationship had never been so close. Far more than the three years he had foreseen have passed and there has been no funeral; he is convinced that his mother's death was averted by his deliberately *not* buying a suit in England like the one he had seen himself wearing at the funeral. His mother still enjoys very good health.

Peter George Hurford was born on September 30th, 1940, in Western Australia. He trained as a schoolteacher and was instructing art at a State High (Secondary) School when I met him in 1959. He has come a long way since then. Today he is the British Airways Regional Sales Manager for the northern (and by far the greater) part of the United Kingdom including Scotland, Wales and Northern Ireland. He pays frequent visits to these countries, as well as to most capitals in Europe and even to the United States. He is tall, just over six feet, elegant in appearance and slim. Rarely at a loss for words, he speaks rapidly yet succinctly. He is also constantly in motion, as he likes to have all of his faculties kept in constant and full occupation.

While I was in Europe in 1972 I told him of the Christos Experience, which he seemed prepared to consider with an open mind. He was curious to try the experiment, but the opportunity did not arise until May 1973, when I was back in Western Australia and he came over for a holiday and reunion with family and friends. He then made a point of finding time for the experiment, which was conducted in my Cottesloe apartment on the evening of Sunday, May 13th, 1973, commencing at 9.02 p.m.

The preliminaries were conducted with exceptional ease and the visualization exercises 'perceived' in great detail, and yet, strangely enough, almost completely lacking the wider horizons achieved by most experimentees. This applied from the time he visualized himself on the roof of his block of flats in London, in Notting Hill (65 Ladbroke Grove), until he accomplished the simulation of a particularly high ascent which, of course, might have been expected from the innumerable international flights he makes in the course of business. Yet strangely enough there was no mention, not even a suggestion, of aeroplanes at any point during his experiment. After twenty-one minutes, most of which was taken up with unusually detailed descriptions of his more immediate surroundings (even when these appeared far below), he descended from cumulus cloud formations to 'everything green, I see sort of green trees, cottonwool type of green trees, and hedges . . . ' which at least was different from the coastline and beach seen by most Australians.

Instead, he found himself approaching a typically European countryside with poplar trees in leaf and the landscape divided into fields of varying shapes and sizes. There also seemed to be a kind of stone-walled quadrangle to which he felt himself being drawn. At the same time he could see a house, a typical rural-Australian bungalow, which was near by but which seemed to have nothing to do with the landscape. It was as though he could see two landscapes at once. Yet, as he descended, the house appeared to recede in both viewpoint and importance. Was it, I could not help wondering at the time, somehow symbolic of his having left his native Australia for a career in Europe? There was, however, no opportunity to suggest this at the time and soon it was apparent it was an unlikely reason for the house's appearance.

Seeing the house for the first time, he had said with surprise, 'I can see something else – the odd shape of a red roof through the trees, corrugated-iron roof. But it doesn't go with the house. I'm about twenty feet above it. It's all safe, and now all I can see when I land is orangey-red soil. It's slightly damp, with grass on it.'

As he looked down, could he see his feet?

'Yes. I have boots on. [His shoes had been removed, as usual, for the preliminary massaging of the ankles.] Sort of dark brown old army boots, with brass eye-holes. And there is a lot of mud spattered over them.' What else was he wearing? 'I've got khaki on – a very baggy, drab, khaki pair of trousers. And I've got a jacket on which is like a safari jacket, and it's darker than the trousers, and it's got a belt around it, tied very badly, not smartly, but tied all knotted-up sort of thing.' Did it have a buckle at all? (I asked this for possible identification of what appeared to be a uniform.) 'It's got a thin little buckle, like one on an old army jacket. It's a battledress-green colour – no, there's nothing on it – and it's got metal buttons – er, funny little dark buttons.' There were no markings visible on the buttons, 'though there might be some very tiny writing on them, but you can hardly see it.' This was no doubt because he had never been in any of the services. Did he see any insignia, or anything else on him?

'Er, funny, I don't know. It doesn't seem logical, but I can see a pip. Small sort of pip on the, er – lapel? With holes in the top of the lapel. [Afterwards, he said he had meant epaulette.] With some sort of sunburst pattern on the pip.' This sounded like the Australian Military Forces insignia. Was there anything on his head?

'I'm terribly afraid I have. It's the sort of thing – I've got a sort of foreign – no, a little cap like *that*.' And he made movements with his hands above his head to describe what was obviously, which he later confirmed, a forage cap, though he had not been able to think of the right term at the time. Did he have anything on his hands?

'I *didn't* have, but I have *now*. I've got grey, knitted, greeny-grey knitted sort of worn-out gloves, but they weren't there till you said it.'

Could he see his features at all?

'I've got a very strong jaw-line. [His own jaw is pointed.] And I'm clean-shaven. I can't see if I *need* a shave or not. I'm *fairly* clean-shaven. A *very* strong jaw-line. Very *angular* sort of jaw-line. Quite a strong jaw-line and, er, darkish.' Afterwards, he said he had meant swarthy; yet his face is usually meticulously clean-shaven and he is very fair-skinned. 'I can't quite work out if I have side-burns or not. [He did in reality.] No, I can't have. A very sharp-cut jaw-bone.' This preoccupation with his jaw-line was expressed with constant surprise, yet it did not occur to him to suggest that he might be seeing someone else entirely; instead he quite clearly identified this visualized person as himself, even though 'he' was so completely different in appearance. What age did he think he was?

'That isn't very important. Thirties. You know.'

Could he look around and see his surroundings?

'I can see a sort of corrugated roof, but it hasn't got any connection with me at all. A corrugated red roof with some bricks showing, and lots of green surrounding. I can see poplar trees, vaguely. I seem to be digging, which is odd. I've got a shovel – a square shovel.'

The shovel appeared constantly during the next seven minutes. He described himself as on the verge of digging something, but he didn't actually set his foot to this shovel.

'I *think* I've started digging, but I'm not sure what I'm at.' Was anyone else with him? 'There *might* be people, but I'm not convinced; but certainly there might be people. They could be there, and they might be digging too. So I might not be able to see them. They might be twenty or thirty feet away, and in little groups. But I am by myself.'

Was the building still not clear to him?

'No. It was all in a kind of flash and I just saw the roof – the red, corrugated-iron roof – and some of the brickwork. But it doesn't fit anywhere. There are some trees at the corner somewhere. It's part of the whole thing, a jigsaw. I'm digging, and just standing, in this outfit. My trousers are tucked into my boots. I'm digging a sort of – *squared-off* digging. Yet I haven't really dug anything at all. I've only put my foot on the shovel in the ground.' What was the ground like? 'Moist and rich.' Was there grass? 'Yes, there's grass where I'm standing.' How far away were the poplar trees?

'Funny, I can't fit it in, the link between the poplar trees and where I'm standing. I haven't built a *frame* of the scenery.' He was still digging? 'I can sort of feel the shovel going through the earth, but I can't get it to dig. And I'm not sure why I'm doing it.' He still hadn't 'actually seen' the other people, but had only sensed them. Did he think that perhaps he was short-sighted? He didn't answer just then, though afterwards he said he supposed this was the sort of visual effect one would have if one did happen to be short-sighted; his own vision, in fact, was near-perfect. Instead of replying to my question, he said, 'I have a vague idea I'm a prisoner-of-war now, working on a farm.'

'Do you have any idea which part of the world you are in?'

'No. It could be France, but it seems to be England. It's not Australia. I really wonder what I'm shovelling around for! It's a very ordinary shovel, with a wooden handle, metal-based,

and squared off. It's a bit shiny. I'm not working very hard.
There might be someone around with weapons, guns. There
might be people fighting or something.'

Was this uniform his own? 'I've certainly had it for some
time.' Did he see animals, or birds, or any other people yet?

'No. I *can* call them up if I want to, but they're not coming
to me naturally. [When he said this, I wondered if he knew
just how pertinent this was to the very nature of the
experiment; you *can* 'call up' things, but if you do you
immediately feel, as he said, that such things had not 'come
naturally'.] The grass is very green and the earth is very clear.
It changes from time to time when I come to think of it. There
is a white cloud coming.'

How did it move? 'It moves quite quickly.' Did he feel the
wind or not? 'No, not really.' Was he warm or cold? 'I'm cool,
actually.' But 'actually', lying on my apartment floor, he was
comfortably warm. He did not know what the cloud was; it
was not in the sky, he told me afterwards, but was
approaching him from low on the ground. I asked him if it
could have been some kind of gas, and he said it could have
been. He still wasn't sure what he had been digging, possibly
a grave or simply a trench for the farm, or perhaps *said* to be
required for the farm. Returning to the experiment, I asked
him if he could still see his surroundings.

'If I go up again, do you mean?'

'No,' I told him. No experimentees had ever suggested
before that they ascend again, particularly not when they
appeared to be in the middle of a scene. I asked him again
what he could see of his surroundings.

'It's very hard,' he replied, 'because I find my logic is
changing all the time. All of a sudden I'm in Australia,
because I can see a red corrugated-iron roof. [This, he said
afterwards, was what he had no doubt been 'visualizing'
before, but from the viewpoint of the person he – his real self –
had merely visualized as being himself.] And it is on a house
with a sort of hump to it, which has got a sort of angle to it, I
don't know, with a little pattern of woodwork on the asbestos.
And it's got a red brick fence and all that sort of thing.'

'You're in one part of the world and seeing another?'

'I don't know really.' Afterwards he said this might have
been the case, yet somehow he felt as though he had been

almost instantly transposed from one locality to the other, but as though the self in the army uniform no longer existed. Had he perhaps died, and returned to see an Australian home? He said he didn't know, giving a nervous laugh at the same time.

If he looked down at what he was seeing, was there anything more than the house? He couldn't see anything else. Was the house inhabited or empty?

'Yes, it looks inhabited. The windows are open, with curtains.' Were there any people? 'No, not in view.' Could he go inside? 'I could do, but it is like I'm putting it all together, *with* people, with that sort of house. They're somehow not *real* people. I'm building up pictures of *that* house. I get an old lady with an apron on, you know – hanging the washing up. I mean, that's what you'd see by that sort of house in the country. I'm not sure she's really there. I think I'm creating these things because they fit, like gum-trees and kookaburras.'

If he went into the house, could he describe its interior?

'The problem is I would watch and tell what I know would be in that sort of house. I don't think my reaction is – well, all right, I will tell you what is there. I'm going through the door. There's linoleum on the floor, a shiny one with a floral pattern. It has a beige colour. There's the dark wood of floorboards. I open the door to the right and I'm going inside, and there's a browny type of room with dark wood on the walls, waist-high, you know. Then there's the white-plastered wall. And there's a big, polished, quite old-fashioned dining-table, round, very heavy-legged, and it's got sort of nice old-fashioned chairs, dark woodstained with nice patterns on the backs, leather-type backs. They're not kitchen chairs; they're rather grand, polished. There is a sofa in the lounge; there's a lounge suite which is all brown velvet. I'm starting to see my grandparents' place, really, and I suddenly see the three-piece lounge suite they had when we were children – that sort of thing.' Then he said nothing for some time.

Did he want to go on with this?

'No. The house has more or less gone.'

'Would you like to go up again?'

'All right.' And he ascended again, very quickly and quite easily, very high into clouds, then descended again. I'm coming down again, and it's much darker, very grey sort of clouds. Quite bright blue light is left in the sky. It's really

quite a dramatic sky. And it's almost dark, stormy, overcast
sort of – and I'm coming down, and . . .
  He was silent for a while, then:
  'There's a big square tower, like a castle tower, a very big
square one, a very high one, and it's got things on it. [He
made descriptive gestures suggesting squared turrets.] I
haven't got to it yet, but I can see it. It's on a hill. It's got a lot
of pointed roofs.' Was he going towards it? 'I'm at the foot
somewhere. Er, it's very grey and dark. I can only see the
ground now. Well, it's very wet and slushy, the ground. It's
got *some* grass on it, but it's very damp, with pools around in it,
that sort of thing. This castle is sort of up above me, all dark
grey granite, and wet looking. There is a very moist air, and
wet, cold, and nasty.'
  Was he near an entry?
  'I can't see an entry. There must be one, of course, not very
far away. It's slightly spongey with lots of grass, the ground.'
What was he wearing? 'Funny leather shoes, sort of like
pasties wrapped up – yes, pasties, or maybe purses – very
sloppy, and they're very wet. Wet and sloppy. Legs are bare,
which is very cold.' What sort of legs did he have? 'Very white
sort of legs, with hair on them. Nasty sort of colour, all cut
about and with smudges on them.' Could he see what he was
wearing above that? 'Like a jerkin thing, skirt and jacket
thing, you know. A belt with a pouch, or a purse, hanging
from it.' What colour clothes? 'Brownish, greyish, darkish.
Really wet. It smells damp.' Did he know what kind of
material? 'Very coarse, sort of woven, quite full. And it's
ragged at the sleeves. The belt is quite nice, quite a good belt.
The purse on the belt I can't quite see all that clearly. I've got
something of a hood-thing on, which is made like a chamois
sort of thing, leathery. I can't quite see who it is. I'm both
looking at him and yet I'm supposed to be him. There's a
thing around the neck holding the headgear. And I have a
staff, wooden. When I'm bent over, I have the sensation of
seeing the feet. Scungey [dirty] sort of shoes in the grass. How
muddy! Lot of footprints all around. I'm bent over, and I can't
see the face. The castle isn't very clear. It's rather bad in a
way. There's a path sort of going between two banks, a very
squelchy sort of path, with a crude stubby sort of grass. Water
everywhere, and all sort of squelchy. It has dirty squelchy

mud. I can feel it as though I have no shoes on.'

Was the path leading anywhere?

'I'm looking down into a lot of forest, sort of a recess on a hilltop, and I think there's some cattle. There's a cart with a great wooden thing, and great lumps of wood make the wheels. It makes a noise. There's a sort of pudding-thing on top of it.' I wanted to ask what this could possibly be, but he would not be stopped. 'I think there are a few other people around here. It's difficult to see their faces. There are some white figures walking along with a staff. Others are brownish. Monkish-looking, maybe. Going down towards the flatter area, the ground is getting a little harder. Quite firm now. I can hear a sound when I'm listening, but I can't hear any voices. [Afterwards, he said the sound was rather like a bell, but he wasn't sure; he was certain he was not confusing it with any noise in the apartment.] I'm going on. I can't see any animals now. It's about five-thirty, six. The path is now wide; it's well-established. Can we stop, do you think?'

It was a pity, but of course I complied. He appeared to have become agitated, though not at all distressed – perhaps it was more a kind of impatience. However, he had opened his eyes after only 53 minutes; 22 minutes of preliminaries, 20 minutes 'digging' as a possible prisoner-of-war, and 12 minutes of something that sounded medieval and bleak. However, he did not stop talking.

'I want to analyse what's happening,' he said. This desire to analyse the mechanics of the experiment, rather than *observe* the experience of it, usually does immediately terminate it. 'What's happening,' he averred, 'is that my imagination is taking over. I'm going on to things, things I'm well, scared of. I'm scared of [them] if I create things, I create enormous – I'm trying to be very honest with myself. If I were to say I want to see a lovely beach or a French palace, I can do it. What I'm trying to do if one gets a flash of something, I'm bringing in other things that sort of go with it. And that's the difficulty. When I see a red corrugated-iron roof, I immediately put [into it] all the figures of one's memory that fit that sort of house. And all I'm doing is building up a theme. Is that thing still running?' He had pointed to the tape-recorder. 'Can we switch it off?' I did.

After this, he said he certainly hadn't chosen either the

scene or the person which had appeared to him; but he was not at all sure that his imagination didn't concoct the accoutrements for such scenes. At the same time he had to admit that he had not liked either of them; there had been something sinister about both. He had the feeling that he had been in danger when he had been a prisoner-of-war, and he didn't like the 'feel' of the second experience either. It had been 'so medieval, twelfth-century'. He could easily concoct from memory and historical knowledge what buildings and garments would be like, but he hadn't expected the dampness, the mud, the feeling of actually participating – as in a dream – in what he was probably merely imagining. He did dream vividly, often of periods long before he was born, but normally such dreams did not distress him. This experience did not exactly distress him either, not the experience in itself; but he was distressed by what had been depicted so far. Perhaps he would try it again some time, but not now.

A few days later he returned by air to London, as hurried and apparently agitated in temperament as ever. The experiment did not seem to have given him any of the calm which it has apparently brought to other experimentees.

Bryant McDiven
Leo van de Pas

Despite, or perhaps because of, the complete failure of his first experiment (see page 54), Bryant McDiven wanted to make another attempt as much as I wanted him to. We decided that he should be the only one to attempt an experiment on the day or evening selected and that the only others present would be Leo and myself, to run the experiment, and his wife, Tedye, whose own experience almost two years before had been so successful (see pages 25-43). Bryant preferred to attempt the experiment in the accustomed surroundings of his own home, rather than in my apartment, as he was so poor at visualization.

When he first failed with the experiment, almost two years ago, Bryant and his wife had just read the book *Creative and Mental Growth* by Viktor Lowenfeld and W. Lambert Brittain. Tedye had come to the conclusion that Bryant was a 'haptic' rather than a visual type of person and, in spite of the highly 'visual' or *seemingly* visual type of paintings for which he is renowned, Bryant reluctantly agreed with her.

The word 'haptic' derives from the Greek *haptikos*, meaning 'able to lay hold of'.

Lowenfeld and Brittain describe a 'haptic' type of person as one who is primarily concerned with his own body sensations and the subjective experiences of a direct participant, in which he accordingly feels emotionally involved. The 'visual' and much more usual type of individual on the other hand registers his experience by starting objectively with his environment, or the surroundings which he sees, much as a spectator, using his eyes as intermediaries for such experience. This visually minded individual becomes disturbed, or at least inhibited, if he is stimulated only by means of haptic impressions, that is if he is asked not to use sight at all but to orient himself only by touch, bodily feelings, muscular sensations and kinaesthetic fusions. This is much like the distress felt by a recently blinded person trying to reorientate and adjust himself to a sightless world of darkness. Lowenfeld and Brittain write . . .

This much is clear, but what is not as obvious is that 'seeing' may also become an inhibitory factor when forced upon an [haptic] individual who does *not* use his visual experiences. An extreme haptic type of individual is normal-sighted but uses his eyes only when compelled to do so; otherwise he reacts as would a blind person who is entirely dependent upon touch and kinaesthesis. An extreme visually minded person, on the other hand, is entirely lost in the dark and depends completely on his visual experiences of the outside world.*

The results quoted by Lowenfeld and Brittain, in which 1,128 subjects were studied by means of specifically designed tests for visual or haptic aptitude, revealed that 47 per cent were clearly predominantly 'visual' and as much as 23 per cent were predominantly 'haptic'. The remaining 30 per cent

* Viktor Lowenfeld and W. Lambert Brittain, *Creative and Mental Growth* (Macmillan, New York, 1947 and Collier Macmillan, London 1964, 2nd edition).

scored below the level where clear identification was possible
or discernment of the aptitudes were so combined as to be
unidentifiable. In other words, about half reacted visually
while just less than a quarter reacted haptically, while most
people, or 70 per cent, tended to be of either one or the other of
these two extreme types. Thus apparently one in every four
individuals depends more upon his subjective experiences
such as touch and kinaesthesis than upon his vision, and 30
per cent vary between the two. When one considers the
enormous degree to which we depend upon purely visual
means for signalling, at traffic lights for instance, it is
alarming to think that only about half the population is being
catered for.

This, however, does not mean that haptic types have
inferior vision. Even inferior visual *awareness* is not necessarily
determined by a physical defect of the eyes. On the contrary,
the psychological factor of having the *aptitude* to observe was
found to be of deciding significance. A haptic type can have
perfect vision but nevertheless his aptitude is to experience
things by touch or feel, whereas a visual type may have
inferior vision but can still be constrained by this aptitude to
experience only, or predominantly, by visual means.

This state of being haptic apparently concerns the Christos
Experiment, and is of importance to the preliminary exercises,
as it implies that for a haptic type to be forced to observe and
experience anything visually can create inhibitions. Indeed,
under these tests it was found that such inhibition frequently
amounted to considerable psychological distress, which both
Leo van de Pas and Bryant McDiven experienced when
suddenly deprived of their media of touch and kinaesthesis
and required to rely on only their visual experiences in the
preliminary exercises for the Christos Experiment.

The visual tests of combined memory and imagination
distress the haptic type simply because he has no aptitude for
them; even if he was accustomed to them it would not help.
On the other hand, the stretching and shrinking exercises
which come at the very beginning of the experiment are
perfectly suited to haptic types, and both van de Pas and
McDiven accomplished these not only with ease but with
great 'feeling' and speed, frequently averring that they
stretched or shrank much further than was required. Other

experimentees, obviously of the visual type, frequently have difficulty with these particular exercises; some are unable either to visualise or to feel the sensation in any way whatsoever.

The haptic type usually also finds the massaging of forehead and ankles very much more stimulating than other experimentees; van de Pas considered that he could actually feel himself stretching and shrinking in both the knees and the head, although he could not visualize it, and McDiven felt that his ankles moved up to join his forehead so that the massaging of the two extremities of his body felt as one. McDiven found it pleasant to be massaged on the forehead to the extent that 'it felt as though it was boring into him', whereas van de Pas, who seems haptic to a lesser degree, found it verging through the pleasant to the unpleasant – much as pleasure can become pain, or warmth become searing heat – and became apprehensive about it, even when I used a far lighter touch than usual.

It therefore seems essential for haptic individuals wanting to attempt the Christos Experiment to have an entirely different set of preliminary exercises, which will not inhibit or distress them. Under any such inhibiting circumstances, it is very understandable that they cannot achieve the final results of visualizing the ultimate experience of revelation. Theoretically, nothing should prevent them achieving this desired result as, haptic or not, they still have dreams in the normal procedure of sleeping. Both McDiven and van de Pas dream frequently and vividly – at least, they *remember* having dreamt frequently and vividly, which many people do not, even though psychologists say that we *all* dream as much as four times a night.

However, if the haptic types should become distressed just prior to the actual process of dreaming consciously (let alone the possibility of visualizing such a thing as a past life or incarnation), satisfactory results can hardly be expected of them, in the same way that satisfactory results could hardly be expected of the visual type if, instead of being *relaxed* by the kinaesthetic exercises in the very beginning, they were distressed or inhibited by them. But if the massaging and stretching exercises help to relax a visual type and accustom him to a feeling of flexibility within his own body before attempting the remainder of the experiment, why shouldn't the visual exercises equally relax and prepare the haptic type for what, by visual projection, is immediately to follow? Thus, the answer may lie in the reversal of order of the exercises, in the elimination of the visual exercises or in their replacement by other exercises suitable to the haptic aptitude. In this chapter I intend to explore these theories with both Leo van de Pas (whose three failures are recorded in *Windows of the Mind*) and Bryant McDiven.

Before proceeding, however, I would like to investigate the haptic person a little more closely. Lowenfeld and Brittain have written that 'the main intermediary for the haptic type of individual is the *body self*'; this is the very sensation of experience that must be eliminated from the conscious mind to prepare for the predominantly visual experience of the Christos Experiment. As it is 'muscular sensations, kin-aesthetic experiences, touch impressions and all tactile experiences that place the self in value to the outside world', it is likely that this also applies to the 'inside world' – probably to an even greater degree. So perhaps the Christos Experiment is still denied to the haptic type who . . . 'is primarily the subjective type; he does not transform kinaesthetic or tactile experiences into visual experiences but is completely content with the kinaesthetic or tactile modality itself'.

For instance, when acquainting himself with an object in darkness the haptic type remains satisfied with his tactile or kinaesthetic experience of the surface structure of the object, or even obstacle. This also applies, though to a very much lesser degree, with merely the partial impressions of those areas or *parts* which he has touched. Tactile impressions within themselves are only partial, as are all impressions of objects which cannot be embraced with a single touch of the hands. Consequently, the hands must move over the object, which is entirely visible to the visual type, for the haptic individual to arrive at a synthesis of such partial impressions. This he can do only when he becomes emotionally interested in the object itself.

Another difficulty to be overcome with the haptic type is that normally he will not build up such a kinaesthetic synthesis, but instead will remain satisfied with his haptic experience. Since the haptic type uses the self as the true projector of his experiences, his pictorial representations (when asked, for instance, to draw an object, or more specifically a collection of objects) are highly subjective. His proportions, perspectives and distances *between* objects are depicted very differently from the readily recognizable proportions, perspectives and distances depicted by the visual type, as the haptic type has an emotional value of his own which is nevertheless as valid as the more familiar 'pictorial' or merely illustrative values to which most of us are accustomed. The work of Marc Chagall, who is a haptic artist, clearly shows the difference between the haptic projection or depiction and the much more predominant visual or 'illustrative' artist.

So it seems quite obvious that if a haptic type is to have any degree of success with the Christos Experiment, he must be subjected to a different approach to it and, equally important, be spared the inhibiting and distressing visual exercises.

At the same time as I reached these conclusions, Peter Hurford (see pages 140-48) arrived from London and told me of a procedure for transcendental meditation he had come across in Europe, but which he thought was derived from Yoga or other Hindu procedures. First, one lies on the floor with one's legs up against a wall, which stimulates the blood in the head in a rather subtler way than the massaging in the preliminaries for the Christos Experiment. Then, to achieve the flexibility and, in this case, complete separation from the body, one progressively imagines or auto-suggests the gradual disappearance from the body, beginning with the toes and working down through feet, ankles, lower legs, knees, thighs, loins, abdomen and chest; then from fingers through hands, wrists, forearms, elbows, upper arms and shoulders; then from neck to chin, face, occiput (back of head), forehead, to the top of the skull – thus leaving only the mind to float freely wherever it will.

I decided to try this process with van de Pas and McDiven in the near future, both with and without the massaging and stretching and shrinking exercises, which appear to be completely haptic in themselves, providing that the experimentee is asked to simulate only the tactile and not any visual sensations of them.

It was a pity this procedure was not tried on Peter Hurford

himself, but it only occurred to me after he had returned to London, while I was writing up the account of his experience, that he was probably a haptic type himself, without knowing or perhaps even suspecting it; or, if not exclusively haptic, then at least predominantly so. I should have suspected this from the beginning when he said that the massaging stimulated him pleasantly, and certainly when he accomplished the stretching and shrinking exercises so rapidly without necessarily 'visualizing' them but merely 'feeling' them.

These, then, are the most significant points for the person conducting the experiment to watch for, as they are the first indications of whether the experimentee has visual or haptic aptitudes. The applicable aptitude can be quickly discerned when the visual-memory exercises begin, for a few questions should easily reveal to the conductor whether the experimentee sees a picture of an *entire* door and its immediate surroundings, as does a visual type, or merely a single detail at a time, looking from one to the other much as if the hands were moving from place to place before being able to assess the entire object, as happens with a haptic type. The final exercises invariably confirm a haptic type, for when looking at his surroundings from a roof, perhaps of a building several storeys high, he can 'see' only close details – no wide horizons or panoramic vista. He also shows distress at being asked to attempt such exercises, a distress which usually increases with his dismay at being unable to perform them when he knows, or at least conjectures, that the majority of people can do them with ease.

Although Peter Hurford *appeared* to visualize the front door of his London flat, it was soon apparent that he was seeing not the entire door but only details of it at a time. For instance, when he had seen the lock on one side of the door, he did not see the number six in the centre, though its distance from the lock was little more than a foot. From the roof of the flat-building of at least six storeys, he saw only details of gardens, trees and shrubs in the immediate vicinity, and no further than the next-door houses. He even had to be prompted to see 'across the road', and then could only visualize a vague sensation of buildings without being able to determine what kind of buildings they were or any details of them. When he saw himself as a prisoner-of-war, his vision was again restricted to one separate detail at a time; he could not even associate the red corrugated-iron roof with the house it was on, let alone 'see' the whole building, no matter what it might have been supposed to be. He could not associate it with the surrounding landscape either, nor with himself. In the case of a much more concentrated object of vision, such as his own face, he could become preoccupied with a mere detail of it – like his jaw-line – without being able to see the rest of his features until he looked at them one at a time. He could *sense* (haptically?) people digging near him; but although they were only 'twenty or thirty feet away', he could not see them. He *sensed* people with weapons, guns; *sensed* that he was a prisoner-of-war and in danger even though there were no *visible* signs of proof of this. The same restriction of vision applied even when he was before the medieval castle-tower (*only* a tower, note; not an entire castle), or following a path, or seeing his own apparel, or discerning animals (some cattle) and other monkish-looking people, one of whom was ploughing. Another figure was visualized some half a minute or more later, exactly as if he could not see the entire group in the field only several yards away from him but had to look from one to the other in much the same way as his hands would have to feel their way over a large object before being able to identify it; his eyes, like his hands, seemed unable to embrace the whole.

Time and again Peter Hurford used expressions which now convince me he is predominantly haptic and not visual, such as . . . 'I just saw the roof – the red, corrugated-iron roof – and some of the brickwork, but it doesn't fit anywhere.' Immediately afterwards he said, 'There are some trees in the corner somewhere – it's part of the whole thing, a jigsaw.' Still later, when asked the distance of poplar trees, he said, 'Funny, I can't fit it in, the link between the poplar trees and where I'm standing.' Then came what to me is the most pertinent statement of all . . . 'I haven't built a *frame* of the scenery.' This seemed exactly the same as the statement of Bryant McDiven that he can never visualize any of his own paintings (and many of them are large, say three feet by six feet or even more), but only the details as he progresses from one small section to another, never knowing how the entire picture will turn out no matter how 'visual' most of his work may appear to the viewer. Only now does Bryant McDiven realize that he has never been able to conceive any of his paintings in their entirety, but only section by section. He, too, cannot 'build a frame' of his own imaginatively conceived scenery, but only details of it from an imagination or aptitude that is haptically instead of visually orientated. For him, as for Peter Hurford in his experiment, details are always vivid (consider Hurford's shovel, buttons, pips on epaulettes, etc.) whereas the entire picture as an integrated whole evades him. With the visual type of person it is of course the reverse: the whole picture can be seen immediately, but the details are elusive.

Bryant McDiven is haptic to an extreme degree, and this explains the complete failure of his attempt at the Christos Experiment. McDiven was born on September 11th, 1923, in the state of Victoria, where he was educated. He served in the Australian Air Force during the Second World War, married and came to Western Australia. About six feet in height, he is of moderately solid build with pleasant and immediately recognizable features, made even more distinguishable by a thick – though now thinning – thatch of hair.

I have already said that the massaging of his forehead and ankles made him feel as though his ankles had sprung up to join his forehead. At the forehead the massaging seemed to have a sensation of boring deep into his head, yet pleasantly so. The stretching and shrinking were accomplished not only with ease and speed, but were also carried well beyond their required distance in a matter of seconds instead of the minute or more usually required. But almost immediately afterwards, when asked to describe his door, the difficulties commenced. He was unable to 'see' the door, and could merely remember it laboriously detail by detail. He had a similar problem when asked to imagine himself on the roof of his bungalow-style house. The first thing he said was that he planted his feet on either side of the central beam of the roof and could *feel* 'a good solid footing'. If it had been difficult for him to see details of his front door, it was even more difficult for him now. Almost as though he was actually trying to discern details and objects in near dark, he screwed up forehead, eyes, the rest of his face. Just as with Leo van de Pas, he became distressed at his obvious inability to do what he had seen two other people – his

wife and a very close friend, Dr Minc – perform with apparent
ease. When the ascent was to begin, vision disappeared
entirely and he merely 'floated' up high into the sky, *feeling* the
entire process but unable to see anything but opaque and
monochromatic densities.

'I seem to be just simply suspended in the sky,' he said.

What colour of sky?

'Well, it changes. Like a . . . grey . . . er, void.'

As he had risen to what he thought to be clouds, I asked
him if he also thought this could be like being *inside* a cloud.
The suggestion seemed to please him, even giving him relief, if
only because it supplied an explanation.

'Could be, yes. Could be inside a cloud.'

If he went higher, could he come *through* the clouds?

'I'm just floating upwards. I'm not exactly *letting* myself
float upwards.' Did he feel all right, safe? 'Yes.' Was there
anything else he could see? 'It's grey. But it's whiter, I think.'
Was it *dark* or a *light* grey? 'It *was* a very *dark* grey, but now
it's a *light* grey.' Was it a luminous grey, or was it . . . 'A warm
grey. Almost an orange grey. But that is maybe because a
light is coming through my eyelids.'

We switched out a near-by standard lamp even though the
room was already much dimmer than usual, as there is no
need whatsoever for what might be considered 'theatrical' or
appropriate lighting for 'atmosphere'. Normal light is all that
is required. With this particular light switched out, the grey
was 'now opaque'.

'It's almost as though it's composed of dust, but pleasant
dust.'

Did he still feel as though he was high up, or where?

'I don't feel as though I'm any particular height, really. It's
almost as though it's just space. I'm not in any relationship to
anything.'

Could he see any part of his own body?

'No.'

Could he see his own feet?

'No, I can't.'

Was there any change in his surroundings? Was there any
glimmer of light, or anything? (His wife had just moved over
and switched on another, but more distant lamp; but he did
not notice this.)

'No, not really. I've lost it a bit. I've suddenly become aware of my own body again.'

So we started once more from the roof of his house which he could again immediately 'feel' under his feet. But could he tell us its colour?

'No. I can't see it.'

He couldn't see the roof at all?

'No, I can't.'

Could he visualize any part of the house or grounds?

'No. I'm *almost* getting images, but not quite.' And his face again contorted as though he were striving to see through a dense fog. What kind of images did he *almost* get?

'It's not clear to me, but I can just see them – almost.'

I suggested his trying to visualize his front garden again, and immediately his face resumed its former contortion.

'But I don't *want* to,' he protested, with considerable vehemence. 'I want to try to find this – this *other* thing.'

'Oh, you do?'

'Yes.'

What did he think this 'other thing' might be? Just colour, or some kind of being, or what?

After some moments' silence, he said, 'I had it almost. It's exciting! But I can't quite grasp it.'

'Is it a visual thing?'

'It's almost *becoming* visual.'

'Any predominant colour at all?'

'Blue. It's a very, very dark blue.'

But again he could make no progress; he could not arrive at even a vague semblance of anything, let alone any particular definition. So I told him I thought it necessary to do one more exercise if any results at all were going to be achieved, and he agreed. I then told him to forget this blueness and again concentrate on looking from his roof.

'All right.'

'Can you see the garden? The fishpond? The walls?'

But instead of replying in any instance, again his face became contorted as he asked, 'Can you put something under my heels? It's getting a little, er . . .'

His wife lifted his heels to place a cushion underneath them, although he was lying on a very thick-piled rug that was in turn on a thick-piled carpet with foam-rubber beneath it. But

Could he see from a distant height?

'Not at present.'

He could both feel that he was at a great height and yet also on his living-room floor. I told him to disregard the feeling of height, open his eyes, and we ended the experiment.

How long did he think he had been trying? Ten minutes, perhaps. He had been fifty minutes seeing almost nothing. He was incredulous. At least this much of the experiment still applied – the incredible speed of time even when he had 'seen' so very little.

It was not entirely a failure, but it was certainly no success.

For his fourth attempt my assistant Leo van de Pas, who has witnessed every experiment I have tried and usually massages experimentees' ankles and manipulates the tape-recorder, had Mrs Ruby Beecham (whose experience is recorded in *Windows of the Mind*) to massage his ankles while I massaged his forehead and conducted the 'run'. This was attempted in my apartment on May 29th, 1973, commencing at 9.15 p.m.

Leo was born in De Bilt near Utrecht in The Netherlands on October 28th, 1942, the fourth of five children. He has had various occupations – from bookshop assistant to customs officer and banker in The Netherlands – and he did his national service with the Dutch Army mostly attached to the Dutch Navy in what was then Dutch New Guinea. Just as writing has been a common accompaniment to my own various occupations, he has always been interested in geneaology. In the little over four years he has been my assistant, he has completed four comprehensive and highly complex volumes of genealogical collections about the monarchies and aristocracy of Europe since the sixteenth century.

In the beginning, even though he had witnessed several experiments, he was reluctant to try one himself, feeling convinced it would not work for him. It didn't, and each successive attempt 'revealed' less to him. Asked to try the new method, he said he preferred to follow the usual procedure and, if it did not work again, then he would try the new method. He said he was no longer apprehensive about the experiment, as he had been in the beginning, and he even seemed hopeful of it revealing something to him this time; he had seen it reveal so much to so many others.

Perhaps he was too anxious for it to work, for he completed the preliminaries much too quickly, in just fifteen minutes, especially the very first and possibly more 'haptic' exercises of stretching and shrinking. However, he was then able to give excellent descriptions of the front door (except for the one omission of the doorbell) of my apartment in which he has lived for four and a half years, so I felt encouraged with his progress. This encouragement seemed even more justified with his descriptions from the roof of my apartment-building, although here again he missed one section of the street immediately in front of him and stretching as far as the ocean on the right. However, he said afterwards that he had been so high up on the building's roof that he had 'looked over' these one-storey buildings to the golf links and sea beyond rather than having 'overlooked' them.

He was then able to accomplish the ascent, without any difficulty this time, although instead of going straight up as do most experimentees he slanted towards the north-east to the suburb of Claremont some three miles away. However, he was soon at cloud-level but, like Bryant McDiven, he then found himself in such dense cloud that he could not see through it. It had become an opaque monotone of an indeterminate grey which, he said, he found unpleasant. Yet he was eventually able to rise above it and see all this cloud beneath him, much as he could from an aeroplane. He could also see clear blue sky above. Then he was able to descend through it again – and I really thought he was going to be successful this time when he said that, far below, he could see ocean.

Indeed he could. But he saw ocean through a pattern of small and regularly spaced clouds like balls of cottonwool. And through them, down on the ocean, he could see a ship. It was quite stationary, with no smoke emerging from either of its two funnels. Except for the calm and glittering sea, there was no motion whatsoever, no sign of people on the ship, no other vessels in all the expanse of water, no islands nor even sign of land. It was, he said, almost as though he were looking at a coloured postcard, but in actuality this was something he had seen in the first week of April 1962, from the window of a plane between Tokyo and New Guinea when he had been in the Dutch Army. No matter how long he watched it, there was no sign, no movement, no change. Eventually he said he wanted to 'return above' again and so reluctantly I let him. He was soon back into dense cloud, then above it, then descending once more.

Again we were hopeful as this time instead of the ship in the ocean he saw land, and he almost immediately landed on a beach. It had fine white sand and the sea behind him was again calm and blue and glittering in the sunlight. Before him were coconut palms, some of them bearing coconuts. Perhaps what happened next was my fault, but I wanted to ascertain the amount of detail he was visualizing and so I asked him to look at any one particular tree and tell me how many coconuts there were on it. Without any hesitation he said 'Three', and that he could see them quite clearly as his focus had become concentrated on the top of one tree with its three coconuts. But then, quite abruptly, the entire picture vanished and almost automatically he returned up into the dense cloud again.

At least he persisted. He descended once more, only to see the ocean empty except for the same ship he had seen on his first descent. But now there was smoke coming from the only funnel he could see; perhaps the second funnel, which he had seen previously, was now hidden by the smoke. Apart from this one small detail, there was no change. And there was still no change after watching this lone ship on the ocean for some moments, so he ascended again.

Each time he rose it was into dense cloud through which he could not see. Above would be brilliantly clear sky and at least he was always able to descend through the cloud again. Yet having passed down through it, it obviously lifted or dissipated, for then he would see whatever confronted him, in relatively bright sunshine, not at all as though it were an overcast day.

Our hopes were raised again when this time he said that he could see, to one side of the ocean, a large island with central mountain peaks and a long narrow peninsula that was green with trees. As he descended, however, he could not bring himself directly down to it, but only to about a mile away from its shore, exactly as though he were on board a ship – although there was no sign of a ship. Yet he also seemed to be at about the height of a boat-deck on a large passenger-ship.

And then he realized that he was looking at an island he had seen in reality – Rarotonga in the Pacific to which our ship, returning to Australia from Europe via Panama, had called on Christmas Day of 1972 without going into harbour or even anchoring, but merely remaining stationary about a mile from shore.

He could not, however, see any of the habitation we had seen in actuality, nor the boats which had put out to sea that afternoon bringing Rarotongans in their mauve and white regalia to sing hymns and Christmas carols to the passengers. Indeed, he did not even see this part of the island, but only the area to the north which we had seen when the ship departed only a few hours after arrival. Once more it was all quite stationary, exactly as though it was a coloured postcard he was looking at rather than any actual, or visualized, scene. Yet, when prompted, he did actually manage to visualize having almost landed on this narrow peninsula with palm-trees so thick he could not see through them, but he could clearly see the part of beach below him where he thought he might land if he were able. However, he couldn't; and the attempt only made him retreat to where he had been formerly, even though there was still no ship there. After that, he felt that he could not approach land again and that there was little point in his seeing any more of an island which he had obviously seen in reality and only recently at that. He was still hoping to see something much more distant in the past, and so he ascended once again.

But again it was to find himself in 'thick, thick cloud'. And even though he could actually visualize himself kneeling on hands and knees and trying to peer down through all this density of cloud, he could still see nothing. Even the ocean had now disappeared.

And so he consented to attempt Peter Hurford's procedure of trying to both visualize *and* feel progressive parts of his body disappearing. Almost from the beginning he had an odd, even comical reaction: asked to imagine his toes as vanished from his feet, he said he could lose all but his two big toes, which made an unexpected and rather remarkable sight. To my surprise, he seemed able to 'lose' the rest of his body quite easily, continuing with his feet, which also removed his ankles, then lower legs, knees, upper legs and thighs. But when he was asked to 'lose' his thighs he said he immediately visualized a mess of blood all over where his left leg had been. He did not feel any pain, however, and was quite willing to continue. Abdomen, chest and neck disappeared. Then when I suggested he lose his fingers, he said that his entire arms and shoulders had already gone and only his head was left; then he 'saw' his head fall forward and become upright, as though standing on its own base. He quickly disposed of the back and top of his head, only to have his head appear to change into stone; and although he could not discern any change in size, it reminded him of the heads erected on Easter Island. At the same time, it was still his own face and he was unable to 'lose' it. Try as he would, it would not go. So I asked him if he felt that his mind was now free to travel wherever it would take him; but he said no, not with his face still attached to it. He tried, but nothing happened. And so he opened his eyes, feeling that having tried his hardest for a little over half an hour was as much as he could do. He had been an hour and fifteen minutes, though like most experimentees he was quite incredulous at having been 'away' so long.

Naturally, he was still disappointed at not having seen a more cinematographic visualization, let alone something approaching a remembrance of a past life. He did feel now, however, that he had not so much a blockage, nor even his former apprehension towards the experiment, but that being haptic he had a deficiency, almost like actual blindness, that prevented him from 'seeing'. It was like a wall through which he couldn't penetrate, 'and that was that'. He had not been aware of any deficiency prior to discovering that he was haptic, but pointed out that one could hardly be aware of even such deficiencies as deafness or colour-blindness if one had always been deaf or colour-blind. He also still suspected that his blockage was possibly due to a violent end in a previous life, which the subconscious did not want to experience again – an explanation for failure which had been put forward in an article in the magazine *Open Mind*.

He had no objection to trying it yet again, he said, but hoped that if he did it could possibly be after talking the matter over with the authoress of the article in *Open Mind;* perhaps she would even witness, or conduct, the experiment. He pointed out that she had mentioned using music during the procedure, which 'speeds up the process of learning within some individuals as well as helping them to remember past lives', and as he could not accomplish anything through the *visual* preliminary exercises, he hoped that, being haptic, music might help him instead.

At least he had the consolation of having 'seen' much more than Bryant McDiven, and was therefore not as haptic as Bryant. By the same degree, however, he was probably more haptic than Peter Hurford.

Richard Chaney

Richard Gerard Chaney, twenty-five and single, one of seven children, was reading for his Ph.D. in Aesthetics in the French Renaissance at the University of Western Australia when he undertook the experiment in my apartment on June 1st, 1973, commencing at 9.10 p.m. He had travelled extensively throughout Australia but had been overseas only once – he spent exactly one year in France (December 1970–December 1971) undertaking research as a guest of various French universities, or as *un auditeur libre*. Naturally he speaks French fluently. The experiment was witnessed by a French friend of his who had been in Western Australia a little over a year.

Richard is just a fraction under six feet tall but is very slimly built. He says he dreams profusely and is frequently able to recall his dreams. He has one recurring dream, set in sharp-peaked and snow-laden mountain country where he is a teacher in a large school that is built on a mountainside with grounds bound by a tall spiked fence. For some reason or other, he knows he should not venture beyond this fence; however, he frequently does and, when he returns, always feels relaxed and relieved and able to resume being the 'respectable schoolteacher'. What disturbs him about the dream is that each time he goes over the fence he is accompanied as far as its tall spikes by half a dozen or so of his students, who wait and watch for him until he returns – at which point he invariably awakens or else the dream ends.

Like the rest of his family, Richard is Roman Catholic; but he says he has an entirely open mind about such matters as reincarnation.

Before commencing the experiment, I tried him with a

simple test and a few questions which showed him to be
probably more haptic than visual, and so I did not expect
much from his experiment. He identified large and small
articles as quickly by touch as by sight, said he was untidy but
nevertheless knew where everything was (confirmed by his
French friend) and did not need to switch on a light if he got
up during the night for anything, whereas his flat-mate did.
He said he was very ticklish in the feet, but he soon became
accustomed to the massaging of his ankles; he then
accomplished the preliminaries in almost exactly the average
twenty minutes, giving excellent descriptions of the front door
of his flat and the building's surroundings from its roof, before
making an easy ascent.

At first I thought he was indeed going to prove haptic, as
after the descent he could see 'almost nothing – a big disc of
the horizon' which was 'all land, flat, a dark browny-
red-yellow colour' with a few stunted, isolated trees.
There was no water whatsoever but there was a road bisecting
the whole wide flat area from one horizon to the other, though
this was not quite in the centre of the picture; it was a blue
sealed road with a broken white line down the middle. The
landscape was so empty and uninteresting, he said, almost
hostile, that he did not want to land there. It was, he
admitted, sketchily suggestive of landscapes in Central
Australia, but it did not resemble any actual landscape he had
ever seen.

He was able to ascend again easily, returning through cloud
over which he traversed fairly rapidly before descending
again. This time he found himself over much greener country,
on a fine day, with more vegetation and with some roads that
were neither straight nor long. Off-centre of this second
'picture' he saw a roughly circular lake, about two-thirds
surrounded by thick trees. On the other side of the lake was a
village of rather old-fashioned, two-storeyed, steeply gabled
houses spaced well apart but without fences or even gardens
between; there was no sign of any people.

For some reason he felt he did not want to land in this
village and instead chose the other side of the lake, near the
trees, where the land was 'quite safe and firm, flat', and green
with what he presumed to be grass or possibly moss – as he
could not discern leaves. The trees around him were in leaf

and were largish oak or plane trees, richly green in colour and
with thick, dark brown trunks. Apart from the village across
the lake, he could see no other sign of habitation; and there
were still no people, nor even animals.

Asked to look down at his feet, he found he was wearing soft
neutral-coloured shoes which, although we witnesses thought
they resembled the ones he had removed, he said afterwards
were very different from any he had owned. However, he
said he was wearing his own green trousers, whereas in reality
he was wearing dark brown trousers with a beige sweater. He
said he was quite definitely *not* wearing a sweater in the
'picture' but only a light-coloured shirt that was 'half-hanging
out at the back – I don't quite know how I can *see* that!'

He was clean-shaven and had fairly long hair that was in a
mess – which was odd, he said, because there was no wind.
(His real hair is auburn and of medium length.) He thought
he was about the same age as in reality, or possibly a little
younger. His hands were bare except for a ring on his middle
finger; I wanted to ask if it was the same ring as he was
wearing but he had immediately expressed his surprise at the
appearance of his hands which he said were 'red, a rough kind
of red, scrawny – they look awful'.

The day had now become a little darker and the horizon
lower, he said. The landscape had not changed and there was
still no sign of people; but now he could see two animals,
white ones, with short hair or fur, one larger than the other,
either cows or sheep, he couldn't tell as they were on the other
side of the lake where the trees began. They were just drinking
from the edge of the lake and did not take any notice of him.

Apart from these and the village, he could see nothing
until he discovered 'a couple of roads, of white earth, with no
signposts or guides of any kind' which did not go anywhere;
they appeared just to start somewhere near him and finish
again without leading anywhere. 'Either that or I can't see
where they end, because of a bend or their going over a hill or
something.'

Eventually he decided to approach the village by a rather
complex yet precise route around trees, etc., which was
evidently perfectly clear and logical to him if rather vague to
his audience. When walking, he was surprised to find the land
beyond the trees not quite so flat and open as he had thought,

but overgrown with grass and weeds and lined with furrows at
right-angles to the direction he was taking.

The houses in the village were still two-storeyed with
steeply gabled roofs, white walls and dark wooden struts or
beams, which made them 'look like boxes wrapped with
masses of dark ribbons'. The angled roofs of forty-five degrees
or more were studded with many chimneys, but he could see
no signs of electric-light wires or lamp-posts. Each house had
'small windows, which is surprising; each is made up of six
panes of thickish glass, two horizontal by three vertical'.
These, like the small doors to each house, were all closed.
There were still no fences or gardens around the houses, but
only a maze of white narrow roads running between them all.
And the houses were laid out symmetrically like a kind of grid,
all facing the same way but not, as one might expect, facing
the lake.

One house, however, was slightly bigger than the rest and
instead of a door had only a large doorway. It was closer to
him and the lake than most of the other houses and was a
different colour, a kind of dark red or dark brown. He was not
particularly happy going into this village because he was
worried by the complete absence of people. But if he was
compelled to go to any one particular house, he would go to
the big one with the open doorway, as all the other doors were
closed. He didn't particularly want to go in, but he did once
he was asked what he could see of its interior.

The room or hall he entered was bare, dark and rectangular
with 'sharp corners everywhere'. The floor was of dark, heavy
timbers and the walls of dark, compressed stones and earth.
The only furniture was 'a long – a very long – table, very
heavy, made of big beams of wood, two of them, made
together to form a top and supported at either end by two
cross-beams'. Apart from that there was nothing, and still no
sign of people. There were no chairs, but only 'something *on*
the table, actually – they're two goblet-things really, one of
which is standing up and the other lying down next to it . . .
they look like old chalices, actually, made of silver with gold
lined inside . . . they look extremely nice.' Had they been lying
there long? 'No. They're both empty.' He could not tell how
long they might have been lying there and there was certainly
no other sign of people having been there.

Asked to look around, he said, 'There are very, very high ceilings; plain, oddly enough, when from outside with all the woodwork you'd expect beams to be inside as well.' The ceilings were dark grey and too high to make out any details. Asked what lighting would be used if it were night, he said, 'I can't imagine, but there's no kind of lighting anywhere around.' There was quite definitely no form of electric light. These houses, he said, were made like those in old Norse tales of very large, stark houses with little in them, large empty rooms 'where heroes and people used to have banquets and that sort of thing there, stark rooms, rather a barn of a house.'

As there was at least one other storey in this house, was there a staircase somewhere? 'Yes, there's a staircase which is really part of the wall. It's not a free, er, a free-moving staircase, it's built against the wall and it sort of forms a diagonal line right from the floor up through the ceiling where there's just a hole, a big rectangular hole in the corner. The staircase forms a long diagonal, as though it's been cut with pinking scissors if you look at it side-on.'

He did not mind going upstairs but found only two very wide, empty rooms; the one which he came into from the stairs was larger than the other, but both had the same windows with three vertical by two horizontal panes. These admitted little light as, despite it being quite bright outside, *inside* it was terribly dark. There were still no lights nor even provision made for lighting; but when he looked up at the ceiling – still flat, so that he thought there might possibly be attics above – he saw a huge, round, dark-metalled holder for large candles, but without candles in it. There was no furniture whatsoever in the room. The floor was made 'not of planks, because they're smaller than that; they're dark brown and they're about three inches across, and they seem to go right across the room without a join, each one.'

There was still no furniture, and now that he was by the window he could see that it was really quite a big window and that it was closed because it couldn't be opened – it was a fixture. It was made of fixed panes of glass still in the same two vertical columns each with three panes. Again, the room had sharp corners and thick walls made of heavy timbers with dark dried mud jammed between. He did not feel at all familiar with the house, and had to look for everything as though he was exploring it for the first time.

There was still no sign of people, nor of people having ever been there, and he could not think of any reason why such a house, let alone the entire village, should be deserted. He didn't think it had been evacuated because of any tragedy or threat. Except for the two goblets downstairs, there was no sign of anything having been used, or even which *could* be used. 'I don't think the goblets have so much been left behind as simply just put there, totally incongruous as that might be. I don't get the impression of people having *left*. I don't know, but perhaps people just come in here every now and then, people just passing through. I don't know.' The only signs of any kind of life were the same two animals across the lake, which were 'rather stylized, white-coloured, like I haven't seen animals before, and they don't move a great deal, only drink. And that's all.'

Still looking out of the window, he was perplexed by the obvious grid-pattern of the houses. He didn't know in which direction he was facing – he didn't know which was north – but the houses were all facing say north or south, or perhaps north-west or south-east, 'but anyway all facing the same way, yet *not* facing the lake. And the roads joining them *don't* form a grid but run in all directions, not a tangle of roads, but enough to join every house to every other house. They're meandering roads, in gentle curves, not sharp-cornered.'

No gardens, no fences, no trees – except those by the lake. He had no idea in which part of the world he could be; it was 'bucolic, countrified', but could be anywhere. 'There are no birds, nor anywhere for them to sit, except on the houses, or the trees over beyond the lake.' He had never seen a place like it, but the houses did slightly resemble those you sometimes saw depicted in children's books – except that these seemed real without his ever having seen them in reality. It was quite a pleasant locality, he said, 'not arid or unfriendly, but it doesn't seem to have any reference point.'

If he had to stay there for any length of time, so that he got hungry or thirsty, what would he do or where would he go? Like Ken Redman and D'Arcy Ryan before him, he said without any hesitation, 'The whole idea of being hungry or thirsty just simply doesn't occur to me. I'm *not* hungry and I'm *not* thirsty, so I don't *feel* the problem. No, it doesn't apply.'

Would he never see any people, no matter how long he stayed there? Very diffidently he replied, 'Well, there *are* those two cups [goblets], which rather make me think I might.' But there were definitely no other signs of people, not even footprints anywhere.

He did not exactly feel content being there, but wasn't apprehensive either. 'I feel a bit intrigued, really, but not ill at ease.' Despite the emptiness and loneliness, he didn't feel boredom either. If he had to spend some time there, he didn't think he would return to the lake but would stay there in the town and 'follow the funny roads from house to house' – even though, from the closed doors and windows, he didn't think he would be able to enter any of them. In any case they would be empty; there was nothing in them to show that people had ever lived there, no curtains at the windows. If he had to sleep somewhere, he would stay in, or return to, the same large building with its open doorway, so he couldn't see the point of trying any of them. It was a clear day, quite clear, with a little cloud here and there, and it was now late afternoon. It wasn't warm, but also it wasn't cold; it seemed to be either late spring or early autumn, and no breeze.

Asked about his clothes again, the shirt and shoes were still the same but the trousers were different. 'They're not mine any more. They're dark red, and they're torn in one leg, the left, a vertical tear from just below the knee to right down to the bottom. But the curious thing is that right down to about three inches from the bottom, or the hem, they've got a kind of embroidery, white and yellow, in sort of swirling patterns that are a bit difficult to describe. And in the middle of each swirl, about six times around the bottom of the pants, are sort of, I don't know, sequin-things, like sort of flat silver plaques but very small.' And he then went into a considerably detailed description of the embroidery – 'looks like cotton, obviously hand-done and not by machine' – which held him fascinated, 'because it has been worked by someone who obviously knew what the pattern was intended, was *going* to be.' And then subsequently his attention became focused on the one metallic, 'yellowy' button at his waist which kept the trousers done up, and which had a face in profile etched on it, but almost upside-down so that it looked the right way up when viewed by him from above. The profile was just a simple outline and was not worked in relief; the head, depicted 'with its hair down to the bottom of the neck', could have been either male or female. He had no belt, but 'two shield-shaped pockets on the front' of the trousers with, however, nothing at all in them.

The only other thing he could see now that he hadn't seen before was something revealed by the tear in his trousers; this was white, either a bandage or a sock, but as it didn't come very high above his ankle (as a sock normally would) it was probably a bandage. Yet he didn't *think* he had been injured. For the rest of it, his clothing hadn't changed at all.

I tried again to see what he would do if he needed to sleep, or if, as with eating and drinking, he didn't need to sleep at all. 'I'd go back inside, and I'd go up into the smaller room and – and – stand by the window.' Sleeping didn't seem relevant either, he said, and it would be rather uncomfortable if he had to sleep on only the bare boards. Yet he then thought that he *would* want to sleep, and that he *would* lie down, 'but the prospect doesn't thrill me a great deal because it's just floor boards, really – planks – small planks.' However, he wouldn't look for some better place, he would stay up there, even though it occurred to him that he would no doubt be much more comfortable on the ground near the lake.

If he had to leave this place, where would he go? 'Back up in the air where I came from.' Could he do that? 'Yes. No trouble.' And he had already done it.

Did he want to descend again, to try to see somewhere or something else? Yes, because he was already travelling. After twenty-five seconds, he gave a little chuckle and then, at the thirtieth second, said, 'I've come down – and it's a very different place, in a town, a big town, and I'm right above a lot of people. Actually I'm right above a big, an extremely big, kind of square, full of loads of people, mainly women, biggish women, with shawls and things, big bulky dresses made of printed cotton, and they all look the same except that they're different.' He couldn't possibly count how many women there were, but 'they are all selling things – some of them have got pigs, geese, wicker baskets, things like that.'

He hadn't yet landed, but was floating just above them. The surrounding buildings were 'fairly ramshackle, dark, made of wood, in fact *wet* wood'. Asked, then, what kind of day it was, he said, 'Oh, it's cloudy, but it doesn't look like rain; it doesn't look as though it has been raining.' Asked more about the buildings in the square, he said it was not easy to tell if they were one- or two-storey, as the ones that were taller did not have windows at the front but only at the sides. 'In front they've just got façades, and they must have skylights up the top from what I gather. But even the two-storey ones definitely haven't got any windows in front. They seem to be rather more like a set for a film than an actual town. That's the effect they give from what I can see of them, although they're *not* a set for a film, they're definitely three-dimensional buildings.' Were there streets going off from the square? 'Very, very small streets, narrow streets, quite a lot of them, full of people. One woman has a donkey.' Any vehicles of any kind? 'No *motorized* vehicles, no. A couple of, well — bicycle-looking things, but they seem to have a type of basket attached to the back part where the driver sits, and they've got three wheels, not two wheels; they're like big tricycles really. They're trolley-type things. They pedal like a bike, apparently. Nobody rides *in* them, they just pedal from on the side. Bit like a bicycle with a side-car, but the two wheels at the back are much smaller than the one at the front. The wheels are like bicycle wheels with small round tyres and spokes. The front one is much bigger than the back two. A bit like a penny-farthing with a basket between the two wheels.'

Could he see what the people around him were selling? 'Yes, fruit and vegetables. And there are some barrows with clothing.' Did he recognize any of these people? 'Not individually, but they're the sort of people one sees in market squares in Europe, except these are of some while ago.' Was it any particular place in Europe? 'No, because none of the market squares I saw were anything at all like this one.'

No part of this particular square was at all familiar to him, nor was this particular situation. He 'felt' he lived not far away and had gone to this square because someone had told him about it and about all the women who were there on market day; and so he had gone to see it. He was just a spectator, a bystander looking at everything for the very first time, both from the point of view of himself in the dream and himself as the dreamer. He would do no more than stand and watch all this bustling activity from where he was standing on very uneven cobbles at one corner of the square. 'And you know, these cobbles are more or less regular and they are cut right through, as far as I can see, from one side of the square to the other, by a kind of drain, straight, that is also made of cobbles, grey, that takes all the water away.' There was then a complicated description of how three of these drains were parallel to each other and in line with three important-looking doors on one side of the market, although he was not certain if these drains had any association with the doors or merely coincided because they were the same space apart.

Asked to look at his clothes again, he was surprised to find that he was still wearing the same trousers but not the same shoes. Those he was wearing now were 'rather more flamboyant, moccasin-kind of things, but made of cloth, with a top flap that bends over to touch the toes with some sort of obvious decoration, very strange, bit like a Christmas decoration really, awful looking things, although of no particular colour.' He couldn't make this decoration out very clearly except that it was 'rather like an ornament in very bad taste'. He thought it was made of both metal and wood. The shoes did not tie or lace or button but were just pulled on. They were between a brown and a dark red colour, and were 'wet, too, like the cobbles had been, because there are dark wet stains in a ring all around coming up from the soles, making them darker there, not in a *regular* line all around, but as though I've stood for a little while in a puddle and the water has been sucked up by the shoes. The rest of them is quite dry.' Yet it definitely wasn't raining, he said, although there were still the same clouds above. The rest of his clothing remained the same as before: the same embroidered trousers, still torn at the left leg, and the same light-coloured shirt, the fairly large collar too stiff, but open. No kind of hat.

But he wanted to watch the activity in the square, he said. Beyond it on one side was the town; and behind him, a street or so away, were fields much like those he had seen in his previous 'view' of the strange deserted village, 'yet somehow a bit different'. There were still only women in the square, and people no longer came out of any of the small streets, nor went back into them. There were definitely no men or children, only women. 'All the ones I can make out are women.'

Would he stay there? No. Where would he go? He had no

choice but to go up. He had no desire to press through the 'fairly packed crowd of all those women' and there was nothing familiar anywhere else. Behind him was just the flat landscape, then nothing. He was happy to stay where he was, but if he *had* to go anywhere else he would go up again.

'It's quite clear, what you see?'

'Oh, absolutely.'

'And you like to watch what you see?'

'Yes, very much. I'm not doing very much, I suppose; but I'm enjoying it all anyway.

'Would you live there at all?'

'No. No.'

Had he ever lived there? 'No.' Was he just a visitor? 'Yes. But I've come specifically to see it, as I told you.' Did he know where he had come from? 'Yes, from a town really much like where I was living in France, in a three-storey average middle-class building in a French town, of about the same period as that of the square, although the square didn't seem to fit into any logical, countryside pattern – I mean a geographical pattern. The time factor isn't the problem, just the geographical factor. The town I live in just doesn't seem to fit in with that other one with the square in it, nor with the landscape I saw before that. It doesn't seem to be situated anywhere you would expect to see such a place.'

Reverting to the time factor, was it possible that the town in which he lived was in the present time and the square in the past? And he could go backwards and forwards between the two, illogical as that might sound? 'No, it's an indefinite time, really. The only way to pinpoint it would be by the clothes, which are cotton, *printed* cotton; and the thought that comes from seeing them is presumably that they have been pretty much the same for – well, centuries. The time, if it's to be taken into consideration without any anachronisms, could be five hundred years ago. Yet somehow it doesn't *seem* that. It seems like now. I'm not conscious of being part of *real* time altogether; it's so long ago; it's just the feeling that – that it's *there*, and that I've come *through* – from space.'

'And you can see quite clearly?'

'Oh, yes. Mm.' He could not have sounded more definite.

Asked if he wanted to stay there, he said there was no point in his staying any longer as he had come to the square to see it, and he *had* seen it. 'I'm not involved in it at all. I came as a spectator, and I'm there as a spectator, and that's all.' So he decided to stop.

Before opening his eyes, I asked him how long he thought he had been seeing these three landscapes or dreams. He thought about it carefully, then said, 'Ten minutes, quarter of an hour. I don't know.' When he looked at his watch, he thought it was merely a quarter of an hour; I told him to look again, for he had been an hour and twenty minutes. He could not believe it.

Afterwards he asserted that he could not possibly have been so occupied with any film or even similar but real events for so long; he would have quickly become bored, whereas in this he wasn't bored at all. In fact, he said, he had been far from bored, he had always been intrigued. And, when asked, he thought it was exactly like having a dream, but a dream with so much more reality in it. Yet all the time he had been quite conscious of sounds in the room – my voice, the tape-recorder, the turning of pages (both Leo and Alain were reading magazines) and other occasional noises.

Asked what he felt about the experience, he said it was 'incredible, most enjoyable, but in retrospect I find it disturbing – that such a thing can happen at all.'

'And what you saw was quite vivid?'

'Yes.'

'And you *were* conscious of the room here the entire time?'

'Oh, absolutely.'

He hadn't been asleep, he said; he hadn't been hypnotized. Had he had any experience like it before? 'No, not at all.' What did he, in fact, think he had been doing? 'For an hour and twenty minutes, I can't imagine!' Did he think he was just daydreaming? Did he ever daydream as vividly as that? 'No' to both questions. 'And I don't ever daydream fictitiously in that sense. When I daydream, I daydream about situations I will conceivably be involved in.'

'All those details you saw – the trousers, their motifs, the button and so forth – could you deliberately concoct details like this yourself?'

'Well, there'd be no point in it really, would there?'

'You did see them?'

'Yes.'

'You didn't concoct any of it expressly for *my* benefit?'
'Oh, no. There'd be no *point* in *that!*'

Author's Note, January 1976

I spoke to Richard only last night, New Year's Eve, when he had just returned to Western Australia after yet another two years of academic research in France. He told me that the last village he had seen in his 'experience' had later been encountered in reality in August 1973, when he had been able to travel in other European countries during the academic summer vacation. However, this village had not been in France as he might have expected, but in Scotland. It had been identical – and so immediately recognizable to him – in almost every detail; so its 'timelessness' had indeed persisted into the present as it had in his experience. More miraculous, however, was that – in this *conscious* or *induced* dream of precognition (for scientific investigation of which see *An Experiment with Time* by J. W. Dunne, Faber, 1939) – it had been projected by over two months into his actual future (or projected back from the future into his previously experienced 'dream'?). This subsequent experience of seeing dream manifested into reality, he said, had been quite shattering.

Kathryn McNaughton

At nineteen, Kathryn McNaughton is a tall, fair girl with long, straight hair worn below her shoulders. Her good figure is enhanced by her erect posture, especially when walking. This gives her a dignity rarely seen these days, and then mostly found in the grace of Indian women dressed in saris. This unusual posture of hers has become a natural characteristic, but had to be developed in the first place between the ages of eight and ten – for it was then that Kathryn became blind.

She is not completely blind, only partially; more specifically, she does have some peripheral sight. She can discern light from dark and, having been blinded by retina pigmentosis, can detect a certain but very restricted amount of detail and even colour – but only the brightest of colours, and even then in only the brightest of light, at the very edge of what was once her normal vision but is now obliterated. The area where she can barely discern such detail is on the edge of a normal person's vision, just where it blurs into non-vision. This means that by staring straight into the dark void ahead of her, she can just discern her feet and where she is walking; but should she look down at them, they are immediately obliterated by her blindness. To endeavour to see an object (and she was able to give me some description of the pattern of another man's tie in bright light), she must turn her eyes at a ninety-degree angle away from it, almost as though she were seeing with an ear instead of an eye – which is, of course, much how the blind do see.

Kathryn is the eldest of five children, born on April 18th, 1954, in a small Western Australian country town called Little River. She has three sisters and a brother; none of them, nor either parent, is blind – and there is no other blindness in her family. During pregnancy, her mother did not suffer any of the illnesses usually associated with blindness, so that, apart from accepting it as hereditary from a distant source, the reason for Kathryn's blindness remains unknown.

She works as a switchboard operator in the city office of a commercial bank and takes down cables in braille. She commutes by bus or train, using her white stick only when necessary and mostly to warn people around her of her blindness rather than to feel her way. She dresses neatly with good taste and a sense of colour she can now remember only from childhood. She parts her hair immaculately by 'feeling' where the parting should be and thus keeping it straight. She has lived for a while in apartment-buildings for the blind; but, a week before this experiment, she moved with her sister and two other sighted girls into their own apartment, as she prefers to be away from the atmosphere of entirely blind people. She needs the help of sighted people only to locate something she has misplaced. Otherwise she can do her own housework, laundry, ironing, sewing to a certain degree and many other chores. Like many of her fellows, she has a cheerful and charming personality and apparently enjoys the almost constant teasing which I found characteristic of the dozen completely and partially blind people I have come to know.

Kathryn can remember and still visualizes colour, but only

the brightest of colours. Shades and tints, let alone the nuances between, elude her. 'Things like pinks and purples', she says, 'are beyond me. They just fade into a blur – a sort of murky grey.' She still has a conception of both dimension and perspective, but only in relation to things familiar to her before going blind. The congenitally blind, on the other hand, not only have no conception of colour but find it very difficult and sometimes impossible to comprehend dimensions once objects become too large to be felt by their hands. Perspective, that optical illusion of the sighted, is quite beyond their comprehension.

Kathryn is also aware that she does dream, as everyone must, but can rarely recall her dreams. This, however, is the only time when she can see both objects and colours clearly, though the memory of it all is mostly gone as soon as she wakes up. In her dreams, she often sees people she knew, especially her family, as they were before she went blind; but people and places known to her only after she was blind do not appear visually, but more as a 'sense' in the case of places (much as though she were finding her way around in them in reality), and people are known as they are known in the reality of her everyday living, predominantly by their voices.

Previously, I had approached two other blind people to try the experiment, but both had declined. The third, working as a Public Relations Officer for the Blind Institute in Perth, arranged a preliminary meeting with about a dozen interested in the experiment, some partially blind and others congenitally. After a discussion of about two hours, Kathryn was the first of several volunteers. I would, in any case, have decided to try her first, if only because I should find the procedures simpler to follow with someone who had seen long enough to remember shapes and colours.

I found, however, that I did not have to be as selectively careful with my questions and phrasings as I had anticipated, for, contrary to being sensitive to the sighted person's inadvertent references to 'seeing', the blind frequently use such expressions themselves. For instance, they talk of having 'seen' a film at the cinema (and frequently go to 'see' films about the blind, such as *Dark Victory, Butterflies Are Free* and *Wait Until Dark*); they also say they 'watched' television. On the other hand, the congenitally blind are mostly impatient with even well-meaning doctors who ask them if they can see the five fingers of a hand held up before them, or if they can see colour.

Colour is what frustrates the congenitally blind most of all, and it is difficult to give them a conception of it. One can associate colours with warmth (reds, oranges and yellows) and cold (blues and greens), but this association is more with the mere ideas associated with warmth and cold rather than with the colours themselves.

Dimensions of small objects can be comprehended, but mostly disappear once objects become larger than the blind themselves. Consequently, dimensions are usually quite incomprehensible when it comes to buildings and mountains, even in many cases to rooms and automobiles.

Perspective is even more elusive. I tried with one congenitally blind by suggesting that a bottle standing close to him on a table would 'seem' to be its actual size, but if placed further away it would then 'seem' to shrink to a certain extent, so that, if placed behind a nearer bottle of the same size, it would not only 'seem' to be smaller but the vision of it would be obliterated by any nearer bottle of the same size. Carrying this procedure further, a bottle 'seemed' to shrink until it became no bigger than, say, a little finger – a dimension readily comprehensible to the blind. Finally, it would 'seem' to disappear altogether. However, even the more intelligent of the congenitally blind found this difficult or even impossible to grasp. To most, the suggestion of an object 'disappearing' merely because of being distant and even before reaching that other incomprehensible definition, the horizon, was quite incomprehensible.

I did not know what results to expect from something so visually orientated as the Christos Experiment, if any results could be expected at all. Indeed, I was even apprehensive that the complete failure of such an experiment would only cause distress to people who have more than enough of it to cope with as it is. But once assured of their eagerness to investigate any possibility, no matter how tenuous, of being able to see even the vaguest of images or colours, let alone dream consciously in their usual manner of 'sensing' and hearing things, I decided to make the attempt.

The experiment was held in the apartment of congenitally

blind Paul Bell on the evening of November 29th, 1973, commencing at 8.24 p.m., with myself conducting and Leo van de Pas assisting as usual with the massage and tape-recording. It was also witnessed by some half a dozen other blind people.

At first I thought we were going to be onset with failure from the very beginning. After the massaging of forehead and ankles, which Kathryn found 'very pleasant and relaxing', she appeared unable to obtain any sense of even feeling herself stretching through her feet and ankles, let alone visualizing it. Almost a minute passed without result, so that I was about to try *feeling* the procedure (as for haptics), instead of visualizing it when she said that a vague image of her feet had at last appeared and that she could indeed 'sense' herself stretching. Even then, she 'felt' it was only about a quarter of an inch or so instead of the two inches I had asked. Again I was reluctant to urge her further when she added that her legs had suddenly stretched out quite rapidly. She could even 'feel' it in the muscles of her legs.

I expected even more difficulty with the stretching through her head. However, she managed this more easily, feeling the 'growth' being confined to her neck. The remainder was accomplished, if anything, a little faster than with the average sighted person. This I had expected from the blind if only, whether haptic or not, because they have had to adjust themselves to haptic senses to find their way around.

As Kathryn had been normally sighted until the age of eight, I decided to ask her to remember – and, if possible, visualize – the front door of the house she had lived in as a child. Were this to fail, I would then attempt to have her describe the door of a more recent residence, even if such a description was confined to 'feeling' instead of seeing. However, she recalled – and *saw* – the door of her childhood home with remarkable detail. I will record this here almost completely verbatim from the tape.

'From what I can remember of it, it seemed to be one of those very big doors [But wouldn't all doors be 'big' when remembered from childhood?] with a kind of cross on it. Yes, it was a wooden door. The cross was formed by the four panels on it.' Did she remember what colour it was? 'I think it was grey.' Did it have a door-knob? 'Yes, on the right-hand side.' And a bell? 'Not that I know of – I think one just knocked on the door, because no one used it very much.'(Later on, I learned that this house had been in a small country town where life was informal and, in any case, the house rather isolated.) What were the walls around the door? 'They were wood.' Colour? 'Also grey.' What was she standing on? 'The verandah. Cement.' Colour? 'Just very ordinary old cement.' A door-mat? 'I don't know. I can't remember.' If she looked up, would there be a roof over her head or not? 'Yes.' What was it? 'Tin.' (Meaning galvanized corrugated-iron.) Colour? 'Silver, I think.' Could she see any of this now while she was thinking about it? 'Yes.' She could? She could see the colours? 'Yes.'

She could see both the details and colours of these surroundings much more distinctly than when she recalled them or 'daydreamed' about them normally – and, she said, she was quite addicted to daydreaming, almost like a child. Sometimes what she saw was vague and dim, such as when I had asked her to look up at the roof above her. But when she was asked to turn and look at what was on the right side of her from the door, she said, 'I can see the large window of the front bedroom – my mother's bedroom. A big wide window that you lift up.' A long window down to the floor? 'No, only half way.' Curtains? 'Yes, lacy ones. White.' To the other side of the door? 'Another big window, of the other bedroom. Just one big one.'

If she turned around away from the door, what did she see? 'Green and yellow – the garden. The path going down to the gate, to the fence, and the driveway.' What colour was the fence? 'White.' What kind of fence? 'One of those three-beamed wooden ones.'

She was then asked to imagine herself on the roof of the house, looking down and all around her. What could she see? 'I can see the road and the paddocks behind it. And it goes a fair way, I should think. I can't tell you exactly how far it goes. I can see the front garden, the trees and flowers in it.' What kind of road was it? 'Oh, it's a bitumen road in front of the house, but it's sand after that.' Were there houses? 'Only slightly to the right, there's one house.' What kind of a house?

'A weatherboard one.' Any colour? 'Green roof. Light yellow, I think it was. A driveway and trees going up to it.'

Could she see what she was describing? 'Partly, not the whole lot of it.'

Turning to the right, 'I can see the road going up, and it's like an X-junction in front of the house. And you look to the right of that house and there are some trees on the other side of the road, and you look past those and you can see our school.' The road was still asphalt – and the school? 'Oh, it's a wooden one, with a green roof.' Any trees around it? 'Yes, especially one particularly big one. Dark green trees, very big leafy ones.' (Probably Moreton Bay Fig trees.)

And as she turned further towards the rear of the house? Her words came so fast, then, that it was difficult to transcribe them from the tape. 'There's the paddock where we had all our swings and that. And a big orange – orangey-green, that's losing its paint – wagon-wheel. There's the long swing, and the short swing. And there's one big tree which has been made into the posts. And if you go around further, there's the outhouse and a sandpit which has got a big tree in front of it. And then the garage behind the house. And if I keep going around further, there's the chook-yard [fowl-run].' Did she see 'chooks' [fowls] in it? 'Yes, white ones.' Had she seen any people or animals as she had looked around? 'Only when I had seen my brother and sister on the swings, that's all.' Were the swings moving? 'No, they were stationary at the time. But I could see the chooks moving around in the yard.' She could? 'Yes.' Turning further to the front of the house again, 'There are more trees, and the garden, and then the bitumen road again. That's all.'

While she had been looking at all this, and obviously remembering it all, was it night or day? 'Oh, day-time.' What kind of day? 'Very bright and sunny.' Any clouds at all in the sky? 'Oh, a few, not many. Small ones.'

Next came what I thought might be difficult for someone blind, but I was quite mistaken. When I asked her could she go straight up into the air, she hesitated for a while; but then suddenly there were the rapid eye movements (REMs) on her eyelids which had been much less discernible before, and almost immediately the words came rushing back, 'I can see a whole lot more houses, and the green paddocks all around them, and behind there I can see a big church, brick, corrugated-iron roof I think, and another church beyond that.' *Were* they big or small churches? This confused her for a moment, and again she hesitated, frowning. Then she said, 'Well, I know they're quite big, but they *look* small.' Could she actually see them? 'Oh, yes!' Also their colours? 'Yes.'

She was so definite, it could clearly be seen in the expression on her face, even with her blind eyes still partly open but with the lids twitching with the rapid eye movements characteristic of dreaming. And I felt almost too excited to contain myself for mere rational interrogation. However, I knew that I must.

What kind of day was it now? 'Still bright and sunny.' Any clouds? 'No, it's clear.' How high had she gone? 'Nearly as high as a plane, I think.' And if she looked down now, what did she see? 'Oh, all the land going off, and the paddocks and the house, and other houses, and the little town.' Did she know what town it was? 'Little River.' This was the country town where she had lived as a child.

She was then asked to change what she could see to night instead of day, and almost immediately she said that everything had gone black. She could see nothing. Even when she looked up, there were no stars. *Everything* was black, and she felt as though she was nowhere. Her face clearly expressed the disappointment at having been deprived so abruptly of what she had been seeing. Even the rapid eye movements had stopped. But when I asked her to change the scene back to day again, they immediately resumed. Could she see again? 'Yes.' What time of day was it now? 'Day-time.' And what kind of day? 'Overcast.' What kind of clouds? 'Thick, grey clouds.' Was there any sun coming through at all? 'If there is, I can't see it.' Could she see what was underneath? 'Just my house.' Could she go above the clouds?

But now there was a lengthy pause. I asked her if she had ever done this as a child. 'Yes.' She could remember having done it? 'Yes.' Could she, then, go above *these* clouds and see what it was like?

When I asked her to do this, I believe I held my own breath. The room, with its two sighted and half a dozen blind witnesses, was quite still. There was not a movement from any of us any more. Moreover, there is not a sound all this time from any of the others on the tape. I wondered if there would be any response from Kathryn.

Then she said, 'All the clouds are like great big fluffy balls of wool.' And above them? She found it difficult to express herself. 'It's just clear. Bright. I don't see any colour.'

But she was able to move across the clouds in any direction and for as far as she liked. The clouds changed all the time, she said; and yet overall they didn't change much. Her eyelids flickered rapidly. Then I asked her to descend through the clouds and tell me what she saw below.

The eyes continued to flicker, but words did not come. Was she seeing anything? 'No.' It had all gone black, once she had come below the clouds. There was nothing. She realized that she would *have* to come down to land eventually, but it wasn't there. She was nowhere. There *could* be land, but she could no longer see it. Everything, even her house, had disappeared. It was all dark – and her face showed her obvious disappointment, even apprehension.

Were there people around her? 'Oh, no. I'm alone.' She did realize that there were still people around her in the room; but up there she was alone. She felt neither warmth nor cold, nothing. Yet she was *there*. Did she have any clothes? A long silence. Could she see her feet? I thought she was again not going to answer when she said, 'Sandals.' What kind of sandals? 'Leather.' Colour? 'Brown.' How many straps? 'Three.' Buckles, or buttons, or what? 'Buckles, on the outside of the feet. No socks, just bare feet. Could she see them? 'Yes.' What else was she wearing? 'Shorts.' Colour? 'Yellow.' (In reality, she was wearing a blue dress.) Anything else? 'A blouse – orange.' She had these clothes in actuality, but the sandals belonged to her sister. Because of what she saw herself wearing, she thought it must be somewhere hot; yet she did not actually feel heat. Did she feel as though she was anywhere in particular now?

'The only place I can think of, presumably, is in the Nullarbors – the Nullarbor Plains.' Had she ever been there? (I thought this was going to be yet another remembered place.) 'Yes.' When? 'About four or five weeks ago.' So it was not a place she had seen before going blind? 'No.'

Her eyelids were again moving rapidly, but she was silent. I couldn't draw her out, and yet I wanted to as her expression was becoming distressed again, or at least perplexed. It is a pity I did divert her, as afterwards she said how she had *seen* this empty, arid, brown land that she had never seen in reality, so vast and forbidding that it had frightened, even appalled, her. There was practically no growth and only a few stunted trees, such as she had never seen in the area where she had lived as a child. She was alone, and the experience was frightening. She didn't at all like being alone. Then, reverting to what had been taped, I had asked her if she still felt as though she was over the Nullarbor Plains, as the REMs had slowed. 'No, it's gone muggy.' And she was obviously relieved, even though for quite some time she found herself left in a complete and lonely void. Then, when I asked her if she would like to attempt going above the clouds again, she was immediately and enormously relieved, and had 'returned' there without any further suggestion. She liked being 'up high'. Was she there already? 'I can get up there as easy as anything.'

She had returned, in a kind of ecstasy, to seeing the clouds 'stretched for miles and miles'. Was it quite vivid? 'Oh, yes!' And could she see the sunlight and the shapes of clouds. 'Hm – hm!'

I asked, 'The way you're seeing all this now, consciously, can you see anything as vivid as this normally?'

'No.'

'No? Can you remember it from dreams?'

'No.'

'Is this, then, about the most vivid thing you've seen since you went blind?'

She thought this over for a while, then said, 'Oh, it's certainly much further and brighter than anything I could ever see. It brought all the clouds near.'

Could she see like this when she was daydreaming? 'Yes, but that's more like just remembering.' She thought for a while. 'But this is more like seeing it with pictures, I think. I mean, it's more like seeing it like as it *was* – like before I went blind. Now I can see it as though I'm *not* blind.'

She was obviously very content, and her eyelids were again moving rapidly; so I did not have the heart to disturb her for a while. Then I asked her what she could see now? Was she still up high? 'Yes.' Were there still clouds? 'Yes.' Was she above or below them? 'I'm going *through* them.' Up or down? 'Just flying straight.'

She was flying in a straight line through the clouds around her. Did she feel anything from them? 'I feel a bit wet.' Was she still above them, or below? 'I'm coming down.' Could she see what she was coming down to? I think we all bated our breaths, but, 'No. When I come down, it all just goes dark again.' If she couldn't actually see anything, could she *sense* anything? 'I think it's just that I don't *want* to go down there. You can do just whatever you want to up here, up above the clouds.'

As she wanted to stay in this obviously pleasant experience, I did not press her to try to see more. I merely asked her what she could do there. 'Just walk, and sink through it all the time.' And she was quite happy doing that? 'Oh, yes!' And that 'yes' was so very definite. 'They're all going clomp, clomp, clomp!' 'And you can actually see yourself walking there?' 'Yes. It's like flying over these great big balls of cottonwool, and coming down through them, and then coming up on top of them again.'

Had she ever dreamt or daydreamt something like this? She considered for a moment, then, 'Oh, I *have* daydreamt it, but I only *think* about it then. I don't actually see it.' She *didn't* actually see it? 'No, but I always thought it would be fun to do it.' And now she could see herself doing it? 'Yes.'

'What time of day is it?'

'It's a clear day, because all the clouds are white and fluffy.'

'And they're all beneath you, are they?'

'Yes.'

'And the sky above them is clear?'

'Yes.'

'Can you see any colour in the sky up above?'

There was a long pause while she was considering. Then, 'There's just the clouds below me, and up above it's clear.' Was this how she remembered it, from before she had been blind? 'No, because I would look *up* at it then, and the clouds would be *above* me. The sky was always blue, with the clouds up *in* it. Now the clouds are all *below* me. And now there's much more cloud.'

'And you still feel alone there, where you are?'

'Yes.'

Had she changed any of her dress?

'I don't know.' She was obviously a little perplexed. 'I don't see myself with any clothes on, and I don't seem to *feel* them on either.'

'And no sensation at all?'

'Just the feeling of going through cottonwool all the time.'

'Is it still wet now, or what?'

She was again surprised. 'No, now it's quite dry.'

'And you're quite happy bouncing around on all that cottonwool?'

'Oh, yes!' And I wish it were possible, on the printed page, to reproduce the contentedness in her voice.

Again I hadn't the heart to disturb her. She was blind – but her rapid eye movements indicated clearly to me that she was at least seeing something, no matter how little mere clouds might seem to the sighted. And yet at the same time I remember all too well the tremendous sense of exhilaration and wondrous awe I myself had felt the first time I had seen the tops of clouds from an aeroplane – an unforgettable experience. That was what Kathryn was now experiencing. Yet after a while I did ask, 'And you see nothing else, I suppose?'

She again considered for a while, then said, 'Not unless I go adventuring?' And she said it in such a tone as to indicate that she was more than ready to do so. Naturally I told her to do whatever she liked, wondering where adventure might lead her.

She followed long lines of clouds and flew over great tufts of them. 'They all look the same, yet they're all so different!'

'Do you see them as very far, or close to you?'

'Oh, miles and miles! As far as I can see!'

'All fluffy clouds?'

'All fluffy clouds. It's a funny thing, but I'm seeing the sun just above the top of them.'

'Are you going towards it, or away from it?'

'Going towards it.'

And the expression on her face now, were it not for the rapid eye movements, was something approaching rapture. So again I let her enjoy herself. But after a few moments, I felt obliged to make her talk again.

'And is the sun up high, or what is it?'

'It's in the afternoon.'

'Is it getting close to sunset, or is sunset still a fair way off?'

'No, it's a fair way off.'

Again a long pause; and so, 'Do the clouds change colour at all, with the sun like that?'

'No. In a way they seem to get darker.'

She was perfectly content to do no more than this for quite some time, and I hadn't the heart to spoil her happiness just for the sake of perhaps finding something more interesting to recount in my book. But after a while it did occur to me to ask, 'As you go towards the sun, do you see any parts of yourself?' 'My head and my body.' Was she wearing anything? 'My orange shirt.' Anything else? 'I've chucked my sandals away.' She had bare feet? 'Yes.' Could she see them, or only feel them? 'Feel them.' Anything else?

'Yes. I feel lonely. I want someone to come along with me.'

'There isn't anybody else there at all? You're just alone up in these clouds?'

'Yes.'

'When you saw your head and your body, was it as you are now? Or when you were younger, or older, or what?'

'No. I had short hair, I think.'

'And what age were you?'

After pausing to consider, she said, 'Nowhere near as old as I am now, anyway.'

'What would you say? Fifteen? Twelve?'

'Oh, twelve or under, I think.'

'Did you have short hair then?'

'Yes.'

'Straight or curly?'

'Straight.'

There was again a pause and, as she had now developed a puzzled expression, I asked her, 'And is there anything else? Is there anything on your hands?' And back came the spontaneous and unexpected reply, 'Oh, I've taken my doll with me!'

'A doll, yes? What kind of doll?'

It was almost whispered, 'A one-legged doll.'

'Is it a gollywog doll, or a cupie doll, or . . .'

'No. It's a proper doll.'

'A proper doll. Does it close its eyes? Or say Mama? Or . . .'

'Yes.'

'And what's it dressed in?'

'It's got one leg off.'

'One leg. Do you know if it's the right leg? Or the left?'

'Right leg. And it has a dress on, I think. It's got a lot of dresses like that. And lovely golden hair. Blue eyes.'

'Can you see that doll now?'

'Oh, yes.'

'And did you have that doll once?'

'Yes.'

'Well, you could hardly have *seen* it recently, but have you imagined seeing it recently?'

'No.'

'But you see it clearly now?'

'Yes.'

'Almost as though when you did have that doll?'

'Yes.'

'And is there anything else about it that you can tell me?'

'She's got a right ear missing.'

'Her right ear missing! Yes? And you're still up there in the clouds?'

'Yes.'

'Are you holding the doll in your hands?'

'Yes.'

She was holding it in both hands, she said, and could see it quite clearly. So I then asked her if she saw herself from the viewpoint of being beside herself or behind herself, and she answered instantly, 'From behind myself.' So she could see her whole head and body? 'Yes.' She was still wearing the orange shirt that could also have been an orange dress, for she couldn't see herself wearing anything else with it. Her feet were still bare and she could see nothing on her hands or fingers. 'Just my doll.' Did the doll have a name? 'Lucy.' And was that the only doll she had ever had, or had she had others? 'That was my first doll.' She did have other ones afterwards, she said; many of them. But this one had remained her favourite. She had always looked after this one more than the others, which was probably why she had 'brought' it with her. When she had wanted to have someone or something with her, the doll had 'just been there'. It had just come into her hands, from nowhere. And what was she doing now? 'Playing with my doll.' Was she still up in the clouds? Or had she come down?

'Um – when I was concentrating on my doll, I was back home, indoors, in my bedroom. But when you ask me where I am, I'm back up in the clouds.' Could she see other things in her room? 'No, only the doll.' And when she was asked where she saw herself to be? 'Up in the clouds.' And when she was back in the clouds, she could see them, could she? 'Yes.' Did she realize when the settings changed? When she moved from the room to the clouds, could she see when it changed from one to the other? 'Oh, yes.' It didn't disturb her when moving from one to the other so quickly? 'I wish it wouldn't.'

When she was in her room with the doll, the doll was its normal size. But when she was back up in the clouds, the doll became much smaller – smaller and less distinct.

And what kind of day was it now? 'Well, when I was down in my room it was night-time. But when I'm back up in the clouds, it's day-time again.' What kind of day? 'Still bright and sunny.' What time of day? 'Morning.' And there were still all the clouds? 'Yes.' Did she feel that, if she wanted to, she could go anywhere or not? 'No. I feel as though if I did get up and go, I wouldn't get anywhere anyway. So I might as well stay here.' Was it pleasant just being able to see the clouds? 'Oh, yes!'

I wondered if it was getting tiring for her, and so I reminded her that, if she wanted to, she could always stop. Was she still aware of being in this room? 'Oh, yes.' And that I was talking to her? 'Yes.' She could, she said, hear one of the blind witnesses, who had known her since childhood, giggling now and again; she could also detect the whirr of the tape-recorder. She heard a train pass by on the near-by railway and, although there had been little other traffic, the occasional car. Had she heard anything else?

'The wind.'

I had not even noticed it myself. But when I listened, I wondered how I could *not* have heard it, blustering just outside the window. And now, while I am transcribing this, it can be clearly heard on the tape. I again reminded her that she could stop at any time, and she said yes, she knew. Did she want to stop? 'No. I'm enjoying the clouds.' It really was enjoyable for her just to see those clouds? 'Oh, yes.' Even though she didn't see anything else? 'Yes.' As she had partial peripheral sight only, could she see anything like this normally? 'Oh, no. I can only see the *grey* of clouds, not the clouds themselves. And I can never get high enough to see above them . . . '

'So this is clearer than anything you can see normally?'

'Yes.'

'Is that why you find it pleasant?'

'Probably. Normally I don't usually see anything in such strong sunlight, you know.'

'Do you think this was purely imaginative? Or through the imagination you just saw them?'

'Oh, no. I'm really seeing them.'

'You are?'

'Yes.'

'And quite vividly?'

'Yes.'

Did she still want to go on? Or would she stop? She wanted to go on. Did she still have the doll with her? 'Yes.'

I could understand her reluctance to stop, when it had been ten years since she had seen *consciously*. So, 'Is there any change in yourself at all?' 'No.' Age? Dress? 'No, I'm just a kid, I think. I think I'm only about four or five or so.' Could she see any other people? 'No.' Did she see herself in a plane? 'I *was* looking out the window at one stage. [This was from a plane she had been in as a child, when she had also been gazing out the window.] In this, though [meaning the Christos Experience], I just got out through the window and walked on the clouds. And I never did *that* in reality!' Had she been seeing anything else that she hadn't wanted to stop seeing in order to take the trouble to tell us? 'Only all the different *kinds* of clouds as they went rushing past me.' They did rush past her, did they? 'Yes, when I jumped out the window. Otherwise the clouds were still.'

She talked happily of the clouds again, and also of her doll, yet rather wistfully of the fact that she was always alone. Then, in another pause on the tape, the wind can clearly be heard in a rising whine, and I remarked, 'Yes, I can hear the wind myself now.' And she said, 'Yes, that's probably what's making the clouds seem to rush past me.'

She still didn't want to stop, but next time I asked her she agreed. Before she did, however, I asked how long she thought she had been on the entire 'trip'.

'Twenty minutes – half an hour?'

She had been just four minutes under the hour – which made her laugh with incredulity. Then she opened her blind eyes and, in an entirely different voice – her normal voice and volume, instead of in the soft and rather childish voice she had quickly assumed at the beginning of the experiment – she said, 'Ooh, that was really weird! But is that all it is?'

On the tape, there is relief from all the others who had kept both quiet and still for so long – raucous laughs came in a sudden rush, then their teasing of Kath, Kathy, Kay, or Kathryn. Such as, '*You* were really weird!' Or, 'You were *really* up in those clouds that time, Kathy!' But Kathryn was now sitting up, excited and exhilarated. 'That was really weird,' she said again, 'until I woke up!' I promptly told her that she hadn't been asleep. 'But I must have been,' she said, 'to have seen all that!'

I was about to remark that she may have opened her eyes, but she hadn't been asleep, when I realized that for the blind there was little difference between having their eyelids closed or open. The eyelids might be open, but the eyes themselves remain sealed. They always would.

I was afraid she would be disappointed – as the blind witnesses mostly seemed to be – at not having had any of the experiences some of my sighted subjects had known; but she soon reassured me that for her to have seen anything at all, after ten years of blindness, had been much, much more than she would ever have dared to hope for.

This time, because of Kathryn's special case, we did not switch off the tape as soon as the experiment was ended, even though I knew most 'post-mortems' to be much the same as what we had already heard during the experience – most subjects regard it as an ordinary dream and feel they must recount it when they 'wake up' in order for it to become known.

Over the noise of all the other excited and sometimes derisive voices, Kathryn said, 'When I came down from the clouds, I felt lost – so back up into the clouds I went.'

Only then did it occur to me that of course her eyes might be open, but the light and surroundings had not exactly come flooding in as it would for a sighted person. So I asked her if she was still seeing those clouds? Was the 'dream' still going on?

'I'm still seeing them as they *were,* but they've gone now.'

Could she ever see them as brightly as that, through either the pathetically limited fringes of her peripheral vision, or when daydreaming?

'Oh, no!' And she could hardly have been more adamant. 'You know, it's really weird! Once I'd opened my eyes, it was as though I had woken up.'

She had clearly seen the doll as though she had sight again. She still possessed this doll, although she hadn't 'felt' it for months. If she were playing with it now, would she see it as she had? 'No, I don't think so – I just 'feel' it. I don't *see* it . . .'

'But you did in that dream you've just had?'

'Oh, yes. And you know? Seeing the chooks moving was really great! They were actually *moving* . . .'

I wish the tape-recorder had still been functioning while I was driving her and a purblind couple home, for it was then that she told us that the only unpleasant thing about the 'dream' had been her loneliness. And then she said that she had been anxious all the previous week, since she had moved into a new private flat with her sister and friends and they had committed themselves to the purchase of a car. The car-salesman had blatantly tricked them into a price increase of three hundred dollars, and this had hurt and infuriated her so much that she had felt herself starting to withdraw from people, even from her family, because somebody had been able to do such a thing. The 'dream', she felt, had had its significant point after all, if only in giving her a taste of the loneliness she could expect if she did withdraw from people altogether. It had been like a warning, she said. She knew, now, that it would be quite the wrong thing for her to do. After all, it was bad enough being blind . . .

The best thing she had to say about the experience, however, *was* taken down on tape. I asked her if it was more vivid than anything she could either imagine or daydream, and she said instantly, 'Oh, much more vivid!' Moreover, she said it in a voice implying that there was really no comparison.

'Is there any difference, any benefit in this dreaming?' I

then asked her.

'I think the childhood dream is like giving you your full sight back.'

I was so astounded, I could only echo, 'You really think it was like giving you your full sight back!'

'I think so,' she said, 'because when I was seeing the trees and all that, the school, the swings – I definitely saw them *straight on*. I didn't realize it at the time, in the dream. But I do realize now that I definitely wasn't looking sidewise at them.'

And then, just before we did switch off the tape, of all things, she thanked me for giving her such an experience, and hoped I would have the time to let her try it again. She had seen no past life, but she did think that the 'mood' of the dream's loneliness had been a clear warning to her. It had been the point of the dream itself which would otherwise have seemed quite pointless, like so many dreams. It was more than enough, she again assured me, merely to have *seen* as she had. She couldn't remember when she had experienced anything that had been anywhere near so . . . exhilarating.

Part Three
The Parkhursts

Leo van de Pas
The Parkhursts

After the impact the Christos Experience had had upon my life, I tried for some time to contact the one person who knew most about it – the authoress-editor of 'Open Mind' Publications – when I returned to Western Australia. But I no longer had a copy of the original *Open Mind* magazine as I had returned it to the people who had first shown it to me, Joy and Ray H–, before leaving for Europe well over a year before; nor could I remember the authoress's name for certain.

Yet, by coincidence, find her I did. While I had been in Europe, she had remarried. Her present husband was Nick Parkhurst who, like her, was English, and who was even more interested in the Christos Experiment than her first husband had been. They were still living in the same district up in the 'hills', or Darling Ranges, about twenty miles or so from the city of Perth where Nick works as an engineer.

To my surprise and pleasure, Mrs Parkhurst was not only pleased but enthusiastically excited at the imminent publication of my book, *Windows of the Mind,* for she had been trying for a number of years to have her own findings about the Christos Experiment published on a wider and more substantial basis than in the magazines privately printed and circulated by 'Open Mind' Publications. But apart from one article in an Australian women's magazine, which had provided our contact, she had met with no success.

I told her about the several experiments I had experienced for myself and performed on others (to my surprise more than she herself had performed) and described the complete failure I had experienced with Leo van de Pas, and the apparently partial failures with others, including Bryant McDiven. She had also experienced a number of failures when using the Swygard procedure (see page 200), and she told me of alternative methods which I could immediately see would be more compatible with haptic people than the visually orientated procedure I had learned from *Open Mind* magazine. Leo, with quite magnanimous patience, agreed to undertake yet another experiment involving an alternative method using music, or even a combination of methods, and so we made an appointment for Leo and me to drive up to their home in the hills above the city one evening.

Naturally – as this also applies to haptic as well as visual people – the preliminary massaging of forehead and ankles was used to begin the procedure, but there was none of the imaginative and memory exercises that are obviously orientated towards the visually inclined. Instead, Leo lay relaxed on his back on the floor of the dimmed living-room, while music was played on a specially recorded tape. As each piece of music – from Gregorian chants through various Oriental music to modern-day jazz – was played, Leo was asked for his reactions to it, and especially if any images or sensations were becoming manifest to him. In most cases there seemed to be no reaction whatsoever; but soon it was obvious that he had a pronounced affinity with Middle Eastern or Arabic music – unexpected for a Dutchman. Yet perhaps I should have expected it, for shortly before we had met in The Netherlands he had made a sea voyage around the Mediterranean coast of North Africa and he had often told me how he had liked the various countries there, particularly Tunisia where he had a strong sensation of feeling very much at home.

However, although we persevered for almost two hours, Leo experienced no more than he had done when using the normal procedure. He tried – and this was all too obvious. No doubt he even tried too hard, for I think he was more concerned with not being a disappointment to any of us than with achieving any positive results from the experiment itself. When we decided to abandon this fifth attempt with him (although we did resolve to try again) he was obviously disappointed; Jacqueline Parkhurst tried to reassure him, pleading with him not to feel discouraged as most people required several attempts using either procedure, and other techniques, before even the first faint results were obtained. This was surprising and interesting to me, as both my experiences had been achieved so easily and vividly, without even completing the visual-type preliminaries. This had also been the case with most of the experimentees I had conducted.

On our way home that evening, I said to Leo that I felt that an experimentee did not always experience a glimpse of what was possibly some past life, but merely had an ordinary dream *while conscious* – surely extraordinary enough in itself – with some of these dreams giving indications of a possible disturbance of the dreamer's psyche with, perhaps, a solution as well, even if in the mysterious and sometimes quite baffling symbolism peculiar to dreams.

In Leo's case, I felt that this had been what had happened. When he asked me to explain what I meant, I reminded him that he had seen himself back in his native Dutch village of De Bilt, near Utrecht, and at one stage he had been riding on the pillion-seat of a motorcycle, unable to determine whether the rider was his young brother, Gerard, or a school friend from many years ago. And when I had asked him to try to determine who the rider might be, both rider and machine had suddenly disappeared, leaving him to make the remainder of the journey 'home' by himself and with only his own resources. In this case, he had walked home; and he had made the rest of the journey surprisingly quickly and with none of the difficulties or delays he had at first anticipated.

'What was the point behind that, if any?' he asked me. I explained that it appeared to me that the motorcycle which had provided him with the means of transport wherever he had wanted to go might possibly represent his present position as my assistant, and in this case it would be neither his brother nor his school friend who had been the rider, but I myself. And if authorship did not prove more lucrative than it had over the last few years, then it was all too clear to me that machine and rider would indeed disappear from under him, leaving him to continue his life and earn his own livelihood with nothing more to depend upon than his own resources.

To my surprise, he did not agree with me; he even seemed loth to consider it. But we already have the benefit of hindsight, and I feel more convinced than ever that this is the meaning behind what little 'dream' he experienced in his very first experiment. Economic pressures have finally forced me to do without Leo's tremendous help as my assistant, and now that his machine and rider have, if reluctantly, disappeared from beneath him he is employed with the local Western Australian airline as a booking-control officer.

Does this seem a reasonable interpretation and outcome of his experience? It does to me. But now I am wondering if, once the possible urgency of this particular message has come through to him and the matter has been resolved, any further attempt would give better and more graphic – perhaps even more pertinent – results, and possibly even a glimpse of some previous life? Yet somehow I do not expect that Leo will ever achieve such a result, for he has always regarded his subjection to the experiment with a considerable reluctance that even amounts to apprehension. He has always felt convinced that the procedure would not work for him. But why shouldn't it, especially when he has seen it work for so many others? Because, he says, he felt that in some previous life he had died a violent death and did not want to be reminded of it.

The work of Jacqueline Parkhurst is very much more than just experimentation with the procedure and experiences of what I have chosen to call the Christos Experience. In fact, this is only one infinitesimal aspect of her work and her dedication to investigating and elucidating a whole new way of life – a philosophy and serious psychological study rather than a religion – which she, in its entirety, calls the Christos Experiment. The procedure for glimpsing past lives is only one very small and comparatively unimportant facet of this, but she has kindly lent me transcripts of some of her experiences with the procedure for inclusion here, which are quite extraordinary in both content and detail.

However, before I set out the transcripts of her tape-recordings I would like to say a word about the procedure, which is often referred to as the Swygard procedure or method. It is apparently named after a Mr Bill Swygard, who had once lived in Miami in the United States, who taught the procedure to Jacqueline Parkhurst's first husband. Where Swygard had learnt the procedure, they do not know. And so it seems by tenuous links indeed that this incredible procedure and the phenomenon to which it leads should have come from Swygard to Jacqueline Parkhurst's first husband, to Jacqueline Parkhurst and then to me before it could be published in some form which might just have the chance of making it widely known.

Jacqueline Parkhurst's experiences took place in early 1972. The first was one of emotion rather than events, and an unpleasant one at that, a resentment that seemed to want to prevent any possible chance she may have had for matrimonial happiness, and which, she said, she had been experiencing over a longer period than just one lifetime, or rather one *ordinary* lifetime. She felt convinced during the experiment, if only intuitively, that she had been suffering this resentment, or else her soul's memory of it, for about a thousand years.

'It's only the *figure* of a thousand years I get,' she has recorded. 'I don't think I have been *actually* resentful for a thousand years, but rather that it was experienced about a thousand years ago.'

She was in an Arabic country; but instead of being a woman, she was a man, young and selfish, relatively wealthy in a life and circumstances where one was either very rich or very poor. She – or rather *he* as she had been then – was always rebelling against something or other, or even against *doing* something, she wasn't yet quite sure what it was. Although she/he had come from a fairly good background, he seemed somehow to be alone now. Yet he was still ambitious, or perhaps greedy, 'always out for whatever I could get'. For some reason or other he envied someone to the extent that this resentment had become a hatred. Then she knew whom it was 'he' resented, it was 'his' elder brother – except that this brother, she was convinced, had been a previous incarnation of Nick, her present husband, who of course was taking her through the experience as well as recording it.

She/he did not envy this brother for any physical or material thing, but rather for a quality or characteristic he possessed. What was this quality he envied? 'I got the word "power",' she said. But a little later on she could quite clearly see that this brother of 'his' disliked 'him' as much in return, and had even tried to kill him. This brother was tall and upright and gave 'him' inferiority complexes. He was such a 'worthy' person, whereas she saw her former self as a sneaky, rather snivelling character – which was probably what had caused the brother to despise him. The brother had tried to kill her/him with a sword, a kind of scimitar. 'You took a swipe and I ducked,' she said to Nick, reincarnated as her present husband. She thought that this had been more in the heat of the moment as Nick, in the previous incarnation of the elder brother, had been too upright to kill her/him in cold blood. She/he had left home, she thought, because there was not the power or position for them both – and she/he being the younger, or the more unsuited, had had to go. This had been deliberated as much by the brother as by her former self.

Why had her former self become as he had, a sneaky and snivelling kind of creature that even she herself rather despised? She thought it had something to do with their mother, who had favoured the elder brother and not her/him. Did this mother resemble anyone in her actual life? (Her own mother had died when she had been very young.) She thought it most odd, but the name 'Eartha', perhaps derivative of 'Mother Earth', seemed to come to her, which did not seem a name of either that time or place. However, she felt quite definite that her resentment had originated because of this mother's favouritism towards the elder brother (the brother was definitely slightly *older,* whereas in actuality her husband, Nick, is a few years younger than she).

Before I proceed further, I must point out that the marvellous detail of these experiences becomes lost in my paraphrasing. To read through the entire transcript of the actual tape-recording not only reveals all the incredible detail and richness of circumstances and settings being glimpsed or dreamed by the experimentee, but also makes it all the more unlikely that any experimentee, let alone so many of them, could possibly concoct it for some kind of sensational or whimsical subterfuge. To hear the tapes, or to actually witness the experiment, is even more astonishing. Those who have witnessed experiments which I myself have conducted seem to have all scepticism and suspicion dispelled from their minds almost instantly and become convinced that the experimentee is indeed recounting a dream – or a revelation from the subconscious – while being perfectly conscious and aware of the *actual* surroundings where the experiment is taking place. To illustrate this, I will transcribe directly some of this particular experiment.

N. In *that* time the name was Eartha?

J. I don't know. It was just a name. Maybe it was 'born of earth', or Earth Mother.

N. So your resentment started because you were not so favoured as I was as a child?

J. Because you were the elder brother, you see – and therefore everything was always given to you.

N. The old story of Cain and Abel?

J. Oh, yes! I think so!

N. Why were you sneaky, then? Something must have been in you. You wouldn't have *developed* that quality?

J. Well, I got the impression that you were – although you were worthy in many ways – you were very, very arrogant. Very proud, you know. And perhaps this was what made you think you jolly well deserved it [the favouritism] or something, I don't know. But you were tending to be a bit sort of smug, which made one feel that one could punch you in the face anyway, which didn't altogether help. About me being sneaky, I don't know. Oh, I think I just got a thought then, that I became sneaky because I now had to steal food, to survive. I didn't get a share of certain things, and I had to live more on my wits to get what I needed, and that ultimately by the time I was twenty-one I was living in a bad way. I mean, I was living the *wrong* way, because I was *having* to be sneaky, and use subterfuge, and whatever else I did to get what I needed to survive, probably because I had left the family by then as well, and it had become a way of life. So I lived in this resentful manner – in a sort of *underhand* manner.

N. Well, what happened to you in this life?

J. What happened in the end? I think I died relatively young. I don't see myself as an old man. And *you* became rich, and powerful, inheriting all the family fortune, all the camels and God knows what else. I was virtually an outcast, I think. I think I got killed by somebody, actually. I don't think I died of disease. I think I got stabbed in some, er, casbah or somewhere. I mean, I went (like I said, at the beginning I was wealthy, or came from a wealthy family) – but I went from there, as though I was an outcast, to a rough area, a 'grotty' sort of district. I think ultimately you always get a knife in you or something, don't you? . . . or something like that happens in those sort of places . . .

N. Do you want to look at anything in that life any more?

J. No.

Was there another life she wanted to look at? Yes, because there were possibly other experiences which might have bearing on the 'resentment' problem.

At first she could only see a woman's veiled face. The veil, however, was not a yashmak, which reveals only the eyes; it was a thin and gauzy veil so that she could see some of the woman's features, which were actually her own. The veil was held by a kind of coronet of flowers, and had things like coins hanging along the bottom edge. She thought she was again in some kind of Arab country; though the clothes, it occurred to her immediately afterwards, were similar to those worn in Georgia in Russia, and she thought that this figure which had appeared to her looked something like a kind of Georgian dancing girl.

N. And this face – *was* it you?

J. I don't know for certain, but I imagine it could be.

N. What time would this be? What country?

J. I think it's one of these Arabian countries, though goodness knows where. Turkish, probably. Before that I got the thirteenth century, but that didn't seem very good. But I would say possibly Turkish, anyway.

N. Was it a happy life?

J. Happy in so far as that nothing happened. I would imagine that I was owned. I never had to *do* anything. I was never *allowed* to do anything. I just *was* . . .

She saw herself standing before an arched gate, or entry of some kind, with heavy wooden doors. She might even have

been *inside* the doors. She distinctly felt that she was the
'property' of someone, perhaps a wife or a concubine or
something like that.

J. I was just a decorative sort of object, I suppose. It seems
I had a creamy sort of skin [which she has in actuality, with
fair hair and a short, plumpish figure; altogether a very
pleasing appearance with a pleasant and friendly
personality]. I said this girl was me, and I suppose it *was*
me, with very black hair falling in kind of ringlets, curls,
sort of *waves* down. Slightly heart-shaped face.

N. And who are you married to?

J. You.

N. And what was I?

J. Some kind of sultan-thing, I think. No, a vizier. And you
were – you seem elderly – but you were perhaps forty.

N. And what was your sexual relationship like?

J. It seemed to be quite good. I mean, one was used to it.
That was the way one was.

N. Do you want to look at that life any more?

J. I see something of the harem, I think, with a sort of
funny inside. A minaret type, with mosaics, and gossamery
veiling hanging from the ceiling. There are sort of reclining
beds with ladies on them. I see one lady, though I can't see
her face. She is lying with her arms up, like that, with sort
of drapery things on them. She seems to be on her own.
Then there is one of those minaret-type doorways (*sic*), sort
of onion-shaped top. The whole wall is covered with
mosaics with scrolly patterns. And there's a door you can't
see, in the wall. It suddenly opens, and you realize only
then that it was part of the wall. And it seems as if two men
– or perhaps men in the sense of their being eunuchs, or
servants – anyway, they open the door and another man
comes in. Then it seems to fade away. It was probably you
coming in. Could *well* have been in Turkey, in the
thirteenth century. It would have been twelve hundred and
something, as we haven't *got* much in that time.

[By this, she meant that of the many experiments which both
of them had conducted, none had appeared to be in this
particular period of time before.]

N. Could be. Were you one of the favourite wives?

J. Yes. One of the *very* favourite wives.

N. Was there perhaps somebody more favourite than you?

J. Funny. I got the thought just as you said that, that I was the second wife.

N. And you were a bit resentful, of course.

J. No, I wasn't actually. I was used to it. This was the way things were. I never knew anything else.

N. And who was the first wife?

J. Pamela. I think you probably had a bit of trouble with her, as she was a very strong personality. I seem to be, at that time, quite submissive in fact. I accepted that this was the law of the land. I never knew anything different, and that was the way it was. I think my difficulty lay more with *her* than with you. In *some* ways. Not that I was difficult, but she was a bit resentful herself, or difficult towards me, because she was the first wife, and the first wife always had more problems because she thought she could always be dethroned, you see. The second wife knew that she could perhaps become the first; but the first always knew that she couldn't go up any further, she could only drop down, so that there was *that* difficulty. And she was older than I was, I think, because I seemed to look young and attractive. And I think she was, well – she *was* your first wife, and she was getting a little bit older, and that worried her probably, too. And so I think that she tended to feel that I could take over her position, not that I seemed to try to; but she always felt that this could be the case as she lost her charms. I think she is what I then called an elderly woman, an older woman in comparison with the other wives and concubines in the harem. She tended to *rule* us, as she was the eldest wife. She would say, 'You should wear this,' or 'You shouldn't wear *this* perfume.' She sort of ruled the roost of the women in the harem. I think. Told the young girls what they should wear, and how they should smell with regard to exotic perfumes. All these sort of things . . .

N. Is there anything else you want to look at in that life?

[In this regard, it seems to me that Nick was more impatient than I had ever been with any experimentees; I had never suggested ending an experience until it had become obvious from the experimentee that the experience had come to its natural end.]

J. I want to see you.

N. Why do you want to look at me?

J. I want to see what you look like. See how you were.

N. Well, have a look then.

J. A most odd figure comes to face me, rather like the Greek Orthodox Church's potentates, with a sort of onion-topped head-dress, like a big onion dome-thing, in white. Tremendous black beard coming right from up above the ears. Do you know what I mean by those pontifical men in the Greek Church, with that type of beard? Somewhat severe. You seem to be dressed in white and gold fabric, luxurious. You seem to be fairly just, but severe, as far as I can see. You just seem to stand there in the picture and survey one, again like the face I saw, the disciplinary face of my father – in the December 25th experiment. The face doesn't look quite the same, but the qualities are disciplinarian – just and fair. But you couldn't step ouside the regulations or whatever limits you [Nick] set. I seem to be young and pliable, and what I would imagine for those times to be pretty. I suppose I would be what I would call twenty today, but I could have been even younger. I think you treated me rather like a pretty little thing, you know? I don't seem to think about anything else regarding that life.

N. Well, we'll move on to the next . . .

'Well,' Jacqueline Parkhurst continues on the same tape, 'all I can see now – it doesn't seem to mean anything – is a man slumped in an old upright deckchair, like you have in England, with two arms and crossbars. Not a sloping one, but an upright square one. Armchair-type. And he is slumped in it, and he looks a bit like Fidel Castro, with a bit of a beard and a khaki-looking cap on, like a Fidel Castro cap, a pull-on one, and a greyish khaki sort of shirt, and he looks rather depressed. He looks a bit like Lawrence of Arabia [in the film of that title] when he got dirty and scruffy; and he has come back from somewhere and just slumped there. He looks as though he has pretty well had it, with his head slumped forward. I don't know what he has been doing. Funny, I think he looks as though he has been in the army, he has on something like an army khaki outfit. It doesn't seem to mean very much at all.'

Nick asks, 'Is this you?'

'I get yes,' Jacqueline tells him, 'but I can't think possibly how.'

'What year do you think it is? What time? And what country?'

'Well, I get a ridiculous answer. I get 1914.'

'Yes?'

'I *can't* have been alive in 1914!'

'Go on – 1914. Tell me about this chap.'

'He is about twenty-six, slim build. I can't see anything else, except that he is sitting in this chair.'

'What nationality is he?'

'Appears to be English.'

'And why is he sitting slumped in a deckchair?'

'Well, he just looks as though he has been on command, and he is just whacked. I mean, he could be symbolic. I don't know what he is.'

'Well, what is he whacked about? What had he been doing?'

'I just get that he had been fighting, and he is now resting. He seems to be a total enigma.'

'He was born when – about 1894 if he was twenty-odd?'

'He was twenty-six.'

'He would have been born in 1888 if he was twenty-six in 1914.'

'But he can't be me!'

'And what does this chap do? I mean, apart from sitting in a deckchair?'

'He appears to be a soldier.'

'What else? Go forward in time. This is 1914.'

'He dies soon after that.'

'What did he die of?'

'He dies a year later.'

'What year is that?'

'1915.'

'And what does he die of?'

'Gunshot wounds.'

'And *where* did he die?'

'On a battleground, because he was sent back to fight.'

'What country was it he died in?'

'I get France.'

'What battle was it?'

'Seems to be the battle of – something like in Holland, or Belgium, on the borders. I think he died in France, and maybe he was taken to a military hospital there. The battle like the "Somme" or some funny word. But it doesn't seem to be quite like that – something to do with song and blossoms. I don't really know. I'm always very bad at names.'

'So he was born in 1888, in England. Whereabouts in England was he born? Where was his childhood spent?'

'I get a ridiculous answer of Sussex.'

'Whereabouts in Sussex?'

'This *is* ridiculous . . . '

'Go on.'

'I get in Lewes. There's a tall street that goes on up a hill, a steep hill, going fairly straight up in front of me. And I can see a lamp-post. There seems to be a very big building at the top. on the left-hand side. It seems to be like a double house, like a semi-detached type of house, a more Edwardian-looking building. There seems to be, on the right-hand side, more trees. [While typing out this transcript, she later remembered that the building was of dark red brick.] Open spaces of gardens belonging to houses that were set back. Or they were back gardens. I don't get anything else.'

'Describe the road. Has it got a footpath?'

'It's got concrete slabs, either side.'

'It wouldn't have concrete in 1914 – or it would be very unlikely.'

'But that's what it looks like now.'

'All right. I want you to tell me what it looked like then.'

'It seems to be rather more countrified, as if it had sort of railings along the side. Wooden railings, with a bar, and a cross-thing on the bar, slats going along horizontally. Not picket fencing.'

'The street, you say, is a hill. Straight or curved?'

'Very straight, the bit I can see.'

It was a short, steep hill with the road about twelve feet wide, she told him. When he said he thought that this was rather narrow, she said that perhaps it was a *little* wider than that, but it was definitely not a very wide road. And she then reminded him that she was not very good at figures, or judging distances. It was perhaps as wide as the room they were in, she said, which he then told her was about twenty feet long; but it was not, she insisted, a very wide street, certainly not a dual-carriageway. More like an English side street.

There then follows an extraordinary amount of detail, and Nick's further questioning about still more details of the road in either direction down this steep incline, the fences on either side, the houses of one period of time where previously there had been fields with cows grazing in green grass. And somewhere not so far away was the sea, to the south.

'Can you tell me what the name of the street is? Can you go and look at a street-name?'

'I get a name – I'm very poor at names – but "Langford" or "Angford". I can't really see a street-name at the moment.'

'Is this the street where you were born, is that right?'

'Well, this *man* was born in it.'

There are a great many more details, of the houses existing both at the time the street was being 'viewed' and when the man who was also being viewed had been born, of a church and other buildings, and far away (from up in the air where she went floating for a while, after Nick told her to go up and view the scene from the air) the curve of the coastline with the sea beyond.

'Come back to this chap,' Nick suggested, 'as this does not seem to be getting us anywhere.'

'I'm confused. I can't think he can be real. It's more like that you can look upon him as symbolic of something – couldn't you? – than that he was real. Could he be an aspect of you – as it is to do with Sussex? It seems crazy to me.'

'I wouldn't know,' Nick said. 'I mean, the thing is when you first saw him, this chap, you thought it was you, yourself.'

'Yes. But it doesn't seem right. I mean . . .'

'Well, what is the significance of this life?'

'Well, I don't know – except that he was fighting a battle, and I am *now* fighting a battle. I don't get anything else.'

'You come from the eleventh century in Arabia, then the thirteenth century in Turkey, and now you're suddenly a chap sitting in a deckchair in 1914. *Now* what! I don't see that it follows. There must be *some* significance, of step by step. That's what I'm trying to get at.'

'Well, this is why I think it's symbolic. I don't think it can be a real life. It can't be. If you look at it symbolically, this person is fighting a battle, and he is a man. *You're* a man, and you have connections with Lewes in Sussex, don't you?'

'But I wasn't born in Lewes, just because my parents happen to live there. *I've* never actually lived there.'

'But did what I describe seem like Lewes?'

'No, not particularly. But it *could* be like Lewes. But what you describe is so vague – too vague to pinpoint. This is what I'm trying to get at.'

'Well, are there any steep hills in Lewes?'

'There are a lot of steep hills in Lewes. Lewes is built on a hill. You've got hills going south. You can see the sea from certain places in Lewes.'

'Well, is there an old stone church? A peculiar sort of stone.'

'There is at least one old stone church, and there is a stone castle. There are still stone-faced buildings in Lewes. And there is a well-known road in Lewes called something like Langford, and I think it's on a hill.'

'Well, I don't think I have ever been to Lewes as far as I know. And even if I vaguely drove anywhere near Lewes on the way to Brighton, I've never stopped in Lewes and driven round it, or looked at it, or walked round it. I have no notion of what Lewes is like at all.'

'But if it's just symbolic, surely you wouldn't start describing a lot of details that *could* be Lewes?'

'Well, how could I be alive in 1914?'

Here the transcript ends.

Both Jacqueline and Nick Parkhurst have experienced many revelations of past lives. They have also taken numerous other people on 'trips', not only *back* into past lives but also *up* into what they call soul contact, or soul consciousness, and *down* into the subconscious for the purpose of self-analysis to undertake the process of attaining 'karmic clearance' (i.e. the removal of past habit patterns).

Some of the people they have experimented with have experienced extraordinary revelations – one woman, when asked early in the experiment to look down at her feet, found them torn and bleeding after she had been thrown to lions as a Christian in Rome, though she felt no pain at the time.

Another saw and vividly 'felt' herself being burnt at the

stake by Roman soldiers and, apart from knowing and experiencing the horror of this, also had to relive the sorrow of seeing her husband's and child's violent deaths at the hands of the Romans.

One man had the remembrance of being stabbed in the throat after coming out of a tavern in Verona, around A.D. 1500. He was attacked in the dark, quite unexpectedly. At this particular point, Jacqueline Parkhurst writes, he actually began to make choking grimaces and noises, and a large mark appeared on his throat. This experience from the past, the man believed, carried over as a fear of the dark in his present life; but after this revelation, his fear was dispelled.

There are others, many others, too numerous to recount here. Some depict violent incidents and even deaths, others reveal only exquisite beauty and tranquillity, and are crowded with incredible detail. Others are merely dim and misty, and little different from most dreams that people are able to recall – if they are able to recall them at all.

The Parkhursts say they have often been asked what point there is in knowing our past lives, if this is what some of these experiences happen to be. Their answer is . . .

None, unless such experiences have relevance for your present life today. If reincarnation is a fact, traumatic events in past lives can have a detrimental effect on one's present life. If we know this, we can begin to see some of the reasons why we are suffering today. If we know that a character defect we had in some past life is still with us today, we can see that we have not changed much in the intervening time – and that can be quite a shock. We realize that we are 'loafing' in our mental and spiritual progress and are not doing nearly enough about correcting our wrong thoughts and actions.

They go on to say . . .

We can no longer blame a few isolated incidents in early childhood for everything that goes wrong later on. There are 'first time' incidents in this life which do *not* create havoc for this life, and in a large number of cases the childhood incident is just starting off the same old pattern once more.

Some people are indeed able to come to terms with themselves by facing a childhood incident squarely, but a growing number of people find that they want to know more about why this event should have happened in the first place – unless life itself is to be considered as totally meaningless.

Sometimes the cause *can* be found in this life, but sometimes psychologists have found that there are totally baffling cases for which there seem to be no cause at all in this life, or a baby can suffer and die before there is time for even any of such events to have happened. Thus it can be seen that to some extent the knowledge of reincarnation and the process of karmic clearance go hand in hand. It *is* possible to unravel ourselves to a certain point without 'pre-knowledge' – but ultimately, in some life, we will have to know ourselves at a deeper level with regard to our past.

The matter of integration is one of the first steps towards sorting ourselves out and becoming generally more balanced and harmonious, of clearing all past habit patterns and hang-ups and becoming eventually a totally 'complete' person.

These unravellings do not come easily, and much anguish may ensue before 'the coin drops'; but when it does, the sheer joy of 'knowing' has no bounds. Often it has taken weeks of patient revelations under this technique, of just-as-patient analysis, interpretation, questioning and meditation, to find the answer to one's earthly predicament. Even then, having found the answer does not mean that you have an excuse for your behaviour or for what happens to you – far from it. It means that you are spurred on more than ever to know, and conquer, one's *self*.

After the two experiences revealed to me under this technique, to which I at first submitted myself both reluctantly and sceptically, I believe that what the Parkhursts say in their books and what their researches have revealed is true indeed. If you wish to get in touch with them, you can write to 'Open Mind' Publications, c/o Post Office, Mahogany Creek, Western Australia 6072.

Commentary on the Christos Experiment
Jacqueline and Nick Parkhurst

We agreed to these unusual experiments being published because we felt that far more research and information on what people experience while in these altered states of awareness is necessary. Although the material may show personal insights, we feel that unless some people are willing for a few of these types of experiences to be made known, the subject cannot be studied seriously. However, even though the Christos experiences are so interesting in themselves, what is even more pertinent is that an open approach is made with regard to their interpretation.

Since undergoing the experiences to gain our own personal insights, we have continued to study other relevant material about 'altered states of consciousness'. We have given considerable attention to the collected works of C. G. Jung and noted the experiences undergone by John C. Lilly, M.D. in his book *Centre of the Cyclone* (Calder and Boyars, London, 1973 and Paladin, Granada Publishing Co. Ltd., London, 1973) and *The Human Biocomputer* (Abacus, Sphere Books Ltd., London, 1974), some of which have been very akin to some of our own. As well as these two areas, we have studied the facts put forward by Professor Charles T. Tart in his book entitled *Altered States of Consciousness* (John Wiley & Sons, Inc., New York, 1969).

Looking back on the experiences with hindsight, it seems likely that a number of things could be happening in a Christos Experiment. However, only further research will clarify the matter. We will submit here a few ideas out of the many possibilities available.

(a) The experiences are real past life remembrances and should be taken at 'face value'. Some of them indicate such a possibility.
(b) Some form of 'genetic memory' is involved whereby the individual tunes into an action or event of an ancestor, or into a collective 'racial memory'.
(c) All experiences undergone in the experiments are symbolic of changes and stages of growth in the person, or are symbolic of his emotional and mental state at the time

of the experiment – i.e. a woman can see herself as a man and it may be symbolic of events concerning the 'animus' in her own psyche. (Male is also symbolic of the conscious, waking mind and female of the unconscious or unknown areas of mind.)

(d) Certain people can enter a state (such as auto-hypnotic) which can briefly be described as 'wanting to reproduce certain phenomena' to please the interviewer. This is a known factor in psychological research – because the interviewer (or psychologist) becomes a 'trust figure', endowed with authority by the individual concerned. The individual may then produce 'what the psychologist wishes – or what the individual "thinks" the psychologist wishes'. Thus Jungian patients produce Jungian type dreams for analysis and Freudian patients produce Freudian ones. All this, however, is usually a subconscious desire on the part of the individual concerned.

We have found though, with our experiments, that this has not seemed to be the case. All our experimentees undergoing the Christos Experiment had a specific reason or motive in mind, which they revealed to us prior to the experiment taking place. We have never done an experiment 'on spec', with no motive on the part of the individual concerned.

Bearing in mind the factors in paragraph (d), the material produced during the Christos Experiment is still so interesting that it is worth further investigation. Even if labels can be applied to certain experiences, it still does not always give an answer as to 'why' they occur and this remains an interesting area for research.

We feel that these 'dreams', as Mr Glaskin terms them, have beneficial effects on the persons experiencing them, and it is obvious that the unknown area of the psyche is trying to 'converse' and 'express' ideas and wishes which may well be found to be highly important for the future development of mankind.

We cannot ignore the fact that human consciousness is on the threshold of a definite change towards higher levels of thinking and motivation – and that such experiments as the Christos Experience may well be one of the means of finding out more about this 'leap in consciousness'.

We are grateful therefore to Mr Glaskin for bringing the Christos Experiment to the attention of the public in his two books and for this opportunity of expressing our views on the subject.

August 13th, 1974

Part Four
The Procedure

First Stage

The experimentee, or person being 'run', is to lie flat on his back on the floor with a cushion under his head and with his shoes off. Another cushion may be placed under the feet, and even under the small of the back as well, to ensure that the experimentee is comfortable.

With his eyes firmly closed, the person's ankles are massaged for two or three minutes to loosen them and induce relaxation.

Shortly after commencement of massaging the ankles, another person (usually the one doing the 'running', i.e. the suggesting and questioning) massages the 'third eye' position, or lower centre of the forehead between the frontal lobes of the brain, in a circular motion with *the edge of his curved hand,* so that it fits snugly into this 'third eye' position or cavity. The massage should be vigorous rubbing, till the experimentee 'feels his head really buzzing'.

The experimentee must be fully relaxed. If he is still a little tense, he should take several deep breaths and then let himself go limp.

Second Stage

Now commence the mental exercises to make the relaxed experimentee expand his mind beyond the normal limits of his physical body. It doesn't matter if the person is spiritually 'aware' or not, the technique still works (with the exception of predominantly haptic – as against the normally visual – types; for these, see the alternative procedure). But of course the greater the sense of 'spiritual awareness' the person has, the greater will be his ability to see and understand his experience. Also, a deep inner need to find out something of a past life is considered necessary to provide it.

The person is then asked to *visualize his own feet* as he lies there with his eyes closed.

Then, still with his eyes closed, he is asked to visualize himself *growing two inches* (or five centimetres) taller (or 'longer', being horizontal) through the bottoms of his *feet*. He just has to *feel* himself become two inches taller, but some will actually *see* themselves do so at the ankles.

He is then asked to say when he *is* two inches taller, the person doing the instructing waiting till he says he has done so. At this stage, the experimentee should be encouraged to start talking as much as possible, so that he will become accustomed to the idea for later on when it is very necessary for him to describe his experience.

Once he has 'stretched' two inches, he is asked to *return to his normal length* or height, trying to see or feel (or both) his feet returning towards him to their normal position.

Repeat this several times till he becomes accustomed to the process, always waiting for each stretch and return to be accomplished.

Now repeat the entire process, but *through his head*.

Then *return to the feet* and have him stretch and return them a distance of *12 inches* (30 centimetres).

Repeat the same distance through his *head*.

Again return him to his feet and have him stretch and return *24 inches* (60 centimetres). The instructor can tell if the person is having difficulty as this 24-inch or 60-centimetre stretch should be accomplished in under a minute. Have the experimentee repeat it till he does so.

DO NOT have him return from this longest stretch, but have him stretch the same distance, 24 inches (60 centimetres) *through the head*. If he says he finds his feet are withdrawing as he stretches through his head, take some patience and perseverance until he has accomplished stretching in both directions.

While stretched 4 feet (120 centimetres), ask him next to *expand all over,* to feel himself growing in all directions, rather like an enormous balloon. This expands him 'out' of himself. The next step is to start him seeing things – familiar things at first.

Third Stage

Ask him to look at his own *front door* from the outside and describe it in full. Ply him with as many questions as you can about it until he has fully described the door *and* its surroundings, including what he is standing on and what is above him when he looks up.

Once he has managed to look at his front door with what is called 'expanded consciousness', he must then become accustomed to a feeling of free movement while obtaining a much wider range of 'vision', or visualizing. You now ask him to imagine that he is *standing on top of his roof,* and to describe what his garden, or immediate surroundings look like from that height. Keep on asking for details as this makes him accustomed to 'seeing' without the use of his 'actual' eyes.

Now ask him to *go straight up in the air about 500 yards* (500 metres will do just as well) and to keep talking as he looks down, describing all he can see from this greatly increased height. If he should balk at the 'height', remind him that he is still actually on the floor and is only *visualizing* being at that height.

Now ask him to *turn slowly in a complete circle* and describe everything he sees, to accustom him to seeing from an unnatural viewpoint.

This done, *ask what time of day it is* while he is 'seeing' what he is. Usually it is 'day-time', but at various hours and with very different weather; yet neither time nor weather will be related to actual conditions.

Now, if he is seeing during the 'day', ask him to *change the scene to night-time,* and to describe all he sees as it now is.

Then *change back to day-time* and ask him to compare the scene of both 'days'. It does not matter if they differ, but they are usually the same.

Next, to give him assurance of safety for the remainder of the experiment, *ask who is changing from day to night and back to day again.* Most will say '*I* am', or '*I* am, but at *your* suggestion.' It is very important that he realizes that he himself has the control over whatever he is seeing.

Fourth (and vital) Stage

If you are satisfied that the person is content in his newly expanded environment, you now carefully guide him to the 'experience' – and possibly to a past life.

Tell him, rather than just ask him, to *keep the picture in bright sunshine* so that he can see clearly where he *lands, feet first*. If he finds he is merely returning to where he was before, have him *go up again*, but this time as high as possible, till there are no distinct details below – then come down to land. If he should again return to the same place, which is most unlikely, have him *go up again and then move freely in any direction* before once more attempting to land.

While looking down, he should *see his feet*; so you have him commence his description of wherever he finds himself by first *describing his feet*, whether they are bare, or what he is wearing on them (often shoes, though of course in actuality he is wearing socks or is bare-footed from the preliminary massaging).

Go on from the feet to ask him *what kind of ground* he is standing on.

Then ask him to *look around him* a little.

If he says he is in, say, a courtyard, ask him *what kind of buildings and so on* are around him.

Are there *other people* there, or not?

Can he see *what else he is wearing*?

Can he see *his hands*, and what is on them?

Can he see *his face*? His *features*? His *figure* as a whole?

(N.B. As in dreams, most subjects can 'go outside' their bodies and look at them quite objectively.)

Is he *standing still*, or now *walking*?

Keep pressing for details until he is firmly 'locked in' on whatever environment in which he now finds himself. If in a market-place, can he see a fruit-stall? What kind of fruit is on it? How much fruit? Keep questioning him till he either tires of it or else he sees clearly and sharply, and in vivid colour, if he isn't already doing so.

Watch the eyelids for rapid eye and eye-muscle movements. The faster the rate of the flicker, the more successful is the vision or dream.

And from now on you must really *play it by ear*. Try *not* to use suggestible questions, but merely ask what he is seeing or doing, then follow up with relevant questions such as 'Colour?' 'What do you feel?' 'How old is he?' 'What is she wearing?' 'Do they speak to you?' 'In what language, or do you just "understand"?' 'What are their names?' and so on.

Try to have a *tape recorder* going from when he *lands* so that further details can be asked about the experience after it is over.

After a while, usually about three-quarters of an hour, he may say that he has seen all he wants to, or, if he has 'gone quiet', you must ask him if he has seen all that he wants to. If he says yes, you can then ask him if he wants to go on 'up' to the *experience of death,* or return directly to everyday life. He is *not in a trance,* but is absolutely conscious to choose what he likes. It is merely a matter of re-locating his consciousness to return to the present. At the same time, he should at *any* time, if asked, be able to identify sounds around him *in the present* while still seeing his past life or experience.

He himself is able to 'return', or stop the experience, at any time he wishes. However, as in an actual dream, an experimentee usually does not wish to terminate it until it has come to a logical conclusion, and even then he is sometimes quite reluctant to return to the humdrum reality of the present compared with what he has just been experiencing – unless he is impatient to talk about it.

Keep an account of *the time taken*. Usually the preliminary procedure takes about twenty minutes, while the experience itself takes anything from half an hour to over an hour, as with an ordinary dream, so that the entire process should take an hour or more. Usually the experimentee will think he has 'been away' for only a quarter of the time and will be astonished at just how long the experience actually lasted.

Alternative Procedure
(*For the* Haptic *Person*)

Briefly, a *haptic* or subjective person (as against a *visual* or objective person) is one who relates to his environment by touch, sound, smell and perhaps even taste – and kinaesthetic fusions of all four – instead of by sight.

The haptic familiarizes himself with his environment by exploring *outwards* with touch, sound and smell, etc., whereas the predominantly visual person observes his environment by relating what he sees to himself *inwards*.

Complete visual types are approximately one in two, while complete haptic types are approximately one in four; the remaining quarter are a mixture of the two characteristics. Hence, one in four (or a little more than that, allowing for the predominantly haptic among the 'mixtures') will not only fail to respond to the usual procedure, but may actually become baffled and distressed by it, especially when they fail to respond.

Few haptics know that they are haptic, and they are difficult to discern from their visual fellows. Being haptic has nothing to do with the quality of their sight, which may well be perfect; it is simply that they do not relate to experience and environment with sight. They may be brilliantly 'visual' artists, like Bryant McDiven or Marc Chagall; or they can, of course, be blind. If they are haptic as well as blind, then they will be much more adjusted to their disability than, naturally, the visual type who becomes blind, and who is of course distressed for some time by being deprived of his most important faculty, sight, and having to relate by unfamiliar haptic means.

Remember this if you find you have a haptic type as experimentee, and give him the greater patience and perseverance he both needs and deserves. You can tell a haptic type by his failure to perform the third stage of the usual procedure, and by his obvious distress at this failure.

However, you may know if someone is haptic before this stage if you know something about him beforehand. If he is the ostensibly untidy type, living in what appears to be a hopeless chaos of untidiness and disorder, yet is always able to put his fingers on anything he wants amongst all this untidiness, then he no doubt relates by touch and sense of place instead of by sight. If he should need to get up in the night for any reason at all, he does not turn on a light to 'see' as do most people. He may also appear to 'touch' other people more than most, especially when first meeting them, but even more so when, though having known them for some time, they first appear on a visit.

A simple test may confirm a haptic for you. Take half a dozen or so small but unusual objects and, having kept them concealed from your experimentee, ask him to close his eyes and identify each one by touch. A haptic will name them almost instantly, whereas the visual type will take some time feeling the object, perhaps turning it over and over, or weighing it, before venturing a guess which even then can be wrong. This applies to smaller objects; with larger ones, the haptic's hand will move immediately over the surface with more speed and assurance, and again he will identify the object faster than the visual type who may not be able to identify it at all. It may not even occur to the visual type to let his hand roam over the object to 'experience' it by progressive touch as does the haptic.

Sometimes, however, a person is almost equally haptic and visual, and the two characteristics are difficult both to discern and determine. In these rare cases, either procedure should work to a certain degree, but a combination of the two will, of course, almost invariably achieve a far greater and much more graphic success.

First and Second Stages
Follow the first and second stages of the normal procedure (see pages 216-18).

Third Stage
Once the final expanding exercise has been completed, the haptic experimentee is to remain lying relaxed in a dimly lit room while various (and as many as possible) kinds of *music are played to him*, ranging from Gregorian chants and excerpts of music from early 'old masters' (if possible, played on the instruments of the time) to ballet and dance music such as the minuet and polka, etc.; include the many Oriental and Middle Eastern styles of music, and progress through to more recent classics, light classical and even near-modern music, including the waltz, the tango and modern jazz.

However, try to *avoid vocal music* unless it is either *purely* vocal, or without words as in some choral music, or is sung in a language which the experimentee does not understand, then he will not be distracted by, or become suggestible to, any of the words. It is, of course, essential to include as much 'native' music as possible, from all countries and continents.

Fourth (and vital) Stage

Let the experimentee *listen to each piece of music* for a few moments and then *ask him his reactions to it*. Does he find it pleasant or unpleasant? Why? Does it suggest any thing or place to him? An emotion, perhaps? Or a person, or persons? Then, as even a haptic person dreams in the ordinary sense of doing so while asleep, images may gradually appear to him. If they do, *keep him talking* about these images by plying him with pertinent but not suggestible questions. After all, there is no point in having an experimentee distracted by what *you* think he should see, or even think he *may* be seeing, as you can prevent him from continuing or even attaining the experience altogether.

He may not actually *see* details, but merely *feel* or *sense* them. But should the sensations fade and perhaps disappear, even when you have asked him if there is anything else he wants to try to experience after hearing a particular piece of music, then *proceed to other music* until, eventually, he proclaims himself 'attuned' to a particular piece or type and wants to talk about it.

Gradually *'lock' him into the newly experienced environment* as in the previous procedure. He will tell you when images are appearing to him, but you will be able to tell this for yourself by watching for *rapid eye movements,* or eye-muscle movements. As before, the faster these become, the more vivid are the experimentee's images or visualization.

From here on the method is exactly the same as before, and the *music may be switched off* or allowed to end of its own accord – unless the experimentee finds it necessary for his visualizing, in which case it can be replayed or replaced by similar music. But for the sake of tape-recording his experience, it is of course preferable to, gradually, fade out the music from the background.

(N.B. Yet another procedure may be found on page 153.)

Conclusion

I had thought that one book on this subject would be all that I would ever write, and until recently I was convinced that there would most certainly be no more than two. But like so many matters in life, as soon as you decide that an investigation is completed it becomes all too apparent that it has only just begun.

Several of the experiences recorded here, particularly those of Jacqueline Parkhurst, have shown me the need to submit myself to ten or twelve such experiments, to see if the experiences from them can be collated into some kind of pattern which might possibly reveal more of the meaning and purpose of life, and of the universe, than is apparent from the experience of a mere lifetime. This is what I now intend to do.

Such a phenomenon may bring a new and very desirable dimension to the lives of a great many people who, through some disability or lack of a faculty, are denied some other dimension of life that is possessed and taken for granted by the majority of us. This, too, I feel compelled to investigate. For it has now become clear to me that the 'windows of the mind' have not only revealed the 'worlds within' which all of us have – but perhaps, too, a door to eternity.